Quest

Second Edition

3

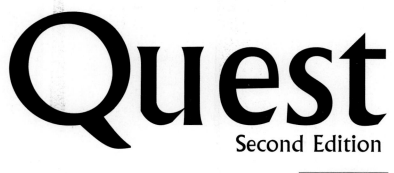

Listening and Speaking

Laurie Blass
Pamela Hartmann

McGraw-Hill

Quest 3 Listening and Speaking, 2nd Edition

Published by McGraw-Hill ESL/ELT, a business unit of The McGraw-Hill Companies, Inc. 1221 Avenue of the Americas, New York, NY 10020. Copyright © 2007 by The McGraw-Hill Companies, Inc. All rights reserved. No part of this publication may be reproduced or distributed in any form or by any means, or stored in a database or retrieval system, without the prior written consent of The McGraw-Hill Companies, Inc., including, but not limited to, in any network or other electronic storage or transmission, or broadcast for distance learning.

ISBN 13: 978-0-07-325331-2 (Student Book)
ISBN 10: 0-07-325331-6
5 6 7 8 9 VNH/PCC 12 11

ISBN 13: 978-0-07-326962-7 (Student Book with Audio Highlights)
ISBN 10: 0-07-326962-X
6 7 8 9 VNH/PCC 12 11

Editorial director: Erik Gundersen
Series editor: Linda O'Roke
Development editor: Jennifer Bixby
Production manager: Juanita Thompson
Production coordinator: James D. Gwyn
Cover designer: David Averbach, Anthology
Interior designer: Martini Graphic Services, Inc.
Photo researcher: PoYee Oster
Illustrator: Tim Jones

McGraw-Hill

www.esl-elt.mcgraw-hill.com

The McGraw·Hill Companies

ACKNOWLEDGEMENTS

The publisher and author would like to thank the following education professionals whose comments, reviews, and assistance were instrumental in the development of the Quest series.

- **Roberta Alexander,** San Diego Community College District

- **David Dahnke,** North Harris College (Houston, TX)

- **Mary Díaz,** Broward Community College (Davie, FL)

- **Judith García,** Miami-Dade College

- **Elizabeth Giles,** The School District of Hillsborough County, Florida

- **Patricia Heiser,** University of Washington, Seattle

- **Yoshiko Matsubayashi,** Kokusai Junior College, Tokyo

- **Ahmed Motala,** University of Sharjah, United Arab Emirates

- **Dee Parker and Andy Harris,** AUA, Bangkok

- **Alison Rice,** Hunter College, City University of New York

- **Alice Savage,** North Harris College (Houston, TX)

- **Katharine Sherak,** San Francisco State University

- **Leslie Eloise Somers,** Miami-Dade County Public Schools

- **Karen Stanley,** Central Piedmont Community College (Charlotte, NC)

- **Diane Urairat,** Mahidol Language Services, Bangkok

- **Pamela Vittorio,** The New School (New York, NY)

- **Anne Marie Walters,** California State University, Long Beach

- **Lynne Wilkins,** Mills College (Oakland, CA)

- **Sean Wray, Elizabeth Watson, and Mariko Yokota,** Waseda International University, Tokyo

Many, many thanks go to Marguerite Ann Snow, who provided the initial inspiration for the entire series. Heartfelt thanks also to Erik Gundersen, Linda O'Roke, and Jennifer Bixby for their help in the development of the second edition. We would also like to thank Dylan Bryan-Dolman, Susannah MacKay, Terry Minkler, Kristin Sherman, and Kristin Thalheimer, whose opinions were invaluable.

TABLE OF CONTENTS

Quest: The Series

Quest Second Edition prepares students for academic success. The series features two complementary strands—*Listening and Speaking* and *Reading and Writing*—each with four levels. The integrated *Quest* program provides robust scaffolding to support and accelerate each student's journey from exploring general interest topics to mastering academic content.

Quest parallels and accelerates the process native-speaking students go through when they prepare for success in a variety of academic subjects. By previewing typical college course material, *Quest* helps students get "up to speed" in terms of both academic content and language skills.

In addition, *Quest* prepares students for the daunting amount and level of listening, speaking, reading, and writing required for college success. The four *Listening and Speaking* books in the *Quest* series contain listening and speaking strategies and practice activities centered on authentic recordings from "person on the street" interviews, social conversations, radio programs, and university lectures. Listening passages increase in length and difficulty across the four levels.

The *Reading and Writing* books combine high-interest material from newspapers and magazines with traditional academic source materials such as textbooks. Like the *Listening and Speaking* books, the four *Reading and Writing* books increase in difficulty with each level.

Quest Second Edition Features

- New *Intro* level providing on-ramp to Books 1-3
- Redesigned, larger format with captivating photos
- Expanded focus on critical thinking and test-taking skills
- Expanded video program (VHS and DVD) with new lecture and updated social language footage
- Test-taking strategy boxes that highlight skills needed for success on the new TOEFL® iBT
- New unit-ending *Vocabulary Workshops* and end-of-book academic word lists
- Teacher's Editions with activity-by-activity procedural notes, expansion activities, and tests
- Addition of research paper to *Reading and Writing* titles
- EZ Test® CD-ROM-based test generator for all *Reading and Writing* titles

Quest Listening and Speaking

Quest Listening and Speaking includes three or four distinct units, each focusing on a different area of university study—anthropology, art, biology, business, ecology, economics, history, literature, psychology, or sociology. Each unit contains two chapters.

Chapter Structure

Each chapter of *Quest 3 Listening and Speaking* contains five parts that blend listening and speaking skills within the context of a particular academic area of study. Listening passages and skill-development activities build upon one another and increase in difficulty as students work through the five parts of each chapter.

Part 1: Introduction

- Thinking Ahead – discussion activities on photos introduce the chapter topic.
- Reading – a high-interest reading captures students' attention and motivates them to want to find out even more about the chapter topic.
- Discussion – speaking activities check students' understanding and allow for further discussion.

Part 2: Social Language

- Before Listening – prediction activities and vocabulary activities prepare students for the listening. Strategy boxes provide students with practical strategies they can use immediately as they listen to conversations.
- Listening – a high-interest conversation (available in video or audio) between students on or around an urban university campus allows students to explore the chapter topic in more depth.
- After Listening – comprehension, discussion, and vocabulary activities not only check students' understanding of the conversation but also continue to prepare them for the academic listening activities in Parts 4 and 5.

Part 3: The Mechanics of Listening and Speaking

- Chapter-specific pronunciation, intonation, language function, and collocation boxes equip students to express their ideas.
- Content-driven language function boxes are followed by contextualized practice activities that prepare students for social and academic listening.

Part 4: Broadcast English

- Before Listening – prediction activities and vocabulary activities prepare students for listening to a short passage from an authentic radio program.
- Listening – a high-interest authentic radio program allows students to practice their listening skills and explore the chapter topic in more depth.
- After Listening – comprehension, discussion, and vocabulary activities not only check students' understanding of the program but also continue to prepare them for the academic listening in Part 5.

Part 5: Academic English

- Before Listening – prediction activities and vocabulary activities prepare students for listening to an authentic academic lecture.
- Listening – an academic lecture written by university professors allows students to practice their listening and note-taking skills. One lecture in each unit is available on video.
- After Listening – comprehension activities allow students to use their lecture notes to answer discussion questions.
- Put It All Together – a longer speaking activity provides students with the opportunity to connect all three listening passages and give a short presentation on the chapter topic.

Teacher's Editions

The *Quest Teacher's Editions* provide instructors with activity-by-activity teaching suggestions, cultural and background notes, Internet links to more information on the unit themes, expansion black-line master activities, chapter tests, and a complete answer key.

The *Quest Teacher's Editions* also provide test-taking boxes that highlight skills found in *Quest* that are needed for success on the new TOEFL® iBT.

Video Program

For the *Quest Listening and Speaking* books, a newly expanded video program on DVD or VHS incorporates authentic classroom lectures with social language vignettes.

Lectures

The lecture portion of each video features college and university professors delivering high-interest mini-lectures on topics as diverse as primate behavior, development economics, and folk heros. The mini-lectures run from two minutes at the *Intro* level to six minutes by Book 3. As students listen to the lectures, they complete structured outlines to model accurate note taking. Well-organized post-listening activities teach students how to use and refer to their notes in order to answer questions about the lecture and to review for a test.

Social Language

The social language portion of the videos gives students the chance to hear authentic conversations on topics relevant to the chapter topic and academic life. A series of scenes shot on or around an urban college campus features nine engaging students participating in a host of curricular and extracurricular activities. The social language portion of the video is designed to help English language students join study groups, interact with professors, and make friends.

Audio Program

Each reading selection on the audio CD or audiocassette program allows students to hear new vocabulary words, listen for intonation cues, and increase their reading speed. Each reading is recorded at an appropriate rate while remaining authentic.

Test Generator

For the *Quest Reading and Writing* books, an EZ Test® CD-ROM test generator allows teachers to create customized tests in a matter of minutes. EZ Test® is a flexible and easy-to-use desktop test generator. It allows teachers to create tests from unit-specific test banks or to write their own questions.

SCOPE AND SEQUENCE

Chapter	Listening Strategies	Speaking Strategies
UNIT 1 ANTHROPOLOGY		
Chapter 1 **Cultural Anthropology** • Social Language: Conversation about privacy and personal space • Broadcast English: Radio program on culture and personal space • Academic English: Lecture on the research of Edward Hall	• Noticing Grammar • Guessing the Meaning from Context • Listening for the Topic and Main Idea in a Radio Program • Preparing to Listen to a Lecture • Having Questions in Mind • Using Abbreviations • Taking Lecture Notes	• Using and Understanding Nonverbal Communication • Expressing Interest and Surprise
Chapter 2 **Physical Anthropology** • Social Language: Conversation about primates and language • Broadcast English: Radio program on Neanderthals • Academic English: Lecture on primate behavior	• Listening for Emotions • Understanding Idioms and Slang • Understanding Stems and Affixes • Listening for the Topic in an Introduction • Using a T-chart • Listening for Lecture Subtopics in an Overview	• Expressing an Opinion • Expressing Agreement or Disagreement • Making Eye Contact • Asking Questions After a Presentation

Mechanics of Listening and Speaking	Critical Thinking Strategies	Test-Taking Strategies
UNIT 1 ANTHROPOLOGY		
• Reduced Forms of Words • Understanding Anecdotes • Expressing Interest and Surprise	• Guessing the Meaning from Context • Making Inferences • Predicting Exam Questions • Deciding on Key Words for Internet Research	• Taking Notes
• Expressing an Opinion • Expressing Agreement or Disagreement • Softening Disagreement • Listening for Intonation to Express Disagreement • Comparing /θ/, /s/, and /t/	• Interpreting Humor • Using a T-chart • Making Connections	• Synthesizing Information

Chapter	Listening Strategies	Speaking Strategies
UNIT 2 ECONOMICS		
Chapter 3 **Developing Nations** • Social Language: On the street interviews about solutions to poverty • Broadcast English: Radio program on Bangladesh • Academic English: Lecture on development economics	• Guessing the Meaning from Context: Proverbs • Listening for Supporting Statistics • Listening for Quoted Material • Noting a Point of Greater Importance	• Managing a Conversation • Using Latin Terms • Negotiating Responsibilities for a Group Presentation • Taking Turns
Chapter 4 **The Global Economy** • Social Language: Conversation about summer jobs • Broadcast English: Radio program on Mister Donut in Japan • Academic English: Lecture on emerging nations	• Listening for the Main Points in an Introduction • Listening for Causes and Effects	• Asking for Confirmation • Offering an Explanation • Interrupting Incorrect Assumptions • Choosing a Topic • Giving a Presentation from Notes
UNIT 3 LITERATURE		
Chapter 5 **Poetry** • Social Language: Conversation about a poetry class • Broadcast English: Radio program with poet Maya Angelou • Academic English: Lecture on American poets	• Listening for Rhyme and Rhythm • Understanding the Passive Voice • Listening for the Main Ideas in a Lecture • Being an Active Listener	• Responding to Negative Questions • Making Appointments and Negotiating Time • Giving a Speech

Mechanics of Listening and Speaking	Critical Thinking Strategies	Test-Taking Strategies
UNIT 2 ECONOMICS		
• Listening for Tone of Voice: Interjections • Giving Advice and Suggestions: *should, ought to* + Verb • Commenting on Past Actions • Reduced Forms of Words: Giving Advice and Suggestions	• Analyzing Solutions • Distinguishing Causes and Effects • Applying Information	• Listening for Details
• Asking for Confirmation • Offering an Explanation • Tag Question Intonation • Reduced Forms of Words: Tag Questions • Interrupting Incorrect Assumptions	• Realizing What You Already Know • Making Connections	• Making Inferences About Attitudes or Feelings
UNIT 3 LITERATURE		
• Questions and Statements • Questions with *Or* • Responding to Negative Questions: Agreeing • Responding to Negative Questions: Disagreeing • The Medial *T* • Making Appointments and Negotiating Time	• Analyzing Poetry: A Poetry Primer • Listening for Inferences • Making Connections	• Taking Notes While Listening

Chapter	Listening Strategies	Speaking Strategies
Chapter 6 **Heroes in Literature** • Social Language: Conversation about movies • Broadcast English: Radio program on mythological heroes • Academic English: Lecture on folk heroes	• Listening for Influences • Listening for Topic Signals • Understanding a Summary in the Conclusion to a Lecture • Comparing Lecture Notes	• Starting a Conversation • Keeping a Conversation Going • Telling a Story
UNIT 4 ECOLOGY		
Chapter 7 **Endangered Species** • Social Language: Conversation about research opportunities • Broadcast English: Radio program on tropical rain forests • Academic English: Lecture on Gerald Durrell	• Listening for Details: Anecdotes • Listening to Fast English • Listening for Signals	• Answering the Phone and Taking a Message • Clarifying Information on the Phone • Using Visuals During a Presentation
Chapter 8 **Environmental Health** • Social Language: On the street interviews about environmental health • Broadcast English: Radio program on a utopian community • Academic English: Lecture on the Green Movement	• Recognizing Figurative Language • Listening to Accented English	• Expressing Concern • Intensifying Concern • Giving Constructive Criticism

The Mechanics of Listening and Speaking	Critical Thinking Strategies	Test-Taking Strategies
• Starting a Conversation • Keeping a Conversation Going • Question Intonation • Reduced Forms Words: *Wh-* Questions • The Voiced *th*: /ð/	• Analyzing Results • Synthesizing • Analyzing a Story	• Listening for the Main Idea

UNIT 4 ECOLOGY

• Answering the Phone and Taking a Message • Clarifying Information on the Phone • *Can* vs. *Can't* • Understanding Outgoing Messages	• Listening for Inferences • Making Connections • Using a Variety of Sources	• Listening for Signals
• Expressing Concern • Intensifying Concern • Expressing Emotional Intensity with Stress • Comparing /ɛ/, /æ/, and /ʌ/	• Listening for Emotions • Making an Educated Guess • Memorizing • Making Connections	• Using a Spider Map to Take Notes

Welcome

Quest Second Edition **prepares students for academic success.** The series features two complementary strands—*Reading and Writing* and *Listening and Speaking*—each with four levels. The integrated Quest program provides robust scaffolding to support and accelerate each student's journey from exploring general interest topics to mastering academic content.

New second edition features

- New *Intro* level providing on-ramp to Books 1–3

- Redesigned, larger format with captivating photos

- Expanded focus on critical thinking skills

- Addition of research paper to *Reading and Writing* strand

- New unit-ending *Vocabulary Workshops*

- New end-of-book Academic Word List (AWL) in *Reading and Writing* strand

- Expanded video program (VHS/DVD) with new lecture and updated social language footage

- EZ Test® CD-ROM test generator for all *Reading and Writing* titles

- Test-taking strategy boxes that highlight skills needed for success on the new TOEFL® iBT

- Teacher's Editions with activity-by-activity procedural notes, expansion activities, and tests

Captivating photos and graphics capture students' attention while introducing them to each academic topic.

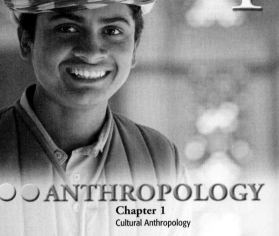

U N I T 1

○○ ANTHROPOLOGY

Chapter 1
Cultural Anthropology

Chapter 2
Physical Anthropology

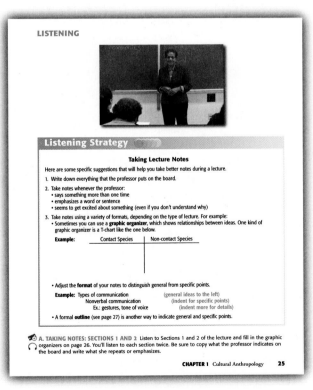

LISTENING

Listening Strategy

Taking Lecture Notes

Here are some specific suggestions that will help you take better notes during a lecture.

1. Write down everything that the professor puts on the board.

2. Take notes whenever the professor:
   • says something more than one time
   • emphasizes a word or sentence
   • seems to get excited about something (even if you don't understand why)

3. Take notes using a variety of formats, depending on the type of lecture. For example:
   • Sometimes you can use a **graphic organizer**, which shows relationships between ideas. One kind of graphic organizer is a T-chart like the one below.

   Example: | Contact Species | Non-contact Species |
   |---|---|
   | | |

   • Adjust the **format** of your notes to distinguish general from specific points.

   Example: Types of communication   (general ideas to the left)
             Nonverbal communication   (indent for specific points)
                 Ex.: gestures, tone of voice   (indent more for details)

   • A formal **outline** (see page 27) is another way to indicate general and specific points.

A. TAKING NOTES: SECTIONS 1 AND 2 Listen to Sections 1 and 2 of the lecture and fill in the graphic organizers on page 26. You'll listen to each section twice. Be sure to copy what the professor indicates on the board and write what she repeats or emphasizes.

CHAPTER 1 Cultural Anthropology **25**

Listening and Speaking Strategies guide students to develop effective academic listening and note-taking skills.

Three high-interest listening selections in each chapter introduce students to the general education course content most frequently required by universities.

🎧 **A. LISTENING FOR THE MAIN IDEA** Listen to the interviews. As you listen, think about this question:
• Do most of the people interviewed worry about environmental health hazards?

🎧 **B. LISTENING FOR DETAILS** Listen to the interviews again. Are the speakers worried about environmental health hazards? Circle *Yes* or *No* in the chart below. If the speaker is worried, write what he or she is worried about.

Speakers	Worried?		What is he or she worried about?
1	(Yes)	No	quality of air and food
2	Yes	No	
3	Yes	No	
4	Yes	No	
5	Yes	No	
6	Yes	No	
7	Yes	No	

🎧 **C. LISTENING FOR EMOTIONS** Listen to the interviews again. Try to determine each speaker's emotional state by using cues such as the tone of voice, how fast the speaker talks, and laughter. If you are watching the video, you can also look for cues in the speaker's facial expressions and body movements to determine his or her emotions. In the chart on page 241, circle the emotion for each speaker or add your own word.

240 **UNIT 4** Ecology

🎧 **C. TAKING NOTES: USING AN OUTLINE** Listen to the lecture. It's in four sections. You will listen to each section twice. Fill in as much of the outline as you can. Don't worry if you can't fill in everything. You'll listen to the whole lecture again later.
There are three main ideas. You'll hear each one three times—once in the introduction, once in the middle, and again in the conclusion.

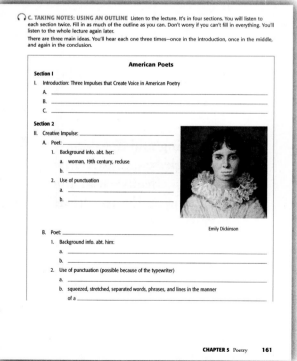

American Poets

Section I

I. Introduction: Three Impulses that Create Voice in American Poetry
    A. _____
    B. _____
    C. _____

Section 2

II. Creative Impulse: _____
    A. Poet: _____
       1. Background info. abt. her:
          a. woman, 19th century, recluse
          b. _____
       2. Use of punctuation
          a. _____
          b. _____

Emily Dickinson

    B. Poet: _____
       1. Background info. abt. him:
          a. _____
          b. _____
       2. Use of punctuation (possible because of the typewriter)
          a. _____
          b. squeezed, stretched, separated words, phrases, and lines in the manner
             of a _____

CHAPTER 5 Poetry **161**

Gradual curve in each chapter from social language, to broadcast English, and then academic listening supports students as they engage in increasingly more difficult material.

Discussion, pair-work, and group-work activities scaffold the students' learning process as they move from general interest to academic content.

Interview six classmates about international hiring. First, think about your own answers to the question below. Then ask six classmates. Write their answers in the chart.
- Many international companies **outsource**—contract out their work to workers in developing countries. Labor is often cheaper in developing countries. Do you think it is a good idea for companies in a country such as the United States to use cheap labor overseas? Why or why not?

Classmates	Yes, it's a good idea because . . .	No, it's a bad idea because . . .
Total	_____ students thought outsourcing was a good idea.	_____ students thought outsourcing was a bad idea.

C. DISCUSSING SURVEY RESULTS In small groups, discuss the results of your survey. Answer these questions:
- Within your group, what is the total number of people interviewed? Count each person just once.
- How many people thought outsourcing was a good idea? A bad idea?
- What were the most common reasons given?

A Chinese seamstress making clothes for a U.S. company

CHAPTER 4 The Global Economy **107**

UNIT 3 VOCABULARY WORKSHOP

Review vocabulary items that you learned in Chapters 5 and 6.

A. MATCHING Match the words to the definitions. Write the correct letters on the lines.

Words	Definitions
_____ 1. advent	**a.** after that
_____ 2. ambiguous	**b.** strong belief
_____ 3. concise	**c.** varied; different
_____ 4. conviction	**d.** long, dramatic story
_____ 5. diverse	**e.** not probable; not expected
_____ 6. perplexed	**f.** confused
_____ 7. saga	**g.** idea that is overgeneralized about a group of people
_____ 8. stereotype	**h.** with few (but well-chosen) words
_____ 9. subsequently	**i.** not clearly explained; possible to interpret in different ways
_____10. unlikely	**j.** beginning; invention

B. WORDS IN PHRASES Fill in the blanks with words from the box.

baggage	herself	way	wits
crowd	life	weight	word

1. Because John was small and weak, he had to use his _____ in order to survive.
2. Sasha's new job was important to her, and she wanted to make a good impression. She knew that she had to prove _____.
3. Gary wasn't sure that he wanted to marry Janet because she had a big family filled with strange people, but he realized that he carried a lot of _____, too.
4. You don't have to take my _____ for it. You can ask anyone. They'll tell you the same thing.
5. From an early age, Cathy had an amazing ability to play the piano. For this reason, she stood out from the _____.

200 UNIT 3 Literature

Unit-ending *Vocabulary Workshops* reinforce key unit vocabulary that also appears on the Academic Word List.

COMPREHENSIVE ANCILLARY PROGRAM

Expanded video program for the *Listening and Speaking* titles now includes mini-lectures to build comprehension and note-taking skills, and updated social language scenes to develop conversation skills.

Audio program selections are indicated with this icon 🎧 and include recordings of all lectures, conversations, pronunciation and intonation activities, and reading selections.

Teacher's Edition provides activity-by-activity teaching suggestions, expansion activities, tests, and special TOEFL® iBT preparation notes.

EZ Test® CD-ROM test generator for the *Reading and Writing* titles allows teachers to create customized tests in a matter of minutes.

ANTHROPOLOGY

Chapter 1
Cultural Anthropology

Chapter 2
Physical Anthropology

Cultural Anthropology

Discuss these questions:
- Where might this woman be? What might the people be doing there?
- In what situations are you in a crowd of people?
- Do you feel comfortable or uncomfortable in a crowd of people?

PART ① INTRODUCTION Place and Space

An American living room in a suburban home.
What cultural values does this room reflect?

A view of an inner courtyard from a Chinese living area.
What cultural values does this courtyard reflect?

A. THINKING AHEAD You are going to read about **concepts** (ideas) of space in different cultures. Before you read, discuss these questions with a partner.

1. For you, what is important to have in a living room? What kind of feeling or atmosphere do you like a living room to have?

2. When visiting a person's house for the first time, a North American guest will often give a **compliment** (statement of admiration) about the living room. What is a typical compliment that a guest might give a host? Is this different in different cultures? Explain your answers.

3. Think about what a typical house was like 100 years ago. What was the basic design of a house in your culture? Is it different from houses today? Why do you think houses have changed?

B. READING Read about two types of houses. Read to understand the main ideas. Don't worry about vocabulary at this point. As you read, think about this question:

• What does each house express about its culture?

Place and Space

What can a house express about its occupants? In an article written in *Harper's Magazine*, Chinese professor Yi-Fu Tuan, teaching in the United States, compared a suburban American house with a traditional Chinese house. In doing so, he was actually comparing one essential aspect of each culture.

5   The focal point of a typical American house, he wrote, is the picture window— usually the largest window in the house, in the living room. A first-time visitor to the home commonly moves toward this window, and a typical compliment that this person gives the host is: "What a nice view!" The guest is complimenting the vista—everything *outside* the house. Tuan explains that this is not surprising because "the distant
10   horizon" is a "symbol of the future."

   Tuan contrasts this with a traditional Chinese home, which is enclosed by "blank walls." Visitors who "step behind the spirit wall" find themselves "in a courtyard with perhaps a miniature garden around the corner." The atmosphere is one of "calm beauty, an ordered world of buildings, pavement, rock, and decorative vegetation," but
15   "no distant view."

   In a Chinese home, Tuan points out, "the only open space is the sky above." He attributes this absence of space to Chinese rootedness to their place. For the Chinese, according to Tuan, "place is deeply felt. Wanderlust is an alien sentiment." Perhaps because there was always "the constant threat of war, exile, and the natural disasters of
20   flood and drought," a common theme in Chinese poetry was nostalgia—a strong and sorrowful desire for home. There is respect for farmers because they are rooted to the land and "do not abandon their country when it is in danger."

   In contrast to Chinese rootedness, Americans usually move from one place to another by choice; "the future beckons, and the future is 'out there' in open space."
25   Tuan attributes American rootlessness to the ideals of "social mobility and optimism about the future." In brief, homes in the two countries reflect the culture of each. *Place*—so important in China—is symbolic of "achievement and stability." *Space*—so important in the United States—"symbolizes hope."

C. COMPREHENSION CHECK Discuss these questions with a partner.

1. According to Tuan, what is important in Chinese culture? What is important in American culture?

2. How do houses in these two cultures reflect the values and beliefs of the people?

1. a point that people focus on (5–10) *focal point*

2. a view (5–10) _____

3. a feeling of having roots—of being attached to a certain place (15–20) *root ness*

4. a strong desire to travel to other places (15–20) *wonder lust*

5. a sad desire (20–25) _____

6. calls; attracts (20–25) *beckons*

7. explains; says that something is responsible for something else (25–28) *attribute*

8. perfect standards or examples (25–28) *ideals*

9. belief that things will be good in the future (25–28) *optimism*

10. a feeling that one has accomplished something (25–28) *achievement*

E. DISCUSSION In small groups, discuss these questions.

1. What do you think about Tuan's ideas?

2. How might a modern Chinese house or apartment be different from a traditional house?

3. What do you think a "spirit wall" is? Do you think these exist in modern Chinese homes, or did they exist just in the past?

4. Does your home express something about your character or beliefs? If so, what?

F. RESPONSE WRITING In this book, you are going to keep a journal. In your journal, you are going to do *response writing* activities. In response writing, you write quickly about what you are thinking or feeling. Grammar, spelling, and punctuation are not very important in response writing. Your ideas and thoughts are important. You will have 15 minutes to write your responses. You can buy a special notebook for your journal, or you can keep your writing in a binder or folder.

Choose *one* of the topics below. Write about it for 15 minutes. Don't use a dictionary but do try to use new vocabulary. Just write as many ideas as you can.

• What is your opinion of the reading on page 5? What did you learn from it?

• What does your home look like? Describe it.

• Do you prefer to travel or stay home? Why?

PART ② SOCIAL LANGUAGE How Close Is Too Close?

BEFORE LISTENING

A. THINKING AHEAD You are going to listen to Ashley and Rachel talk about studying for an exam. Before you listen, discuss these questions with a partner.

1. To prepare for an important exam, do you prefer to study alone or with other students? Why?

2. If you accidentally **bump into** someone as you're walking down the street, do you say something? If so, what do you say?

3. What does the adjective *private* mean? What might the noun *privacy* mean? (If you don't know, don't use a dictionary. You'll hear an explanation in the conversation.)

B. VOCABULARY PREPARATION Read the sentences below. The words and phrases in orange are from the conversation. Match the definitions in the box with the words and phrases in orange. Write the correct letters on the lines.

a. change the subject	c. have to	e. think; predict
b. continue with	d. irritate a lot; bother	f. those things; that information

____c____ **1.** We've got to study hard for tomorrow's test.

____a____ **2.** We don't have time to get off the track and talk about other things.

____b____ **3.** We need to stick to the subject. Let's not talk about movies.

____f____ **4.** I think we should review all that stuff about symbolism from Chapter 1 of the book.

____e____ **5.** I bet this test is going to be hard.

____d____ **6.** Doesn't it drive you nuts when you study a lot for a test, but the professor asks you about something you didn't study at all?

 **A. LISTENING FOR THE MAIN IDEA** Listen to the conversation. As you listen, think about this question:
• What is personal space?

Critical Thinking Strategy

Guessing the Meaning from Context

When you listen to spoken English or read written English, you probably won't understand every word. Usually your goal is to understand the main idea. To do this, it's not necessary to know the meaning of every word.

The strategy of guessing the meaning from context may be easier to practice in reading because you have time to reread and think. Although you don't have this advantage when listening, the speaker's **intonation** (rising and falling voice) can help you. If you can also see the speaker as you listen (as in a lecture or video), you can often guess the meaning from nonverbal communication.

In this book, you'll practice using three different contexts for guessing the meaning of new words:
• the reading context (other words in the sentence; other sentences close by)
• the listening context (the speaker's intonation and tone of voice)
• the visual context (the speaker's nonverbal communication, such as facial expressions and body movement)

1. **privacy** = *time alone without people*

   wonder = *want to know*

2. **personal space** = *the area is privacy*

   boundaries = *distance between two people.*

3. **skeptical** = *dont believe other people*

   unconscious = *dont take care of other people*

👥 Now compare your answers with a partner's answers.

Critical Thinking Strategy ●●●●

Making Inferences

Speakers don't always clearly state what they mean. Instead, they often **imply** (suggest) information. The listener needs to make **inferences** (guesses, assumptions) about information that isn't directly stated.

Example: **You hear:**   "Professor Wang took ten points off my essay exam because I didn't include examples."

   You infer: It's important to include details and examples on exams in Professor Wang's class.

🔊 **C. MAKING INFERENCES** Listen to parts of the conversation again. Then circle the letters of the correct 🎧 answers to the questions below.

1. Who is "she"?

   A. another classmate

   B. a friend

   C. the professor

   D. the teaching assistant

2. What do these two students think about the fact that "some languages don't have a word for *privacy*"?

   A. They're surprised.

   B. They already knew it.

   C. They don't believe it.

   D. They think that everyone knows it.

3. The psychologist from Harvard University _____.

   A. has an uncomfortable chair

   B. is unconscious

   C. needs less personal space than Hall was giving him

   D. needs more personal space than Hall was giving him

Listening Strategy

Noticing Grammar

English grammar is very complex, and you will probably never be able to learn all of it from classes and books. One way to learn more about grammar is to pay close attention as you listen. Begin to notice the grammar that the speaker uses. Sometimes you will hear examples of grammar that you have learned in class. Sometimes you will notice grammar that you haven't learned yet. Becoming good at *noticing* grammar (as well as vocabulary and phrases) and then *using* this in your own English will help you to learn the language faster and better.

Example: **You hear**: "Maybe she talked about this the day you were absent."
            You notice: The speaker doesn't use the word *that* between *day* and *you*.
            You learn: The word *that* is often optional.

D. NOTICING GRAMMAR You heard a student tell a story about Edward Hall and a psychologist. Listen again and pay special attention to the verbs. Write the verbs you hear on the lines below.

And this famous guy _____*is*_____ (1) really skeptical. I mean, he _____*doesn't*_____ (2) believe that there's some, um, specific amount of space that we each need. So during the conversation—and they _____*talked*_____ (3) for about an hour— Hall _____*moves*_____ (4) his chair just a little closer to this other guy's chair. And the other guy _____*moves*_____ (5) his chair a little back, a little farther away. And this _____*is*_____ (6) unconscious; he _____*verbzc*_____ (7) even realize that he's _____*doing*_____ (8) it, right? So a few minutes later, Hall _____*moves*_____ (9) toward him again, and, the other guy _____*moves*_____ (10) back again, to have a little more space. And this _____*h*_____ (11) on for an hour. So finally, when Hall _____*_____*_____ (12) to leave, he _____*points*_____ (13) out to his friend that they started the conversation on one side of the room, and now they're on the opposite side.

AFTER LISTENING

A. TAKING A SURVEY Interview five classmates about personal space. First, think about your own answers to the questions in the chart. Then ask five classmates the questions. Write their answers in the chart.

	How far from another person should you stand?	How often do you need privacy?				
		Never	Seldom	Sometimes	Often	Very Often
Example	about 2 feet				✓	
Classmate 1	about 1 m			✓		
Classmate 2	about 2m		✓			
Classmate 3	about 1.5m			✓		
Classmate 4	~~feet~~ about 3 feet			✓		
Classmate 5	about 1.5m		✓			

B. DISCUSSING SURVEY RESULTS Form small groups. Try not to be in a group with someone you interviewed. Discuss these questions.

1. Were the people in your survey from the same culture? No

2. Were their answers similar or different? Similar between 1m to 2m

3. In your opinion, is a person's requirement for privacy and personal space determined by culture or by individual needs?

PRONUNCIATION

🎧 Reduced Forms of Words

In natural, spoken English, some words become reduced, or shortened. For example, the word *him* may be reduced to *'im*.

Also, when people speak quickly, two or three words are often pushed together so that they sound like one word. For example, *got to* becomes *gotta*.

Examples:	Long Forms	→	Reduced Forms
	Ken moved toward **him**.	→	Ken moved toward **'im**.
	Have you read **them**?	→	Have you read **'em**?
	We've **got to** get serious.	→	We've **gotta** get serious.
	Hailey's **going to** ask about symbolism.	→	Hailey's **gonna** ask about symbolism.
	I was **sort of** uncomfortable.	→	I was **sorta** uncomfortable.
	The show was **kind of** interesting.	→	The show was **kinda** interesting.
	I **don't know** where I heard that.	→	I **dunno** where I heard that.
	Tyler was **trying to** get away.	→	Tyler was **tryna** get away.

Notes:

1. People use reduced forms when speaking but use the long form when writing. The reduced form is not correct in academic writing.

2. In conversation, *him* and *them* usually sound the same. You can know which word it is only from the context.

A. REDUCED FORMS OF WORDS
Listen to the conversation. You'll hear the reduced forms of some words. Write the *long* forms on the lines.

A: Dr. Roberts is _____*going to*_____ give a test tomorrow on the first three chapters.
1

B: I know, and I haven't even read _____*them*_____ yet. I've
2

_____*got to*_____ get busy tonight.
3

A: I thought you were _____*going to*_____ help your brother move tonight.
4

B: Oh no! That's right. I'll just tell _____*him*_____ I can't. He'll be
5

_____*kind of*_____ mad, but what can I do?
6

A: I _____*do not know*_____. You can't do everything. Maybe you're
7

_____*trying to*_____ do too much. You have school and a job and family responsibilities.
8

LANGUAGE FUNCTION

Understanding Anecdotes

The introduction to an **anecdote** (short personal story) is in the past tense, but the rest of the anecdote can be told using either the present tense or the past tense. Using the present forms of verbs to tell anecdotes is more informal and conversational.

Example: You won't believe what **happened** to me yesterday. **I'm walking** down the street and a man in a gorilla suit **comes** up to me and **asks** for directions to the library.

In an anecdote, certain important words are **stressed** (emphasized) for dramatic effect. This makes the story more interesting and helps to hold the attention of listeners.

Example: Of *course* I can give directions to the library. I almost *live* there!

B. UNDERSTANDING ANECDOTES
In Part 2, you heard an anecdote near the end of the conversation. Now listen to another anecdote. Listen for answers to these questions. On a separate piece of paper, take notes as you listen. Then discuss these questions with a partner.

1. What reduced forms of words do you hear? ~~gotta~~ *gonna* *mpha*

2. What tenses are used at the beginning and end of the anecdote? What tenses are used for most of this story? *past* — *past*   *PAO*

3. What words are stressed? ~~really~~
   ~~so~~ *wow* *happy*
   ~~so~~ *realization*

WORDS IN PHRASES

> ### Expressing Interest and Surprise
>
> As you listen to someone telling an anecdote, instead of remaining silent through the story, it's common to say an occasional word or phrase to show that you're paying attention. This occurs in informal situations and not, for example, as you're listening to your professor's lecture. Probably the most common way to show that you're listening is to say *mm-hmm* ("Yes, I see.") from time to time. Here are some other expressions that you can use.
>
> | **To Express Interest** | **To Express Surprise** |
> |---|---|
> | Yeah? | Wow! |
> | So what happened next? | Oh my gosh! |
> | And then? | You're kidding! |
> | That's great. | You've got to be kidding! |

PUT IT TOGETHER

A. PLANNING AN ANECDOTE Think of a very short story to tell a small group. Try to think of a story that is surprising, funny, frightening, or amazing.

1. Choose *one* of the following:
   • a time when you were afraid
   • a funny encounter you once had with someone from another country
   • an unusual experience that once happened to someone you know

2. Think of a way to introduce your anecdote. For example:
   • I'll never forget the time I was . . .
   • I had a funny encounter with someone from . . .
   • The most unusual thing happened to a friend of mine. Last year, . . .

3. Write some notes about your story so that you don't forget any details. Do not write out the story in complete sentences. You want to *tell* your story. You do not want to *read* your story. Although your introduction is in the past, use the present tense to tell the anecdote.

B. TELLING AN ANECDOTE Tell your anecdote to a small group. Don't read from your notes, but **glance** (look quickly) at them occasionally to help you remember. When other students are telling their anecdotes, use some of the expressions from the Words in Phrases box above to show interest or surprise.

BEFORE LISTENING

In the United States, people call this phone a **cell phone**. In England, they call it a mobile phone. In Singapore, it is a hand phone. What do you call it? What other names can you think of for this device?

In English, a **pager** is also called a beeper because of the sound that it makes (*beep! beep!*). In your native language, what do you call this device? What sound does it make?

When listening to music on a **Walkman** or an iPod, people usually wear **headphones**. However, sometimes the sound **bleeds**, and other people nearby can hear it. Do you listen to music on headphones? If yes, when do you listen?

This very crowded subway is a common sight in Tokyo, Japan. Would it bother you to be on such a crowded subway?

A. THINKING AHEAD You are going to listen to part of a radio program. In small groups, discuss these questions before you listen.

1. Look at the pictures on page 15 and read the captions. The words in **bold** are from the radio program. Discuss the questions in the captions.

2. For people who travel to other countries, a common piece of advice is: "When in Rome, do as the Romans do." What does this mean that the traveler should do?

3. Imagine yourself in a big crowd of people leaving a sports event or a theater—a place without much **elbow room**. Does it bother you to be in a crowded place, or do you like it? In other words, would you prefer to have more elbow room, or do you enjoy being in a crowd?

Speaking Strategy

Understanding and Using Nonverbal Communication

We communicate with language, but we also use **nonverbal communication**. Nonverbal communication includes **body language** (movements with the body), **gestures** with the hands, and **facial expressions**.

Examples:

This body language expresses the idea "I don't know."

This gesture expresses "Who? Me?"

This facial expression shows confusion.

When you're communicating in a language that is not your native language, it's especially important to be able to use and understand nonverbal communication. Sometimes it can help you to **compensate** (substitute) for words that you don't know.

B. UNDERSTANDING AND USING NONVERBAL COMMUNICATION With a partner, follow the instructions below.

1. *Without words*, communicate any six of the emotions or ideas in the box below to your partner. Use only body language, hand gestures, and facial expressions. Your partner will guess the emotions or ideas. Then exchange roles.

Yes.	I don't know.	I'm angry.
No.	I don't care.	I'm surprised.
Maybe.	I'm confused.	I'm happy.
Really?!?	I don't like that; it's horrible.	I'm so-so.

2. If you have been in a **heterogeneous** group (one with people from different countries or cultures) or have seen different cultures in movies, you must have noticed nonverbal communication that is different from yours. Discuss different nonverbal communication you have noticed.

C. GUESSING THE MEANING FROM CONTEXT Read the sentences below. The words in orange are from the radio program. Match the definitions in the box with the words in orange. Write the correct letters on the lines.

a. able to allow or accept actions that one doesn't really like	e. going onto property without permission
b. act of entering a place that "belongs" to another person	f. got
c. aware; knowing	g. moving, unwanted, into another person's place
d. crashes	h. relating to space

_____g_____ 1. The sales clerk stood just a few inches from me, and I felt like he was **invading** my personal space. It made me uncomfortable.

_____h_____ 2. There are unspoken "**spatial** rules" in every society that let us all know "how close is too close."

_____d_____ 3. There are too many cars and too few traffic lights in that neighborhood, and this leads to a lot of **collisions**.

_____c_____ 4. I wasn't even **conscious** that the music from my headphones was bleeding and that the woman next to me was bothered by the noise.

_____b_____ 5. Jimmy got in trouble for **trespassing** on government land.

_____f_____ 6. I **acquired** some new ideas and customs when I lived in India for several years.

_____a_____ 7. Mark's never spent much time around children, so he's not very **tolerant** of the noise that they make.

_____e_____ 8. Allison put all her books on my desk, and it felt like an **incursion** of my territory.

LISTENING

Listening for the Topic and Main Idea in a Radio Program

In the introduction to a formal radio program, the host will usually include the following information:
- the topic
- the main idea
- the name of the people being interviewed
- some background about the topic

The host will usually start with some interesting background information about the topic to catch your attention and hold your interest. Then the main idea of the program will be given, sometimes in an introductory expression.

Examples:　Today we're going to explore how . . .
This hour we'll take a look at why . . .
Today's guest is going to help us understand what . . .
In this hour, we thought we'd discuss . . .

The main idea is the general idea about the topic. It's a sort of "umbrella" that covers all of the more specific **points** (details). In a long interview, there may be several different supporting ideas—one for each section—as the conversation moves along. However, *all* of these ideas are still logically part of the larger, umbrella idea from the introduction.

A. LISTENING FOR THE TOPIC AND MAIN IDEA IN A RADIO PROGRAM You are going to listen to part of a radio program called "Talk of the Nation." As you listen to the introduction, read along with the audio script below. Underline the main idea and circle the topic.

Penkava: From NPR News in Washington, this is "Talk of the Nation." I'm Melinda Penkava.

There are unspoken laws out there, boundaries that we can't see, but boundaries that we can feel very much when someone crosses them: someone comes a step too close to talk with you, or plops down in the chair next to you when she could have clearly taken a seat from the other 20 available chairs in the coffee house. We often react to this, not with words, but with body language of our own, which is fitting, because the rules of personal space seem to be unspoken, and therein lies the problem. Different people, different cultures even, set different boundaries for their personal space.

There are more of us on this planet than ever before. And while there are still wide open places you can go for miles without your elbow touching another human being, most of us do live in places where elbow room is harder and harder to come by. And so, this hour we thought we'd take as close a look as we can at this idea of giving each other a little space.

In small groups, compare what you underlined and circled.

B. LISTENING FOR SUPPORTING IDEAS: SECTION 1 Listen to Section 1 of the radio program. As you listen, think about the question below. Write your answers on the lines.

What are two reasons that more people nowadays feel that other people are "invading their space"?

_____

_____

C. LISTENING FOR SUPPORTING IDEAS: SECTION 2 Listen to Section 2. As you listen, think about the question below. Write your answer on the lines.

Why does Rita (calling from Germany) feel that she is giving up her personal space every time she visits India, but when she lived in India, she "didn't feel it"?

_____

_____

D. LISTENING FOR EXAMPLES: SECTION 3 Listen to Section 3. Listen for the answer to this question. Write your answer on the lines.

What is an example of an "incursion" on our personal space these days?

_____

_____

E. LISTENING FOR DETAILS Listen to the whole program again. Write your answers to the following questions on the lines.

1. What does Professor Robert Sommer teach? _____

2. What does Professor Deborah Pellow teach? _____

3. Deborah Pellow says that "culture . . . is about communication." What examples of communication does she mention? _____

_____

4. What three kinds of apparatus (electronic devices) does Deborah Pellow mention that bother some people in public places? _____

_____

5. What is the main way that the radio host indicates interest—that she is paying attention to her guests?

_____

F. MAKING AN INFERENCE Listen to one short part of the program again. Circle the correct answer to the question below.

• Basically, what is Robert Sommer's answer to the interviewer's question?

A. Yes.   C. I'm not sure.

B. No.   D. We saw more in the past.

AFTER LISTENING

A. DISCUSSION In small groups, discuss these questions. Then share your group's answers with the class.

1. In public places, are you ever bothered by the noise of cell phones, pagers, or headphones? If so, what do you do about it?

2. If you could live anywhere, what sort of place would you choose—a big busy city, a less-crowded small city, an uncrowded small town, or a place where there is a lot of "elbow room"? Why?

B. TAKING A SURVEY Read the survey questions in the chart below. Think about your answers. Then interview five classmates. Ask them the questions and write their answers in the chart.

	What are some advantages to living in a big, crowded city?	What are some disadvantages to living in a big, crowded city?
Example	Good shopping	Neighbors don't know each other.
Classmate 1		
Classmate 2		
Classmate 3		
Classmate 4		
Classmate 5		

C. DISCUSSING SURVEY RESULTS In small groups, discuss the results of your survey. Answer these questions:

• What was the most common advantage given?
• What was the most common disadvantage given?
• Which advantages or disadvantages were surprising to you?

PART ⑤ ACADEMIC ENGLISH
Edward Hall and the Concept of Space

BEFORE LISTENING

Walruses don't seem to mind being in very close physical contact.

Parakeets enjoy being wing to wing.

Hawks are solitary hunters.

Swans choose one mate to be with; they don't usually gather in large flocks.

A. THINKING AHEAD You are going to listen to a lecture about the concept of space. Before you listen, think about space in relation to animals and humans. Look at the photos above. In small groups, discuss these questions.

1. What other animals can you think of that like to be in close physical contact?

2. What other animals prefer to have little physical contact?

3. Do you think there is a wide variation in how close people like to be? Explain your answer.

Preparing to Listen to a Lecture

Preparing to listen to a lecture will help you understand more of what you hear. Here are some ways to prepare to listen to a lecture.

- Read the homework assignment before listening to the lecture. The more you know about the subject before a lecture, the more you will understand during the lecture.

- Before each lecture, take a few minutes to review in your mind what you already know about the topic. Look back at your notes or the reading assignments.

In lectures, professors often cover information that is *in addition to* what is in the reading homework. During the lecture, the professor may sometimes confirm your knowledge (say what you already know) and may sometimes correct something you have misunderstood. However, most often the professor will *add* to what you already know.

B. PREPARING TO LISTEN TO A LECTURE In Parts 1, 2, and 4, you learned about cultural concepts of space. Review your notes and the reading. Bring all of your knowledge on the subject together and on a separate piece of paper write what you know about cultural concepts of space. Answer these questions.

1. How does culture influence our concepts of space?

2. What is privacy?

3. What is personal space?

In small groups, share what you wrote.

Having Questions in Mind

Before you listen to a lecture, it's a good idea to have questions in mind. This way, you will be listening for answers to your questions, and you will be a more active and focused listener.

Example: You know: The lecture is about Edward Hall and the concept of space.
You ask yourself: Will the professor tell the same anecdote I heard in Part 2 (page 10)? In what ways does culture influence how we use space?

In small groups, look at the partial outline for the lecture on pages 26–27. What questions do you have? What are you curious about? Write questions on the lines.

Question 1: _____

Question 2: _____

Question 3: _____

Question 4: _____

D. GUESSING THE MEANING FROM CONTEXT Read the sentences below. The words and phrases in orange are from the lecture. Guess their meanings from the context. Write your guesses on the lines.

1. Greeting people is **universal**. In other words, it can be found in all cultures.

   Guess: _____ *sample   not unique* _____

2. Many people can't **afford** such a large house. It's awfully expensive.

   Guess: _____ *have* _____

3. There are **partitions** that break the large office into smaller areas. People have hung things like pictures and calendars on these partitions.

   Guess: _____

4. Jacob and Madison were deeply **engaged in** conversation and didn't notice anything happening around them.

   Guess: _____ *join* _____

5. There are a lot of trees and plants that **screen out** the ugly highway near my house, so I can't see it. Unfortunately, I can still hear it.

   Guess: _____ *hard* _____

6. In a traditional Japanese house, you can **slide** back a moveable wall and see the garden.

   Guess: _____ *move* _____

7. It's going to be very cold tonight, so you'll probably need to sleep under a thick **quilt**.

   Guess: _____

8. Our time is almost **up**, so I guess we'll have to finish next time.

   Guess: _____ *due* _____

👥 Now compare your answers with a partner's answers.

Taking Notes

It's important to take careful notes as you listen to a lecture. Taking notes helps you learn, organize, and remember the information. After the lecture, you can review your notes. Good notes are also important because exam questions come not only from assigned reading but also from lectures.

In standardized tests, you can take notes during the mini-lectures you hear. You'll practice lecture note-taking in every chapter of this book. Here are a few general suggestions:

• Don't "just listen" and not take notes at all. You won't remember the information at exam time and there won't be anything you can study.
• You won't have time to write down everything that is said. Note-taking is not like writing a dictation.
• Write notes, not complete sentences. There probably won't be time for full sentences.
• Use abbreviations whenever possible.

Listening Strategy

Using Abbreviations

Using abbreviations makes it possible to take notes quickly and efficiently. In most lectures, there are many common words you can abbreviate.

Examples:

about	→	abt.	people	→	peo.
and	→	+	something	→	sthg.
especially	→	esp.	typical	→	typ.
essential	→	ess.	with	→	w/
important	→	imp.	without	→	w/o
means	→	=	for example	→	ex.

You can also predict which words will appear often in a lecture and make up your *own* abbreviations for them.

E. USING ABBREVIATIONS Here are some words that you'll hear in the lecture. Write your own abbreviation for each one.

1. culture _____

2. space _____

3. animal _____

4. distance _____

5. privacy _____

6. conversation _____

7. language _____

8. Edward Hall _____

LISTENING

Listening Strategy

Taking Lecture Notes

Here are some specific suggestions that will help you take better notes during a lecture.

1. Write down everything that the professor puts on the board.

2. Take notes whenever the professor:
   • says something more than one time
   • emphasizes a word or sentence
   • seems to get excited about something (even if you don't understand why)

3. Take notes using a variety of formats, depending on the type of lecture. For example:
   • Sometimes you can use a **graphic organizer**, which shows relationships between ideas. One kind of graphic organizer is a T-chart like the one below.

Example:	Contact Species	Non-contact Species

   • Adjust the **format** of your notes to distinguish general from specific points.

   Example: Types of communication   (general ideas to the left)
   　　　　　　　　　Nonverbal communication   (indent for specific points)
   　　　　　　　　　　　Ex.: gestures, tone of voice   (indent more for details)

   • A formal **outline** (see page 27) is another way to indicate general and specific points.

A. TAKING NOTES: SECTIONS 1 AND 2 Listen to Sections 1 and 2 of the lecture and fill in the graphic organizers on page 26. You'll listen to each section twice. Be sure to copy what the professor indicates on the board and write what she repeats or emphasizes.

Edward Hall and His Research on the Concept of Space

Section 1

Topic/term that Hall coined: _personal space → culture influence_   _proxemics_

Definition: _____

_____

_____

Contact Species	Non-contact Species
walrus	horse
parakeet	hawk
	swan

Hediger: _call the them personal distance. vs face?_

_____

_____

_____

Section 2

Both animals and humans: _need movement space_

Animals: _Need space biology_

Humans: _need space · culture_

Distance Zones	Examples
1. intimate,	Touch lot
2. personal	shack hand talk hus hand / not
3. social	work together
4. public	speech

Hall notes that this pattern: _are universal. but many not be found_

in all culture

Section 3: The Use of Space in the Design of the Home

I. U.S. culture
    A. What's important: _privacy – high values_
    B. How the home reflects this: _need s for privacy_
        1. children: _have own bed room_
        2. parents: _share bed room_
    C. What people do to be alone: _close one door - leave to know_

II. Arab culture
    A. The home: _donse home (long space_
    B. What's important: _dony like done alone_
    C. What people do to be alone: _stop talking_

III. Japanese culture
    A. The home: _many ezely_
    B. What's important: _show closeups_
    C. What people do to be alone: _queer_
    D. How language reflects this: _dont have privacy need_

🔊 **C. CHECKING YOUR NOTES** Listen to the whole lecture again. As you listen, fill in any missing information.

AFTER LISTENING

A. USING YOUR NOTES Answer as many of the questions below as you can. Don't worry about the ones you can't answer; you'll have another chance to listen to the whole lecture.

Section 1

1. What does the term *proxemics* mean?

_____

_____

2. What do contact species need? Also, what are some examples of contact species?

_____

_____

3. What do non-contact species do? Also, what are some examples of non-contact species?

_____

_____

4. What did Hediger mean by his term *personal distance*?

_____

_____

5. Which animals have a larger personal distance than others?

_____

_____

Section 2

6. What are the four distance zones that are common in some cultures?

_____

_____

7. In cultures that have just *two* distances, what are the two?

_____

_____

Section 3

8. What is highly valued (very important) in American culture? Arab culture? Japanese culture? How do houses in these three cultures reflect the values of each culture?

_____

_____

9. What do people do in each of these cultures when they want to be alone?

_____

_____

10. What does it mean when an Arab stops talking? What does it mean when an American stops talking?

_____

_____

B. LISTENING FOR SPECIFIC INFORMATION Listen to the whole lecture again. This time, listen specifically for the answers to any questions that you could not answer in Activity A (pages 27–28).

C. DISCUSSION In small groups, discuss these questions.

1. Did anything in the lecture surprise you or interest you? Explain your answer.

2. Was there something in the lecture that you didn't understand? If so, discuss this with your group. Maybe your group members can help you understand it.

D. APPLICATION In small groups, choose another culture that wasn't mentioned in the lecture you heard. If you had to give part of the lecture about this culture, what would you say? What information would you include about:

• the design of a "typical" home (either traditional or modern)
• how a typical home reflects that culture's ideas about space
• the concept of privacy

Share your group's ideas with the class.

Critical Thinking Strategy

Predicting Exam Questions

Students need to be able to predict the kinds of questions their professors will ask on an exam. Making such predictions (a strategy that some students informally call *psyching out* the professors) can guide how and what you study. Here are some suggestions for psyching out your professors.

• Pay attention to what your professors *emphasize, repeat, write on the board,* or *appear to get excited about.*
• Don't be shy about asking your professors what kinds of questions to expect on an exam.
• Consider what kinds of questions appeared on previous exams (if any) in the class.

E. PREDICTING EXAM QUESTIONS With a partner, write on a separate piece of paper six questions that you might expect on an exam about the concepts of boundaries and space. Three of your questions should be about the radio program in Part 4. Three should be about the lecture. When you finish, exchange questions with another pair of students. Write answers to the other pair's questions.

PUT IT ALL TOGETHER

RESEARCHING In this activity, you are going to research and compare the nonverbal communication of two cultures.

Step 1
First, choose two cultures that interest you.

Culture 1: ___Mbx Co___   Culture 2: ___French___

Now choose *one* of these topics to research:
• facial expressions (including eye contact)
• hand gestures
• posture and body movement
• personal distance zones
• the need for privacy (and how it is found)

Critical Thinking Strategy

Deciding on Key Words for Internet Research

When doing research on the Internet, you can use a search engine to help you find useful information and articles. To use a search engine, you type in key words to start your search. It is important to choose your key words carefully. Think of your key words as the topic of your research.

If you are researching a person, you can type in that person's name and a key word. To search for a whole phrase, put quotation marks around the phrase. It is not necessary to use capital letters for key words.

Example: "edward hall"   proxemics
                        name   key word

If you are researching a topic, type in two or three key words for your search.

Examples: "facial expressions"   united states   japan
                        topic   culture   culture

Step 2

Do Internet or library research for information on your topic. For an Internet search, use your topic and the two cultures you have chosen for your key words. Look at several different websites and take notes on what you learn.

Since you are comparing two cultures, you may want to use a T-chart to organize your information.

Example:

Culture 1	Culture 2

Step 3

In small groups, explain your project. Be sure to:
• introduce your topic
• tell where you found your information
• explain similarities and differences between the two cultures
• tell what you were surprised to learn

As you listen to your group members, express interest or surprise when appropriate. Use expressions from the Words in Phrases box on page 14.

CHAPTER 2

Physical Anthropology

Discuss these questions:
- What is the woman doing?
- How might a gorilla and a human communicate with each other?
- Have you ever communicated with an animal? How?

PART ① INTRODUCTION Apes and Sign Language

Eddie Murphy talking with a bear in the movie *Doctor Doolittle*

A. THINKING AHEAD With a partner, discuss these questions.

1. How do animals communicate? What kinds of messages do animals communicate to each other? Give some examples.

2. How do you think apes (such as chimpanzees or gorillas) communicate with each other in the wild? In other words, what kinds of communication do they use?

3. If you need an English word that you don't know, do you sometimes create a new word? If so, can you think of words that you have created? Did people understand them?

4. If you didn't know the word *bear*, what name would you make up for that animal?

B. READING Read about apes and sign language. As you read, think about these questions:
• How are apes able to communicate with humans?
• What types of things can apes communicate?

Apes and Sign Language

Experiments have shown that apes can learn to use, if not speak, true language (Miles, 1983). Several apes have learned to converse with people in ways other than speech. One
5 such communication system is American Sign Language, or ASL, which is widely used by deaf and mute Americans. ASL employs a variety of hand gestures, positions, and shapes, as well as facial expressions to communicate
10 words and meaning. These signs combine to form words and larger units of meaning.

Dr. Roger Fouts teaching Lucy the chimpanzee American Sign Language.

The first chimpanzee to learn ASL was Washoe, a female. Washoe lived in a trailer and heard no spoken language. The
15 researchers always used ASL to communicate with each other in her presence. The chimp gradually acquired a vocabulary of more than 100 signs representing English words (Gardner, Gardner, and Van Cantfort, 1989).
20 At the age of two, Washoe began to combine as many as five signs into rudimentary sentences such as "you, me, go out, hurry."

The second chimp to learn ASL was Lucy, Washoe's junior by one year. From her second day of life, Lucy lived with a family in Norman, Oklahoma. Dr. Roger Fouts, a researcher from the nearby Institute for Primate Studies, came two days a week to test
25 and improve Lucy's knowledge of ASL. During the rest of the week, Lucy used ASL to converse with the family. After acquiring language, Washoe and Lucy exhibited several human traits: swearing, joking, telling lies, and trying to teach language to others. Washoe, Lucy, and other chimps have tried to teach ASL to other
30 animals, including their own offspring.

Dr. Penny Patterson with the gorilla Koko

Because of their size and strength as adults, gorillas are less likely subjects than chimps for such
35 experiments. Lean adult male gorillas in the wild weigh 400 pounds (180 kilograms), and full-grown females can easily reach 250 pounds (110 kilograms).
40 Because of this, psychologist Penny Patterson's work with gorillas at Stanford University seems more daring than the chimp experiments. Dr. Patterson raised
45 the now full-grown female gorilla, Koko, in a trailer next to a Stanford museum. Koko's vocabulary surpasses that of any chimp. She regularly employs 400 ASL signs

and has used about 700 at least once. Asking, in the evening, to get into her bedroom, Koko gestures "Penny, open key hurry bedroom." What she is saying, translated into English, is "Penny, unlock my bedroom door and be quick about it."

50 Koko and the chimps also show that apes share still another linguistic ability with humans—productivity. Speakers routinely use the rules of their language to produce entirely new phrases that are comprehensible to other native speakers. I can, for example, create "baboonlet" to refer to a baboon infant. I do this by analogy with English words in which the suffix –let is used for the young of a species. Anyone who

55 speaks English immediately understands the meaning of my new word. Koko, Washoe, Lucy, and others have shown that apes also are able to use language productively. Lucy used gestures she already knew to create "drinkfruit" for watermelon. Washoe, seeing a swan for the first time, coined "waterbird." Koko, who knew the gestures for "finger" and "bracelet," formed "finger bracelet" when she was given a ring.

60 No one denies the huge difference between human language and gorilla signs. There is a major gap between the ability to write a book or say a prayer and the few hundred gestures employed by a well-trained chimp. Apes aren't people, but they aren't just animals either. Let Koko express it: When asked by a reporter whether she was a person or an animal, Koko chose neither. Instead, she signed "fine animal

65 gorilla" (Patterson 1978).

Source: *Anthropology: The Exploration of Human Diversity* (Kottak)

C. VOCABULARY CHECK Look back at the reading. Find words or phrases to match the following definitions. Write the correct words and phrases on the lines. Line numbers are given in parentheses.

1. not able to speak (5–10)   *mute*

2. uses (verb) (5–10)

3. primitive, basic, simple (20–25)

4. saying vulgar ("bad") words (25–30)

5. goes beyond; is better than (45–50)

6. baby (50–55)

7. comparison (50–55)

8. created or made up (55–60)

9. difference (60–65)

10. movements of the hands to communicate meaning (60–65)

D. DISCUSSION In small groups, discuss these questions.

1. In what ways are apes and humans similar in their use of language? In what ways are they different?

2. What information in the reading did you find interesting? Why?

3. What do you know about other studies of animals and language?

E. RESPONSE WRITING Choose *one* of the topics below. Write about it for 15 minutes. Try to use new vocabulary but don't use a dictionary. Just write as many ideas as you can.
• What did you learn in the reading that was surprising?
• Have you communicated with an animal? Describe the situation.
• If you could communicate with an ape, what questions would you like to ask?

PART ② SOCIAL LANGUAGE Chimps Like Us

BEFORE LISTENING

Charles Darwin developed the theory of evolution.

A. THINKING AHEAD Think about what you know about **evolution**—the scientific idea that animals (including humans) have developed over time from earlier, simpler animals. In small groups, discuss these questions.

1. What do you know about Darwin? Can you name other scientists who have contributed to the study of evolution?

2. What evidence do scientists have to support the theory of evolution?

B. VOCABULARY PREPARATION
Read the sentences below. The words and phrases in orange are from the conversation. Match the definitions in the box with the words and phrases in orange. Write the correct letters on the lines.

a. and other, similar things **b. continue with**	**c. convenient** **d. great; wonderful**	**e. take quickly**

_____ **1.** Ryan is going to **stick with** his exercise program even though it's very hard for him.

_____ **2.** I think two-year-old children can be like monkeys; they often just **grab** what they want instead of asking first.

_____ **3.** A shelf above your desk is a **handy** place to keep your textbooks.

_____ **4.** I enjoy cultural anthropology. I like learning about different belief systems **and all**.

_____ **5.** Emma loves learning about how animals think and how intelligent they are. She thinks it's really **cool**.

LISTENING

A. LISTENING FOR THE MAIN IDEA Listen to the conversation. As you listen, think about the question below. Then write your answer on the lines.

According to Jennifer, in what ways are humans and other primates—such as chimpanzees and monkeys—similar?

_____

_____

1. Why is Jennifer going to take physical anthropology?

_____

2. What do students learn about in a physical anthropology class?

_____

3. What example does Jennifer give of chimpanzees using tools?

_____

4. How does Brandon think chimpanzee tool use is different from human tool use?

_____

5. What is one example of how nonhuman primates use language?

_____

6. How does Brandon think Koko's use of language is different from a human's use of language?

_____

LISTENING STRATEGY

Listening Strategy

Listening for Emotions

When you listen, you can hear both what people say and how they say it. The way people express themselves often shows how they are feeling. Paying attention to the emotions behind the words a person says will give you important information. Speakers can express emotions through word choice, stress, tone of voice, emotional behavior (laughing and crying), and nonverbal behavior (gestures and facial expressions).

Examples: Hey, that's not funny. (Happy)

Hey, that's not funny. (Angry)

In the first example, you can tell the speaker is happy because there is laughter in her voice. In the second example, the speaker has an angry tone of voice.

1. How does Jennifer feel about taking physical anthropology?

    A. She's happy about it.

    B. She's unhappy about it.

    C. She doesn't care about it.

2. How does Victor react to what Jennifer says?

    A. He's interested in this information.

    B. He's a little insulted or angry.

    C. He's not interested in the subject.

3. Which statement best describes how Victor's feelings change?

    A. First, he feels confident. Then he feels less confident.

    B. First, he's angry. Then he's less angry.

    C. First, he doesn't feel confident. Then he feels more confident.

4. How does Jennifer feel when she answers Brandon?

    A. She feels unsure of herself.

    B. She feels sure of herself.

    C. She feels confused.

5. Which statement best describes the way Victor feels?

    A. He is bored.

    B. He wants to talk about a different subject.

    C. He is excited.

AFTER LISTENING

A. GUESSING THE MEANING FROM CONTEXT Read the sentences below. The words and phrases in orange are from the conversation. Guess their meanings from the context. Write your guesses on the lines.

1. We plan ahead. We know we need to accomplish a task, like get food, and we design an **implement** specifically for that purpose.

   Guess: _____

2. Can this gorilla use sign language to make up original sentences? If so, then I would say that's "language." If not, then it's just **imitative behavior**.

   Guess: _____

3. Hey, Brandon, you sound angry. I guess you **take exception** to being compared to a chimpanzee.

   Guess: _____

Now compare your answers with a partner's answers.

Test-Taking Strategy

Synthesizing Information

Standardized tests often ask you to answer questions based on information from two or more sources. For example, you may get information from both a listening passage and a reading passage. Then you are given a question that requires your understanding of both passages. When you need to combine information from more than once source to increase your understanding of a topic, you are synthesizing information.

Example:

You hear:	A passage that gives a definition of art
You read:	An article about a chimpanzee named George who paints pictures
You are asked:	Based on the definition of art that you heard, are George's paintings "real art"?
You synthesize:	To answer, you use what you remember from both passages to explain why George is or is not a true artist.

You synthesize information when you take a test, write a paper, participate in a class discussion, or prepare a presentation.

B. SYNTHESIZING INFORMATION In the conversation, Brandon says:

"Can this gorilla use sign language to make up original sentences? If so, then I would say that's 'language.' If not, then it's just imitative behavior."

Look back at the reading from Part 1 on pages 33–34. Look for information that will help you answer this question:
- According to Brandon's definition, are gorillas and chimps capable of using language, or are they using just imitative behavior?

LANGUAGE FUNCTIONS

Expressing an Opinion

If you have strong feelings about a topic, you may want to give a strong opinion. Sometimes, however, you want to give a softer opinion, for example, if you're not sure or if you don't want to hurt someone's feelings. Strong opinions are often simple statements without anything added.

Example: **Strong:** Dr. Taylor gave a boring lecture today.

Adding an opinion expression (*It seems to me, I think, In my opinion*) tends to soften an opinion statement.

Examples: **Soft:** It seems to me that Dr. Taylor gave a boring lecture today.
I think Dr. Taylor gave a boring lecture today.
Dr. Taylor gave a boring lecture today, in my opinion.

Expressing Agreement or Disagreement

There are many ways to express agreement or disagreement with someone's opinion. Here are some phrases.

Examples:

Agreement		Disagreement
I agree. *	**Softer**	I'm not so sure about that.
I agree with that.		I don't agree.
I agree with you.		I disagree.
I'm with you.		I disagree with that.
You're right.		I disagree with you.
I couldn't agree more.		I completely disagree.
I completely agree.	**Stronger**	You're wrong.

You can soften disagreement by adding *sorry* or *I'm sorry*.

Examples: Sorry, I don't agree.
I'm sorry, but I disagree with you.

*Agree is a verb. It's incorrect to say *I'm agree*.

A. EXPRESSING AGREEMENT OR DISAGREEMENT With a partner, discuss the questions below. Practice expressing soft and strong opinions.

- Are chimpanzees intelligent?
- Can animals use tools?
- Is primate "language" the same as human language?
- Should we put wild animals in cages in zoos for human amusement?

Examples: **A:** Are chimpanzees intelligent?
B: In my opinion, they are very intelligent.
A: I'm not so sure about that.

Softening Disagreement

The most direct way to disagree with someone is to interrupt the conversation and state your opinion.

Examples: **A:** Chimpanzees are intelligent.
B: Wait a minute. I don't agree with that.
Hold on. I'm not sure I agree.
Hold on a minute. I'm not so sure about that.
Well, I don't think I agree with you.

However, such a direct and strong disagreement can seem like a personal attack on the speaker's judgment or ideas. For this reason, you usually want to soften your disagreement. In addition to using the word *sorry*, there are other ways to soften disagreement. You can appear at first to agree, add *but*, and then disagree.

Examples: **A:** Both humans and chimps use tools.
B: I agree, but I think our tools are much more complex.
That may be, but our tools are much more complex.
I understand what you're saying, but our tools are much more complex.

INTONATION

🎧 **Listening for Intonation to Express Disagreement**

Often your intonation alone–not your words–signals that disagreement will follow. This is perhaps the softest form of disagreement.

Notice the subtle differences in intonation (especially vowel length) in these examples.

Examples:	Agreement	Disagreement
	I agree.	I agree . . .
	I agree with that.	I agree with that . . .
	I completely agree.	I completely agree . . .

🎧 **B. LISTENING FOR INTONATION TO EXPRESS DISAGREEMENT** Listen to the conversations. Is Speaker B's disagreement *Soft*, *Neutral* (neither soft nor strong), or *Strong*? Circle the type of intonation you hear. Listen for the use of phrases such as *sorry*, agreement followed by the word *but*, and intonation.

1. Soft   Neutral   Strong

2. Soft   Neutral   Strong

3. Soft   Neutral   Strong

4. Soft   Neutral   Strong

5. Soft   Neutral   Strong

6. Soft   Neutral   Strong

🎧 **C. GUESSING THE MEANING FROM INTONATION** Listen to Speaker B's response in the conversations. In each case, Speaker B *says* he or she agrees, but is this true? Listen for Speaker B's intonation to decide what Speaker B is really thinking; in other words, do you expect Speaker B to add *but* and then disagree? Check (✓) your answers.

	Agrees	Will probably add *but* and disagree
1.	_____	_____
2.	_____	_____
3.	_____	_____
4.	_____	_____
5.	_____	_____

Now listen again to the conversations. Listen to how Speaker B finishes his thoughts. Check your answers.

PRONUNCIATION

🎧 Comparing /θ/, /s/, and /t/

The voiceless /θ/ sounds the same as /s/ to some students and /t/ to others, but these three sounds are pronounced differently. Listen to these contrasts.

/θ/	/s/	/t/
thank	sank	tank
thick	sick	tick
theme	seem	team
Beth	Bess	bet
path	pass	pat

The voiceless /θ/ sound is important in pronouncing many ordinal numbers.

fourth	seventh	tenth
fifth	eighth	eleventh
sixth	ninth	twelfth

Listen to these contrasts.

/θ/	/s/	/t/
fourth	force	fort
eighth	ace	eight
tenth	tense	tent

🎧 **D. HEARING THE DIFFERENCE BETWEEN /θ/, /s/, AND /t/** Listen to the following words. Circle the words you hear.

1. tank   sank   thank
2. tin   sin   thin
3. pat   pass   path
4. tick   sick   thick
5. fort   force   fourth

6. tie   sigh   thigh
7. mat   mass   math
8. tent   tense   tenth
9. eight   ace   eighth
10. bet   Bess   Beth

🎧 **E. PRONOUNCING /θ/, /s/, AND /t/** Look again at the words in Activity D. Listen. Repeat the words after the speaker.

🎧 **F. PRONOUNCING /θ/, /s/, AND /t/ IN SENTENCES** Read along as you listen to the conversation. Then listen again and repeat each sentence after the speaker. Pay special attention to words with /θ/.

A: You have an anthro class on Thursday, don't you?
B: Yeah. Anthro is at three-thirty.
A: Over on North Campus?
B: No. South Campus. It's in Thorne Hall.

PUT IT TOGETHER

👥 **AGREEING AND DISAGREEING** With a partner, choose five topics from the list below. Discuss the topics. Agree or disagree with your partner. Give soft, neutral, and strong opinions, depending on how you feel. Pay attention to intonation and choice of words to soften disagreement. Remember to pronounce /θ/ correctly.

Topics
- teaching language to chimps and gorillas
- whether chimpanzees and gorillas can really communicate
- a course or major you particularly like or dislike
- a musician or actor you like or dislike
- a computer game you like or dislike
- a website you visited recently
- a new TV show
- a movie you saw recently

PART ④ BROADCAST ENGLISH
What Happened to the Neanderthals?

BEFORE LISTENING

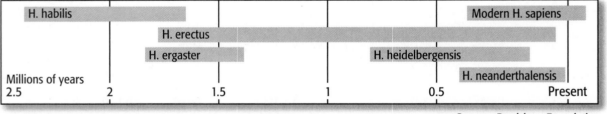

Timeline for Genus *Homo*

Source: Bradshaw Foundation

👥 **A. THINKING AHEAD** You are going to listen to a radio program about Neanderthals. Neanderthals were a **species** (a sub-category) of the *Homo* genus, the group of primates that includes humans. In small groups, see what you already know or can guess about Neanderthals before you listen to the program.

1. Could Neanderthals speak, or did they just **grunt** (make simple noises)?

2. Did Neanderthals have more hair than modern humans?

3. Do scientists think Neanderthals were as smart as humans today?

4. Did Neanderthals walk with bent knees, like chimpanzees?

5. Did modern humans kill all the Neanderthals?

6. Did modern humans **breed with** (have children with) Neanderthals?

This is what scientists today think a
Neanderthal looked like.

B. VOCABULARY PREPARATION Read the sentences below. The words and phrases in orange are from the radio program. Match the definitions in the box with the words and phrases in orange. Write the correct letters on the lines.

> **a. didn't have the right tools and resources**
> **b. disappeared**
> **c. grow well; multiply**
> **d. moving around; wandering around**
> **e. remains of things that lived a long time ago**
> **f. went back to**

_____ **1.** Neanderthals were **roaming around** Europe for thousands of years. They lived in various parts of the continent.

_____ **2.** The ancestors of modern humans originally lived in the north, but they later **retreated** to the south.

_____ **3.** Scientists have long wondered why Neanderthals suddenly **vanished** so long ago. There is no proof of their existence after a certain point in time.

_____ **4.** Is it possible that Neanderthals **were not equipped** to live in a cold climate?

_____ **5.** On the other hand, modern humans were able to **flourish** in the warmer climates of Africa. Their populations grew.

_____ **6.** We can tell a lot about plants and animals that lived long ago by studying their **fossils**.

Understanding Idioms and Slang

Speakers often use informal expressions such as idioms and slang. **Idioms** are groups of words that together have a meaning that is very different from the ordinary meaning of each separate word.

Examples:

adds weight to	→	makes more believable
dress for success	→	dress appropriately to make a good impression
it turns out that	→	we learned that

Slang phrases are very informal expressions often used by certain groups of people, such as teenagers or musicians. Slang is usually popular for a period of time and then becomes less common.

Examples:

can't hack it	→	isn't competent enough
do (someone) in	→	kill (someone)
wimp out	→	become scared; lose courage

While some idioms are acceptable in formal speech and writing, slang phrases are not. In general, people avoid using idioms and slang phrases in written English.

C. UNDERSTANDING IDIOMS AND SLANG The idioms and slang in the box above are from the radio program. Use them in the sentences below. If necessary, change the verb to the past tense.

1. Ethan wants to _____, so he wears a suit to work every day.

2. Sarah was going to ask Tom out on a date, but she _____ at the last minute.

3. The workload at my job has been extremely heavy for months. I'm afraid that this new assignment will _____ me _____.

4. Jack tried to study medicine, but he just _____. It was too hard for him.

5. New evidence _____ the idea that modern humans originated in Africa.

6. Scientists used to think that apes couldn't learn to use human language, but _____ they were wrong.

LISTENING

Listening for the Topic in an Introduction

You can often learn the topic of a radio program from the introduction. The host of the program may tell you the person who is being interviewed, his or her qualifications, and the topic of the interview. Listening closely for this type of information in the introduction will help you to focus and understand more.

A. LISTENING FOR THE TOPIC IN AN INTRODUCTION Listen to the introduction to the radio program. As you listen, write the answers to the questions below.

1. What is the topic of the radio program?

_____

2. What do you learn about the person being interviewed?

_____

B. LISTENING FOR THE MAIN IDEA Listen to the whole radio program. As you listen, write the answer to the question below.

Why didn't Neanderthals survive?

_____

_____

C. LISTENING FOR DETAILS Listen to the whole program again. Listen for the answers to the questions below. Write the answers.

1. What did modern humans in Europe have that Neanderthals didn't have?

_____

_____

_____

2. What did modern humans in Europe do that Neanderthals didn't do?

_____

_____

_____

3. When did Neanderthals die out? _____

4. What is the latest theory on Neanderthals? Did humans descend from them?

_____

_____

_____

Now look back at your answers in Activity A on page 44. Do you need to change any of your answers?

Interpreting Humor

Sometimes humor is universal; it is based on ideas that people all over the world share. Other times humor is difficult to understand, especially when the speakers are not speaking your native language or are not from your culture. Understanding cultural humor can take time. If you are having a hard time understanding humor, ask a native speaker to explain or interpret it for you.

D. INTERPRETING HUMOR Listen to part of the radio program. Then in small groups, discuss these questions:

• Can you explain the humor?
• Is the joke cultural or universal? (**Hint:** In the U.S., women sometimes jokingly refer to men as Neanderthals.)

AFTER LISTENING

DOING RESEARCH Find out more about Neanderthals. What else do scientists know about them? What is the current thinking about whether modern humans and Neanderthals **interbred** (bred between species)? Go to a search engine on the Internet and type in the key words:

Neanderthal "recent research"   Neanderthal extinction
"early humans"   "genus *Homo*"

Now, in small groups, share your research information.

PART ⑤ ACADEMIC ENGLISH
Human and Nonhuman Primate Behavior

BEFORE LISTENING

Dr. Jane Goodall and a wild chimp in Gombe, Tanzania

A. BRAINSTORMING In small groups, share your knowledge of primates and primate behavior by answering these questions.

1. What are some nonhuman primates? Try to think of at least six examples.

2. What do you already know or believe about the following:
    • how primates move from place to place
    • what primates eat
    • which primates use tools and how they use tools
    • how primates care for their offspring

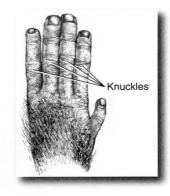

Knuckles

Lemurs, one type of prosimian

B. THINKING AHEAD You are going to hear a lecture about the behavior of humans and nonhuman primates. Before you listen, see how much you already know by answering these questions. Circle *T* if you think the statement is true; circle *F* if you think the statement is false. You'll learn the correct answers in the lecture.

1. Humans, apes, monkeys, and prosimians are all primates.   T   F

2. Humans, apes, monkeys, and prosimians share a common ancestor who   T   F
   lived millions of years ago.

3. Humans and monkeys share a common ancestor.   T   F

4. Most of the time baboons move around their environment by swinging   T   F
   through the trees.

5. Most of the time chimps and gorillas move around their environment by   T   F
   walking on the ground on four limbs but with the weight of the front limbs
   on the **knuckles** instead of the flat hands.

6. According to fossil evidence, our early human ancestors probably began to   T   F
   use and carry tools before they began to walk on two feet.

7. Two early species of humans (which don't exist today) are   T   F
   Australopithecus garhi and *Homo ergaster.*

8. In general, primates provide more parental care to their young than   T   F
   most other **mammals** (warm-blooded animals that produce milk for their offspring).

9. Humans differ from nonhuman primates in that only humans provide food   T   F
   for their offspring after the young are **weaned**—gradually become independent—
   from mother's milk.

10. One thing humans have in common with chimpanzees and gorillas is   T   F
    that all three species hunt for and eat meat.

Understanding Stems and Affixes

In academic English, and especially in scientific language, there are many words that have stems (the main part of a word) or affixes (prefixes and suffixes) that come from Greek or Latin.

Examples:	**Affix:**	pre-	→	before
	Word:	prehistoric	→	before written history
	Stem:	homo	→	human
	Word:	*Homo sapiens*	→	modern species of human beings

Knowing commonly used stems and affixes will improve your comprehension of spoken and written English and will increase your vocabulary.

Note: In addition to the Latin stem *homo*, meaning "human," there is the Greek prefix *homo-*, meaning "same, like." For example, the prefix *homo* is used in the words *homogeneous* and *homonym*.

C. UNDERSTANDING STEMS AND AFFIXES Below are some stems and affixes you will hear in the lecture. In small groups, brainstorm as many words as possible with these stems and affixes. Write them on the lines. If necessary, use a dictionary.

Prefixes	Meanings	Examples
bi-	two	bicycle, binary, bisect _____
quadr-	four	_____

Stems	Meanings	Examples
arbor	tree	_____
erg	work	_____
loc(o)	place	_____
mor(t)	death	_____
mot(or)	move	_____
pater/patr	father	_____
ped	foot	_____
terr	land, earth	_____

D. GUESSING THE MEANING FROM CONTEXT Read the sentences below. The words and phrases in orange are from the lecture. Guess their meanings from the context and from your knowledge of stems and affixes. Write your guesses on the lines.

1. An example of a **terrestrial quadruped** is the baboon.

   Guess: _____

2. The **locomotor** style of humans is referred to as **bipedalism**.

   Guess: (locomotor) _____

   Guess: (bipedalism) _____

3. The human ancestor that first used tools was *Homo ergaster*.

   Guess: _____

4. **Paternal** care involves provisioning (providing food), protection from predators, and infant transportation.

   Guess: _____

5. Young animals that have a large amount of parental care usually have a lower **mortality** rate.

   Guess: _____

Now compare your answers with a partner's answers.

E. TAKING NOTES: ABBREVIATIONS The following box contains some common abbreviations. Below the box is a list of words that you'll hear in the lecture. Write your own abbreviation for each one. Use the abbreviations for taking notes during the lecture.

Common Abbreviations			
approximately	→ approx./≈	relative	→ rel.
depend/dependent	→ dep.	similar/similarity	→ sim.
different/difference	→ dif.	unusual	→ unus.
distinct/distinction	→ dist.	usual	→ usu.
hypothesis	→ hyp.	year(s)	→ yr(s).
identity	→ ident.	million	→ mil.

1. behavior _____
2. human _____
3. nonhuman primate _____
4. primate _____
5. ancestor _____
6. chimpanzee _____
7. *Australopithecus garhi* _____
8. *Homo ergaster* _____
9. environment _____
10. termite _____

LISTENING

🎧 **A. LISTENING FOR THE MEANINGS OF NEW WORDS AND PHRASES** Listen to the following words and phrases in sentences from the lecture. Guess their meanings from the context. Write your guesses on the lines.

1. hand axes: _____

2. hypothesis: _____

3. predators: _____

4. primatologist: _____

5. propose: _____

Listening Strategy

Using a T-chart

As you learned in Chapter 1 (page 25), when taking lecture notes, you should use a graphic organizer that best fits the information. For example, if your professor is contrasting two ideas or two things, a **T-chart** is a good way to organize your notes.

Example:

Monkeys	Apes
tails	no tails
walk along tree tops	swing from branch to branch
deep chest	broad chest

👥 **B. PREDICTING** Look at the T-chart on page 55. With a partner, discuss these questions:
• What will the lecture compare?
• What specific things might be compared?

Listening for the Lecture Subtopics in an Overview

Some professors give an overview of their lecture at the beginning. In an overview, they may give you the main subtopics of the lecture they are about to deliver. They may also indicate the order in which they will discuss these topics. An introduction like this is a kind of roadmap. It lets you know where the lecture is going beforehand so you can be ready for each new subtopic.

When professors give you an overview, they might use one of the following phrases:

Specifically, I am going to discuss . . .
I'm going to cover X, Y, and finally Z.
First, I'll talk about X. Then I'll discuss Y. Finally, I'll cover Z.
I'm going to cover three topics today: X, Y, and Z.
Today, I'm going to cover: one–X; two–Y; and three–Z.

C. LISTENING FOR THE LECTURE SUBTOPICS IN AN OVERVIEW Listen to the introduction of the lecture. In the overview, the professor will mention four subtopics. As you listen, look at Sections 1, 2, 3, and 4 on pages 55–57. At the beginning of each section, fill in the subtopics that the professor mentions. In other words, what four behavior patterns of humans and nonhuman primates is the professor going to compare?

D. TAKING NOTES: INTRODUCTION Listen to the introduction again. In the box below, take notes on the main points in the introduction.

Introduction

1. _____ are primates

2. All 4 shared a common ancestor, _____

3. Will compare _____

E. TAKING NOTES: SECTIONS 1, 2, 3, AND 4 Listen to the lecture. You will listen to each section twice. Fill in as much of the T-charts as you can. Don't worry if you can't fill in everything. (You'll listen to the whole lecture again later.) Remember to use abbreviations.

Baboons use all four limbs to move from place to place.

Human and Nonhuman Primate Behavior

A sifaka with young clings to a tree.

Gibbons use their long arms
to swing in the trees.

Section 1: _____

Humans	Nonhuman Primates
_____ = walking on 2 hind limbs	1. _____ Ex: sifaka
Earliest evidence: _____ _____	2. _____ Ex: baboon
Earliest stone tools: _____ _____	3. _____ Ex: a. _____
One hypothesis: _____ _____ _____	b. capuchin monkeys 4. Knuckle-walking Ex: a. _____ b. _____ 5. Brachiation: _____ Ex: _____

Section 2: _____

Humans	Nonhuman Primates
1. Oldowan tool trad. = _____ _____	1. Goodall observed _____ _____ _____ _____
a. Began _____	
Ended _____	2. Another researcher found _____
b. Created by *Australopithecus garhi*	_____
2. New type of tool = _____ _____	_____ _____
a. Were used until _____ _____	However, tool use is _____ _____
b. Used for: _____ _____ _____ _____	_____ Also, _____
c. Used by *Homo ergaster*	

Section 3: _____

Humans	Nonhuman Primates
1. Dif: _____ _____	1. Dif: must _____ _____ _____

2. Dif: _____
 	
 _____
 	
    a. provisioning
 	
    b. _____
 	
    c. _____
 	
    d. _____
 	
    e. result: _____
 	
 _____
	2. Dif: _____

Section 4: _____

Humans	Nonhuman Primates
Much food provided by father = _____	1. Diet rarely has _____ 2. Exception: _____ _____

Source: Adapted from a lecture by Sharon Gursky, Ph.D, and Michael Alvard, Ph.D.

F. CHECKING YOUR NOTES Listen to the whole lecture again. As you listen, review your notes and fill in any missing information.

AFTER LISTENING

A. USING YOUR NOTES Use your notes to answer these questions. Don't worry about the ones you can't answer.

1. According to fossil, behavioral, and genetic data, at what point in time did humans and all other primates share a common ancestor?

   _____

2. What are five primate locomotor patterns? _____

   _____

3. Approximately, how long ago did the first bipedal human walk? _____

4. Why did early humans become bipedal? _____

   _____

   _____

5. How long ago were the first stone tools used? _____

6. What species of humans used Oldowan tools? _____

7. Until approximately when were these tools used? _____

8. What is an example of a nonhuman primate that uses tools, and what are two tools that it uses?

   _____

   _____

9. What is the main difference between humans and nonhuman primates in their use of tools?

   _____

   _____

   _____

10. What are two differences between human parenting and nonhuman primate parenting? _____

    _____

    _____

11. What is the only primate (besides humans) that hunts for meat? _____

In a small group, compare and discuss your answers.

B. CHECK WHAT YOU LEARNED Look back at Activity B (page 50). What have you learned? Do you need to change some of your answers?

C. DISCUSSION In small groups, discuss what surprised you or interested you in the lecture. Then make a list of everything that you've learned about primates. (Try not to look back at your notes.) When you finish, write three questions that you might expect to see on an exam. Then share your exam questions with your group.

D. MAKING CONNECTIONS Do Internet or library research to find out more about two of the species in the timeline for genus *Homo* in Part 4 (page 44) that were also mentioned in the lecture: *Australopithecus garhi* and *Homo ergaster* (sometimes called *Homo habilis*). Try to find answers to these questions:

• Where did they live?
• How were they similar to or different from each other?
• How were they similar to or different from later *homo* species?

PUT IT ALL TOGETHER

GIVING A PRESENTATION With a partner, prepare and give a presentation on one of the topics below.

STEP 1
With a partner, read the projects below and choose one to do. Then follow the directions for the project.

Project 1
If you have access to a VCR or DVD player, rent the film *Gorillas in the Mist* (1988), a true story about a woman who studied gorillas in their natural habitats in Africa. As you watch the film, take notes. Focus especially on the answers to these questions:

• What nonhuman primate behavior do you notice in the film that was mentioned in this chapter?
• What can you learn (from *Gorillas in the Mist*) about the behavior of gorillas in the wild?

Project 2
If you live near a zoo or wild animal park, spend an hour there observing nonhuman primates—sifakas, monkeys, gibbons, orangutans, gorillas, or chimps. As you watch them, take notes. Focus especially on the answers to these questions:

• What nonhuman primate behavior do you notice that was mentioned in this chapter?
• What behavior is similar to human behavior? What behavior is different?

Project 3
Choose *one* nonhuman primate—sifakas, monkeys, gibbons, orangutans, gorillas, or chimpanzees. Do some Internet or library research on the primate you choose. Find out about the primate's habitat, behavior, and distinguishing features. Take notes on what you learn. Websites that might be useful include:

• Indiana University's "African Primates at Home"
• The University of California Museum of Paleontology's "Primates: Apes, Monkeys, and You"
• The National Primate Research Center at the University of Wisconsin

STEP 2
With your partner, organize your notes and prepare for your presentation. Decide who will give each part of the presentation. Your presentation should be less than five minutes long. Be sure to:

• give an introduction to your topic
• tell how you researched your topic
• explain what you learned

Speaking Strategy

Making Eye Contact

When you give a presentation, it's important to make eye contact with your audience. Good eye contact helps to hold your listeners' attention. Look at the faces of the people you are speaking to. Here are some tips:

• If you are speaking to a big group, move your eyes around the room to look at everyone. Don't keep your eyes on just one member of the audience or one area of the room.
• If you are uncomfortable looking directly into a person's eyes, look at a spot just over the head.
• Try not to look at the ceiling or the floor.
• If you are referring to note cards, glance at them but always look up as you speak.
• If you are using a visual (a picture, diagram, or poster), don't look just at your visual.

Speaking Strategy

Asking Questions After a Presentation

Professors and other speakers often want the audience to ask questions when their lecture or presentation is finished. Sometimes you'll have a question in mind before the presentation begins; other times, you'll think of one while you are listening. While you are listening, write down your questions so you won't forget them when the time for questions comes. Asking questions after a presentation not only increases your knowledge on a subject; it also helps you to pay attention, and it shows the speaker that you are interested in the subject.

Example: **You hear:** *Gorillas in the Mist* is based on the true story of Dian Fossey and her attempts to protect the gorillas she was studying.
You write a note: Where?
After the presentation, you ask: Where was the movie filmed?

STEP 3

With your partner, give your brief presentation to the class. Remember to make frequent eye contact with your audience. At the end of your presentation, ask the audience for questions. As you listen to other presentations, write down questions to ask later.

UNIT (1) VOCABULARY WORKSHOP

Review vocabulary items that you learned in Chapters 1 and 2.

A. MATCHING Match the words and phrases to the definitions. Write the correct letters on the lines.

Words and Phrases   **Definitions**

_____ **1.** bet (verb)   **a.** suggest

_____ **2.** collisions   **b.** disappeared

_____ **3.** get off track   **c.** lost courage

_____ **4.** handy   **d.** theory

_____ **5.** hypothesis   **e.** continue with

_____ **6.** propose   **f.** went back to

_____ **7.** retreated   **g.** think; predict

_____ **8.** stick with   **h.** change the subject

_____ **9.** vanished   **i.** convenient

_____ **10.** wimped out   **j.** crashes

B. TRUE OR FALSE? Read the statements below. Circle *T* if the sentence is true. Circle *F* if the sentence in false.

1. If somebody **drives you nuts**, you probably want to spend a lot of time with him or her.   T   F

2. A person who is **skeptical** believes everything he or she hears.   T   F

3. "**Spatial**" rules are social rules that let us all know "how close is too close."   T   F

4. If you are **trespassing** on government land, you probably have permission to be there.   T   F

5. You might **take exception to** being compared to a chimpanzee if you find the idea insulting.   T   F

6. If you're **dressed for success**, you will probably do better in a job interview.   T   F

7. A primate that is **bipedal** walks on four legs.   T   F

8. A **predator** is an animal that is hunted by another animal.   T   F

C. SENTENCE HALVES Match the sentence halves. Write the correct letters on the lines.

_____ **1.** If you experience **nostalgia**, you

_____ **2. Quadrupeds**

_____ **3. Partitions**

_____ **4.** Scientists who are **primatologists**

_____ **5.** People who are **deaf**

a. study humans, apes, and monkeys.

b. can't hear.

c. walk on four legs.

d. may feel sad.

e. break large spaces into smaller ones.

D. THE ACADEMIC WORD LIST In the boxes below are some of the most common academic words in English. Fill in the blanks with words from these boxes. You will use some words twice. When you finish, check your answers in the readings on page 5 (for items 1–10) and page 33 (for items 11–20). For more words, see the Academic Word List on pages 315–318.

abandon	attributes	constant	culture	theme
achievement	brief	contrast	symbolic	

In a Chinese home, Tuan points out, "the only open space is the sky above." He

_____ this absence of space to Chinese rootedness to their place. For the
　　　　　1

Chinese, according to Tuan, "place is deeply felt. Wanderlust is an alien sentiment." Perhaps because

there was always "the _____ threat of war, exile, and the natural disasters of
　　　　　　　　　　　　　　　2

flood and drought," a common _____ in Chinese poetry was nostalgia—a
　　　　　　　　　　　　　　　　3

strong and sorrowful desire for home. There is respect for farmers because they are rooted to the

land and "do not _____ their country when it is in danger."
　　　　　　　　　4

In _____ to Chinese rootedness, Americans usually move from one
　　　　　5

place to another by choice; "the future beckons, and the future is 'out there' in open space." Tuan

_____ American rootlessness to the ideals of "social mobility and optimism
　　　　　6

about the future." In _____, homes in the two countries reflect the
　　　　　　　　　　7

_____ of each. *Place*—so important in China—is
　　　　　8

_____ of "_____ and stability." *Space*—so
　　　　　9　　　　　　　　　　　10

important in the United States—"symbolizes hope."

Experiments have shown that apes can learn to use, if not speak, true language (Miles 1983). Several apes have learned to _____ 11 with people in ways other than speech. One such _____ 12 system is American Sign Language, or ASL, which is widely used by deaf and mute Americans. ASL employs a variety of hand gestures, positions, and shapes, as well as facial expressions to _____ 13 words and meaning. These signs combine to form words and larger units of meaning.

The first chimpanzee to learn ASL was Washoe, a female. Washoe lived in a trailer and heard no spoken language. The _____ 14 always used ASL to _____ 15 with each other in her presence. The chimp gradually _____ 16 a vocabulary of more than 100 signs representing English words (Gardner, Gardner and Van Cantfort, 1989). At the age of two, Washoe began to combine as many as five signs into rudimentary sentences such as "you, me, go out, hurry."

The second chimp to learn ASL was Lucy, Washoe's junior by one year. From her second day of life, Lucy lived with a family in Norman, Oklahoma. Dr. Roger Fouts, a _____ 17 from the nearby _____ 18 for Primate Studies, came two days a week to test and improve Lucy's knowledge of ASL. During the rest of the week, Lucy used ASL to _____ 19 with the family. After _____ 20 language, Washoe and Lucy exhibited several human traits: swearing, joking, telling lies, and trying to teach language to others. Washoe, Lucy, and other chimps have tried to teach ASL to other animals, including their own offspring.

ECONOMICS

Chapter 3
Developing Nations

Chapter 4
The Global Economy

Developing Nations

Discuss these questions:

- What kind of work might this man do?
- What are some developing nations? What are some wealthy ones?
- In your opinion, is it possible to solve the problems of poor nations?

A hair-braiding salon in the United States

A. THINKING AHEAD In small groups, discuss these questions.

1. What does it mean to be poor? What does it mean to be wealthy?

2. How do economists define *poor* and *wealthy*? What are some other ways of defining these terms?

3. What basic items do people need to live? Why is it difficult for many people to acquire these things? Is it possible for all people to have these basic things? Why or why not?

4. Why might it be difficult for very poor people to receive a business loan from a bank?

5. What is most important for financial success? Rank your answers from 1 to 6.
   (1 = the most important, 6 = the least important)

   ___2___ **capital** (money to begin a business)

   ___3___ luck

   ___1___ hard work

   ___6___ **perseverance** (determination; not giving up)

   ___4___ education

   _____ other: _____

B. READING Read about **microcredit**. Work with three other students. Each student will read about *one* of the people below. Make sure that you understand your section well because you will need to explain it to the other members in your group.

What is microcredit?

Microcredit, a bank loan service that began with Grameen Bank in Bangladesh, is one solution to the problem of poverty. *Microcredit* refers to programs that give small loans to very poor people for self-employment projects. These people become **microentrepreneurs**–people who begin a small business. The money that they earn from their businesses helps them care for themselves and their families.

International Year of Microcredit 2005

At the heart of the Year of Microcredit are the millions of poor and low-income clients that have benefited from access to financial services. Here are a few of the people who have moved out of poverty, thanks to microcredit loans.

Uganda: A Local Call to Success

Fatima Serwoni (center) became one of the first village phone operators in Uganda.

5   Fatima Serwoni lives in the village of Namunsi in Uganda and runs a small store, selling food and household items. She has built her business with the help of a series of loans from FOCCAS, a local microfinance institution. Since
10   becoming a client, she has increased her weekly income by 80 percent and has consistently paid the school fees for her four children. With her most recent loan, Fatima purchased a mobile phone kit to
15   start a pay phone business, becoming one of the first "village phone operators" of MTN VillagePhone, an initiative of Grameen Foundation USA and MTN Uganda. Undeterred that her village has
20   no electricity, Fatima uses a car battery to charge her phone. With the nearest public pay phone more than four kilometers (2.5 miles) away, people in Fatima's community are happy to have convenient and affordable telephone access for the first time. Fatima is pleased with her new business, which has the added benefit of
25   attracting people to her store and generating greater profit to share with her family.

Mozambique: Staying Afloat

Lize Nhaca of Catembe owns a small fishing enterprise and is the winner of the Global Microentrepreneur Awards held in Maputo on November 4, 2004. In 2002, Lize, a widow with five children, was unable to work for three months due to illness.

When she recovered, many of her fishing nets were ruined. Lize decided to apply for a loan with Hluvuku-Adsema Fundo de Credito Male Yeru to cover the costs of resuming her business. Since then she has been granted four loans, the first one in January 2003 for a total of around US$260 and the most recent in September 2004 for around US$690.

With the basic financial services, Lize's commercial activities recovered allowing her to support her extended family of 16 members and start building a new concrete house. In addition, her company has generated four permanent job posts, seven temporary ones, and supports the business of self-employed women that buy her fish to sell in Catembe and Maputo. "The money lent by Hluvuku has given me many benefits," Lize said. "If not for those loans, when I recovered from my illness and found that the nets were ruined, I wouldn't have had the money to buy new nets or repair the boats."

United States of America: Styling a New Start

Fatimata Lonfo fled Cote d'Ivoire in October 2001. Now the proud owner of Windyla's Boutique and Hair Braiding Salon in Staten Island, New York, Fatimata credits her success to God, to perseverance, and to ACCION New York, a non-profit microfinance organization that gave her first small business loan. Her business supports her and her three children, the oldest of whom started community college this past fall. She was chosen as the winner of the New York contest of the Global Microentrepreneur Awards due to the great economic and social impact of her business on her family and community.

Bolivia: Three Children Finishing School

Fortunata María de Aliaga has sold flowers from a La Paz, Bolivia, street corner for as long as anyone can remember. When her children were young, she worked long days to give them the opportunity she never had— the chance to go to school. There were days when she barely had enough money to set up shop. Then, 15 years ago, Fortunata learned about Banco Sol, a bank affiliated with ACCION International. Together with three other women, she qualified for a loan that allowed her to buy flowers in bulk at a much cheaper rate. With a strong repayment record, Fortunata was approved for larger loans and began to borrow on her own. Today, Fortunata is proud to report that she put her savings to good use. "All three of my children finished school," she beams. "And I even had money left to make some improvements to my house!"

Fortunata María de Aliaga

Source: International Year of Microcredit 2005 (Website)

C. GETTING THE DETAILS Fill in the chart with information about the one person you read about. (Each member of your group read about one person.)

People	Countries	Types of Business	Number of People Who Benefit	Additional Information or Vocabulary
Fatima Serwoni	Uganda		many	
Lize Nhaca	Mozambique	fishing	60	
Fatimata Lonfo	US	Salon	3	
Fortunata María de Aliaga	Bolivia	flower sell	4	

Now share what you learned with the other members of your group. Do not simply hand your chart to other students to copy. Instead, *tell* your group what you learned. When other members explain what they learned, fill in the rest of your chart.

D. VOCABULARY CHECK Look back at the reading on pages 69–70. Find words or phrases to match the definitions below. Write the correct words and phrases on the lines. Line numbers are given in parentheses.

1. an organization for a specific purpose (5–10)

2. a business (25–30) _____ enterprise

3. an ability to communicate or connect with or something (20–25) _____ access

4. a woman whose husband has died (25–30) _____ widow

5. effect, impression, or influence (45–50) _____ impact

1. Most people who receive microcredit are women. How would you explain this fact?

2. Two facts about microcredit programs are that the repayment rate is very high—above 90 percent—and that they work well in rural areas but not usually very well in big cities. Brainstorm possible reasons for these two related facts.

3. Compare microcredit loans to giving people **welfare**—help (money, food, or housing) from the government for people in need. What are the advantages and disadvantages of each?

F. RESPONSE WRITING Choose *one* of the topics below. Write about it for 15 minutes. Try to use new vocabulary but don't use a dictionary. Just write as many ideas as you can.

• What was your reaction to the reading?
• What are your ideas on microcredit loans compared to welfare? Which is better? Why?
• What are your ideas on other ways to solve the problem of poverty?

PART ② SOCIAL LANGUAGE Solutions to Poverty

BEFORE LISTENING

A. THINKING AHEAD You are going to listen to Mike interview people on the street. He's going to ask for their opinions on how to end poverty. Discuss these questions in small groups:

• What do you think most of the people will say?
• Will most people think that welfare is a good idea? Explain your answer.

B. VOCABULARY PREPARATION Read the sentences below. The words in orange are from the interviews. With a partner, discuss the meanings of the words in orange.

1. When that airline was going out of business, there was an intervention by the government, which saved the company.

2. During his year of unemployment, Chris had to depend on handouts from his relatives in order to pay his bills.

3. I know Ben's words were harsh, but he's really not as hard and cruel as he sounded.

LISTENING

A. LISTENING FOR THE MAIN IDEA Listen to the interviews for the answer to this question:
• Do most people think that welfare is the solution to poverty?

Test-Taking Strategy

Listening for Details

In the listening section of a standardized test, you may have to listen to short conversations and then answer questions about what you heard. As you listen, it is a good idea to take brief notes. Use phrases and abbreviations, not complete sentences. This will help you remember important details about the conversation, and you will be better able to answer questions that follow.

B. LISTENING FOR DETAILS Listen to the interviews again and take notes in the chart on what the people say. Write short phrases, not complete sentences.

Speaker	What is this person's opinion?
1	
2	
3	
4	
5	
6	
7	

C. GUESSING THE MEANING FROM CONTEXT Listen to parts of the interviews again. This time, listen for explanations of the phrases below. Then write in your own words what you think the terms mean. You'll hear each part twice.

1. **no free lunch** = _____

2. **a safety net** = _____

Managing a Conversation

People often use words and phrases that do not have much meaning but serve an important purpose: they help the speaker manage the conversation. In other words, the speaker uses the words or phrases to gain time to think, to ask for clarification, or to give clarification.

Some words and phrases give the speaker time to think of what to say. They tell the listener, "I'm not finished talking yet. I'm still thinking." When you hear these, you know that you should wait and give the speaker a little time.

To Gain Time

As I say/said,	**More Formal**
Well,	
Uh, (or um)	↓
You know,	
Actually,	
Like	**Less Formal**

Example: A: Do you know anything about that new antipoverty program?
B: **Well, um, actually** . . . not really.

Speakers use other phrases to ask for clarification about something they don't understand.

To Ask for Clarification

Excuse me. What did you mean by that?	**More Formal**
Do you mean . . . ?	
Are you saying . . . ?	↓
So, you're saying . . . ?	
So, you mean . . . ?	
You mean . . . ?	**Less Formal**

These are phrases speakers use to clarify what they have said.

To Clarify
What I mean is . . .
I mean . . .
That is . . .

Example: A: **Do you mean** the government should never offer welfare?
B: **Well, what I mean is** the government needs to be careful about offering welfare to everyone.

Mike:	Hi. I'm doing interviews for Campus TV. May I ask you one question?
Speaker 1:	_____, I guess so. Sure.
	1
Mike:	What do you think should be done to end poverty?
Speaker 1:	_____ here in the States, or anywhere?
	2
Mike:	Anywhere.
Speaker 1:	_____, I think the government has to get involved. The
	3
	government needs to create more jobs.

Listening Strategy

Guessing the Meaning from Context: Proverbs

Every language has **proverbs**—well-known sayings that express some wisdom about life. If you hear a
proverb that is new to you, you can sometimes guess its meaning from the context.

Example: This class is very popular, so I recommend that you register soon. Remember, the early bird
catches the worm.

You can guess from the context that this proverb means you will have a better chance of success if you act as
quickly as possible.

🔊 **E. GUESSING THE MEANING FROM CONTEXT: PROVERBS** Listen to a part of an interview again.
🎧 Write the proverb that you hear. Then guess its meaning from the context. Write your guess on the lines.

Proverb: _____

_____

Guess: _____

_____

👥 In small groups, compare your guesses.

AFTER LISTENING

👥 **A. TAKING A SURVEY** You are going to interview two classmates about their solutions to the problem of
poverty. Read the questions in the chart on page 76 and think about your own answers. Then write
another question above how to solve poverty. Finally, ask two classmates the questions. Write their answers
in note form in the chart.

Questions	Classmate 1	Classmate 2
1. What can wealthy nations do to end poverty in their own countries?		
2. Do you have solutions for poor nations?		
3. Is welfare a good answer to the problem of poverty? Why or why not?		
4. Your question:		

B. DISCUSSING SURVEY RESULTS In small groups, discuss the results of the survey. Then discuss the questions below. (Try not to be in a group with someone you interviewed.)

• Did any of the ideas surprise you?
• Were there any unusual suggestions?
• Did a majority of students share similar ideas?

PART 3 THE MECHANICS OF LISTENING AND SPEAKING

Participating in a study group

INTONATION

🎧 Listening for Tone of Voice: Interjections

In conversation, interjections are words or phrases used to express some emotion. They are very common in conversation and carry meaning. However, the meaning is often communicated through the context or the tone of voice—the way that you say it. One interjection may have many different meanings. The tone of voice can completely change the meaning of the interjection.

Interjections		Meanings
Uh-huh.	→	Yes.
Uh-huh.	→	You're welcome.
Uh-huh!	→	Yes!
Uh-uh.	→	No.
Uh-oh.	→	There's a problem.
Yeah.	→	Yes.
Yeah!	→	I really agree!
Yeah?	→	Really? Is that true?
Yeah . . .	→	I don't think so . . .

Example: **A:** That econ lecture was pretty interesting.
               B: Yeah! (**Agreement**)
               C: Yeah . . . (**Disagreement**)

Sarcasm—saying the opposite of what you really mean—is often expressed through tone of voice.

Come on!	→	Please!
Come on.	→	You're not serious. (**Sarcasm**)
Yeah, right.	→	You're right./I agree.
Yeah, right.	→	You're wrong./I disagree. (**Sarcasm**)

Examples: **A:** I forgot to go to the grocery store.
               B: Come on! You said you wouldn't forget!

                A: I'm going to study all weekend.
               B: Come on. You always say that and then you sleep all weekend. (**Sarcasm**)

                A: We should review this article before the test.
               B: Yeah, right. I'm sure it'll be on the test.

                A: It's going to be an easy exam.
               B: Yeah, right. Maybe for you, but not for me. (**Sarcasm**)

A. LISTENING FOR TONE OF VOICE Listen to the conversations. What does the second speaker mean? Circle the correct letters.

1. A. Yes.
B. No.
C. You're welcome.
D. There's trouble.
E. I really agree!

2. A. Yes.
B. No.
C. You're welcome.
D. There's trouble.
E. I really agree!

3. A. Yes.
B. No.
C. You're welcome.
D. There's trouble.
E. I really agree!

4. A. Yes.
B. No.
C. You're welcome.
D. There's trouble.
E. I really agree!

5. A. Yes.
B. No.
C. I don't think so.
D. There's trouble.
E. I really agree!

6. A. Yes.
B. No.
C. You're wrong.
D. There's trouble.
E. I really agree!

LANGUAGE FUNCTIONS

Giving Advice and Suggestions: *Should, Ought to* + Verb

To give advice, use the modals *should* or *ought to* + verb. *Should* and *ought to* mean "it's a good idea." You can give advice to another person (*you, he, she, they*) or to yourself (*I, we*).

Example: **A:** So what do you think I **should do** about my physics class?
B: I think you **ought to join** a study group.

To express "it's not a good idea," use *shouldn't* + verb*.

Example: I think you **shouldn't worry** about it.

You can make advice even more forceful by adding *really* before *ought to* or *should*.

Example: You **really ought to** join a study group.

Similar to advice, suggestions are given when you want to be helpful. They're less forceful than advice. Use *can, could, might,* or *Why don't you* . . . ? when making suggestions.

Suggestions: You **might join** a study group.
You **could join** a study group.
Well, you **can join** a study group.
Why don't you join a study group?**

Ought to isn't used very often in the negative form.
**This seems like a question but is usually, in fact, a suggestion. Use this structure only with *I, you,* or *we*.

Listen to Speaker A's problems. Choose appropriate cues from the box to give advice or suggestions to Speaker A. Write your suggestions on the lines.

~~ask the teacher~~	**look for a biography on the Internet**
do more research	**start now**
go to the library	**study with me tonight**

1. Why don't you ask the teacher? _____
2. _____
3. _____
4. _____
5. _____
6. _____

Commenting on Past Actions

Often, people make comments about something that happened in the past—when it's too late and when advice can't really be of any help. To comment on past actions, use the same modals as for advice: *should* and *ought to*. To make the meaning past, add *have* + the past participle of the verb.

Example: **A:** What do you think **we should have done**?

B: We **should have started** this presentation earlier.

C: We **ought to have started** this last week.

To make a negative comment about a past time, use *shouldn't have* + the past participle.

Example: **We shouldn't have waited** so long to get started on this.

🎧 **C. COMMENTING ON PAST ACTIONS** Listen to Speaker A's problems. Choose appropriate cues from the box to make a comment about each one. Write your comments on the lines.

ask the T.A. to explain it	**budget your money better**	**study harder**
be more careful	**start earlier**	**use more sources**

1. We should have started earlier. _____
2. _____
3. _____
4. _____
5. _____
6. _____

PRONUNCIATION

🎧 Reduced Forms of Words: Giving Advice and Suggestions

You learned about reduced forms in Chapter 1 (page 12). Here are some examples of reduced forms in phrases for giving advice and suggestions.

Examples:

	Long Forms		**Reduced Forms**
	We ought to do it.	→	We otta do it.
	Why don't you do it?	→	Why doncha do it?
	You ought to have done it.	→	You otto uv done it.
	We shouldn't have done it.	→	We shudden uv done it. OR We shuddena done it.
	Jim should have done it.	→	Jim shud uv done it. OR Jim shudda done it.

🎧 **D. REDUCED FORMS OF WORDS** Listen to these sentences. You'll hear the reduced forms of some words. Write the *long* forms on the lines.

1. Microsoft _____ build the factory here.

2. Microsoft _____ built the factory there.

3. Why _____ take that class?

4. The government _____ started a microcredit program.

5. The government _____ started a microcredit program.

6. They _____ raised taxes.

PUT IT TOGETHER

👥 **GIVING ADVICE AND SUGGESTIONS** Work with a partner. Use the cues in the box below and on page 81. Student A gives advice or suggestions. Student B responds with an appropriate interjection.

Example: **A:** We should do this project together.

      B: Yeah.

Student A thinks it would be good . . .	Student B . . .
to go to the library.	agrees.
for Student B to take a few more classes.	expresses sarcasm.
to take a survey and get students' opinions before doing their class presentation.	strongly agrees.
Student A thinks it would have been good . . .	**Student B . . .**
if Student B had bought a new computer.	indicates "no."
if Student B had not invited so many guests to the party.	is hesitant; doesn't really agree.

Now exchange roles.

Student A thinks it would be good . . .	Student B . . .
to plan a class party.	strongly agrees.
to hire a rock band to play live music.	indicates "no."
for Student B to do all of the cooking for the party.	expresses sarcasm.
Student A thinks it would have been good . . .	**Student B . . .**
if Student B had not overslept.	agrees.
if Student B had gone to bed earlier.	doesn't really agree.

PART ④ BROADCAST ENGLISH Bangladesh Primer

BEFORE LISTENING

A. THINKING AHEAD You are going to hear a radio program about Bangladesh. In small groups, discuss these questions.

1. Look at the map of the Indian subcontinent. When this area was under British rule, the countries immediately to the west and east of India were part of India. When the British left, the country was **partitioned**. What are these two countries today? What do you know about these two countries?

2. What is the major religion of these two countries? What is the major religion of India?

3. What do you know about the climate and seasons in this area? What might be good about the **monsoon** season—a time of heavy wind and rain (often **floods**)? What might be bad about this?

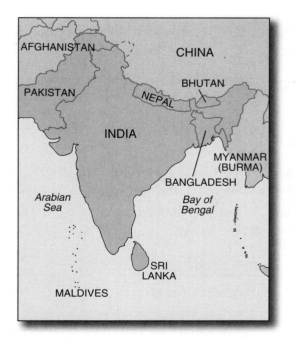

The Indian **subcontinent**, which includes India, Bangladesh, Bhutan, Nepal, Pakistan, and Sri Lanka.

4. Why might a **dam** be especially important in a country that often experiences floods?

B. VOCABULARY PREPARATION Read the sentences below. The words and phrases in orange are from the radio program. Match the definitions in the box with the words and phrases in orange. Write the correct letters on the lines. (There are two answers for each sentence.)

a. amazing	f. everywhere in the country
b. changed	g. having enough to stay alive but with nothing left over
c. clothes	
d. coming from ordinary people and organizations	h. help (often financial)
e. a country or person who receives something	i. people who gain from something good
	j. possiblity

_____ _____ **1.** Xenrovia is a **recipient** of **aid** from the United Nations, but the country soon won't need this money.

_____ _____ **2.** The situation has **shifted**. Economic development used to come from the government, but today there is more of a **grassroots** effort.

_____ _____ **3.** Andrew owns a factory that produces ready-made **garments** that he sells to clothing stores **nationwide**.

_____ _____ **4.** A recent **extraordinary** discovery of a natural resource in Xenrovia has created the **potential** for a new export industry in the near future.

_____ _____ **5.** The **beneficiaries** of this program will be those people living below the **subsistence** level because they are the poorest of the poor.

LISTENING

A. LISTENING FOR BACKGROUND INFORMATION: SECTION 1 In this radio program called "All Things Considered," the host talks with Ambassador Teresita Schaffer.

Listen to Section 1 of the program twice. As you listen, fill in the graphic organizer with information about Bangladesh's history.

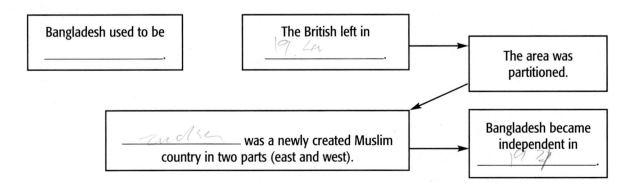

B. LISTENING FOR MAIN IDEAS: SECTION 2 Listen to Section 2. As you listen, check (✓) the answers to the question below.

• Which adjectives can describe Bangladesh?

_____ flat   _____ wet   _____ crowded

_____ normal   _____ abnormal   _____ social

Listening Strategy

Listening for Supporting Statistics

In radio programs, presentations, and lectures, speakers often make an **assertion** (statement) and then give **statistics** (numerical data) to support it. The statistics strengthen the speaker's argument and make it more believable.

Example: Assertion: Poverty has been eradicated in Xenrovia.
              Supporting statistic: For one thing, unemployment is no longer a problem. We've seen the unemployment rate go from 9 percent to 4 percent in just 5 years.

When you hear an assertion, listen for statistics or other facts to support the statement. Be prepared to write down important statistics. You may also need to remember facts and statistics for an exam.

C. LISTENING FOR SUPPORTING STATISTICS Listen to part of Section 2 again and write on the lines the statistics you hear.

Host: In the case of Bangladesh, I suppose, Ambassador Schaffer, it's fair to say that geography is destiny.

Schaffer: Well, geography has certainly marked the place. Uh, Bangladesh is about the size of Minnesota, and, uh, is flat as a pancake. In a normal dry season, about _____ of its land area is rivers. It's the delta of the Ganges and

                1
the Brahma Putra, which come together. And in a normal monsoon season, that percentage goes up to over _____. The floods that you read

                                  2
about in the newspapers are in the abnormal monsoon seasons, when _____ of the country may be under water.

             3

Host: But even a normal monsoon season, you're saying, uh, leaves the country awfully wet.

Schaffer: That's right.

Now discuss this question with a partner:
• What idea do these statistics support?

1. How does social distance in Bangladesh compare to that in India or Pakistan?

   _____

2. What is the reason for this? _____

   _____

This bridge is part of Bangladesh's **infrastructure** (basic system of public works, including roads, bridges, dams, and power supply).

E. LISTENING FOR DETAILS: SECTION 3 Listen to Section 3. Listen for details that will help you answer the questions below. Write your answers on the lines.

1. In the past, what was the economic focus of Bangladesh? What has the focus been on recently?

   Past: _____

   _____

   Recently: _____

   _____

2. What significant export industry does Bangladesh have now? _____

   _____

3. What is an important potential export industry? _____

   _____

   _____

4. What does Ambassador Schaffer say about microcredit programs? Check (✓) the answers below.

   _____ Many people have been affected.

   _____ There are 120 million participants.

   _____ Microcredit programs are almost everywhere in the country.

   _____ The people who participate live below the subsistence level now.

   _____ The people who participate can now earn cash income.

AFTER LISTENING

A. DISCUSSION The host of the radio program says that "geography is **destiny**"—in other words, geography determines a future that we cannot avoid. In small groups, discuss these questions.

1. How has geography been the "destiny" of Bangladesh? That is, how has the economy of the country been affected by its geography?

2. Think of several countries, anywhere in the world, for which geography has been their destiny. How has the geography affected the lives of the people who live there?

B. EXPANSION: INTERNET RESEARCH Think of a country to research on the Internet or in the library. Find answers to the questions in the chart on page 86. Write your answers in the chart.

Questions	Country: _____
What is the geography of the country or region?	
How has the geography affected the economy?	
What are its export industries?	
Are there other potential industries?	
What have been recent major infrastructure projects?	
Are there any programs (such as microcredit) to raise people out of poverty?	

In small groups, share the information you found. Discuss similarities and differences between the countries or regions that were researched.

PART 5 ACADEMIC ENGLISH
Amartya Sen and Development Economics

BEFORE LISTENING

Amartya Sen receiving the Nobel Prize for Economics

A. THINKING AHEAD You are going to listen to a lecture about Amartya Sen, the 1998 recipient of the Nobel Prize for Economics. In small groups, discuss these questions:

- What do you know about famines?
- What causes them?
- Where have famines occurred in recent history?

B. HAVING QUESTIONS IN MIND Look at the outline for the lecture on pages 89–91. What questions do you expect (or want) the lecturer to answer? Is there anything that you're curious about? Write three questions on the lines.

Question 1: _____

_____

Question 2: _____

_____

Question 3: _____

_____

Compare your questions with a partner's questions. Then look at the questions in Activity A on page 92. Are any of these similar to the questions you or your partner wrote?

C. GUESSING THE MEANING FROM CONTEXT Read the sentences below. The words and phrases in orange are from the lecture. Guess their meanings from the context. Write your guesses on the lines.

1. Although Ade was born in a developing nation, he came from a **well-to-do** family and always had adequate food, clothing, and educational opportunities.

   Guess: _____

2. Three million people **starved** to death in the 1943 Bengal famine that occurred in what is now Bangladesh and northeastern India.

   Guess: _____

3. There was no rain for six months last year. This led to a serious **drought** that killed all the crops.

   Guess: _____

4. That part of the country was hit hard by **natural disasters** last year: first a drought, followed by a flood, and then an earthquake.

   Guess: _____

5. In a country with an **authoritarian regime**, only one person (or a few people) has absolute power, and the citizens have little or none.

   Guess: _____

6. When there were food shortages, many people **hoarded** food: They bought all they could, and the market shelves were empty in a very short time. This only made the shortage situation worse.

Guess: _____

7. In order to **avert** a food shortage next time, the government is trying to educate people not to hoard.

Guess: _____

8. If resources were distributed among all the citizens **equitably**, then everyone would have the same amount and no one would be without food.

Guess: _____

9. The **gross domestic product** of a country represents the value of all the goods and services that the country produces, but it's not a good indicator of how rich or poor the citizens of a country are, according to Amartya Sen.

Guess: _____

10. Members of the **press** reported the economic problems in newspapers and magazines.

Guess: _____

Now compare your answers with a partner's answers.

D. TAKING NOTES: ABBREVIATIONS Write your own abbreviations for these words and phrases from the lecture.

1. famine   _____

2. poverty   _____

3. development   _____

4. democracy   _____

5. gross domestic product   _____

6. government   _____

7. percentage   _____

8. society   _____

9. economics   _____

10. quote   _____

11. unquote   _____

12. population   _____

Now, in small groups, compare your abbreviations.

LISTENING

🎧 **A. TAKING NOTES: SECTIONS 1, 2, AND 3** Listen to the lecture. You will listen to each section twice. Fill in as much information as you can but don't worry if you can't fill in everything. (You'll listen to the whole lecture again later.) Remember to use abbreviations. You will listen to Sections 4 and 5 in Activity C (page 90).

Amartya Sen and Development Economics

Section 1

Background information about Amartya Sen: _____

_____

Examples of recent famines: _____

_____

Traditional ideas about causes of famine: _____

_____

Section 2

Causes of famine:

    Not _____

    Instead, _____

Where are there no famines? _____

Why is this the case?_____

_____

    Supporting information: _____

_____

Section 3

Who dies in a famine?	Who is not affected?
Ex:	

Listening for Quoted Material

Speakers and writers use quoted material to support points that they are making. In print, we use quotation marks to indicate quoted material.

Example: Amartya Sen has said, "It is not a question of more or less government but what kind of government."

When speakers refer to quoted material, they often say "quote" at the beginning of a quoted statement and "unquote" at the end. Here is an example:

Example: Amartya Sen has said, quote, "It is not a question of more or less government but what kind of government," unquote.

If the speaker is quoting a short statement, he or she might say "quote unquote" together, at the beginning of the quoted material.

Example: In 1970, Amartya Sen published *Collective Choice and Social Welfare* in which he offered an answer to U.S. economist Kenneth Arrow's quote unquote "impossibility theorem."

B. LISTENING FOR QUOTED MATERIAL Listen to Section 3 again. Listen for a quote. Then write a paraphrase (explanation in your own words) of the quote.

_____

_____

C. TAKING NOTES: SECTIONS 4 AND 5 Listen to Sections 4 and 5. You will listen to each section twice. Fill in as much information as you can.

Section 4

What can be done to avert famines?

1. _____

   Why? _____

2. _____

   How? _____

   _____

Section 5

1. Summary: Two factors that cause famine: _____

2. A mistake: _____

3. Sen's "poverty index" = _____

   + _____

4. Two examples of countries that are taking care of the poorest people:

   1. _____

     How? _____

   2. _____

     How? _____

      GDP per person/average income = _____

      But: life expectancy = _____

       adult literacy = _____

Listening Strategy

Noting a Point of Greater Importance

During lectures, professors often give a list of reasons, causes, effects, events, and so on. When taking notes, you need to write these down in order, with a number for each.

However, sometimes one of these points is more important than the others. The professor will indicate this in one of several ways, among them:

It's most important to note that . . .
However, even more serious is . . .
And here we find the central cause . . .
More importantly, . . .

When the professor indicates a point of greater relative importance, you need to indicate this in your notes. Simply put an asterisk (*) or check mark (✓) next to the number of the point.

D. NOTING A POINT OF GREATER IMPORTANCE Listen to part of Section 4 again. Listen for the point of greater importance. In your notes, mark the point with an asterisk (*) or a check mark (✓).

E. CHECKING YOUR NOTES Listen to the whole lecture again. As you listen, review your notes and fill in any missing information.

AFTER LISTENING

A. USING YOUR NOTES Work in small groups and use your notes to discuss these questions.

1. What was happening in India when Sen was growing up?

2. Where were some famines in recent history?

3. What are some traditional beliefs about the causes of famine?

4. What are the true causes of famine, according to Sen?

5. In which kinds of countries is there no famine?

6. What is Sen's explanation for this? (In other words, what happens in case of a natural disaster in these countries?)

7. How can we prevent famine?

8. Why is it a mistake for economists to use GDP as an indicator of poverty, according to Sen?

9. What does Sen's "poverty index" refer to?

10. Why is Costa Rica an example of a country that's doing things right?

Speaking Strategy

Using Latin Terms

People often use Latin terms in formal speaking situations. The more you hear them, the better you'll understand them. Once you are comfortable with them, using them in academic speaking situations can make you sound more fluent. Here are some common Latin terms.

Latin Terms		Meanings
a priori	→	before the fact
ad hoc	→	for this purpose
ad nauseam	→	to the point of nausea; repeatedly, endlessly
modus operandi	→	way of doing something; method of procedure
per se	→	by itself
pro forma	→	made or done in a routine manner
quid pro quo	→	this for that (you do something for me, and I'll do something for you)
verbatim	→	word for word; literally

Example: According to Amartya Sen, famines are not caused by any natural disaster per se.

B. USING LATIN TERMS Read the sentences and change the words in orange to the appropriate Latin phrases.

per se

1. A country's Gross Domestic Product ~~by itself~~ does not necessarily determine the quality of life of the people.

2. Brad complained endlessly about the way the government handled the problem; we got tired of listening to him after a while.

3. To look at the problem of poverty, the government established two committees just for this purpose. (**Note:** put this phrase before the noun.)

4. The newspaper reported what the president said word for word in order to be completely accurate.

5. Let's study the previous committee's method of procedure. Since they were successful in solving similar problems, we can do things in the same way.

Now say these sentences out loud with a partner.

C. MAKING INFERENCES Discuss these questions with a partner:
- What probably contributes to the high life expectancy in Costa Rica? In other words, how is it possible for people in a poor country to be so apparently healthy?

D. DISCUSSION On a separate piece of paper, write your answer to this question. Then in small groups, discuss your answers.
- What information from the lecture surprised you or interested you? Make a list of everything that you've learned about development economics. (Try not to look back at your lecture notes.)

Critical Thinking Strategy

Applying Information

You frequently need to apply information that you have learned to a new situation. For example, you may need to apply information to an exam question or to a new assignment. Frequently, you need to use this strategy of **application** on an essay exam to prove to the professor that you truly understand the material covered in class.

Example: Your exam question: How can Sudan avoid famines in the future?
You apply the information: According to Amartya Sen, public employment programs can help avert future famines.

E. APPLYING INFORMATION Think of a recent or current famine anywhere in the world. With a partner, discuss possible causes based on what you learned in the lecture.

F. MAKING CONNECTIONS With a partner, write six questions that you might expect on an exam about the eradication of poverty. Three questions should be about the radio program in Part 4, and three should be about the lecture in Part 5.

Part 4 Radio Program (pages 82–85)

1. _____

2. _____

3. _____

Part 5 Lecture (pages 89–91)

4. _____

5. _____

6. _____

When you finish, exchange questions with another pair of students. Write answers to their questions.

PUT IT ALL TOGETHER

GIVING A PRESENTATION In a small group, you are going to research, prepare, and give a short presentation.

STEP 1

In a small group, read the following projects. Choose one for your group's topic; don't do the research yet.

Project 1
Do Internet or library research to find out about hunger in your community. Research these questions:

• Why is hunger a problem in your community?
• What are people doing to correct the problem?
• What are organizations in the community doing?
• Are these efforts effective? Why or why not?

Project 2
Do Internet or library research to find out about microcredit. (**Hint:** Try the website for Grameen Bank.) Research these questions:

• Who started microcredit?
• Where and when did it start?
• How well is it working today?
• What is its future?

Project 3
Do Internet or library research to find out more about Amartya Sen's life. Research these questions:

• What was Sen's career path?
• What stimulated his interest in development economics?
• What else does he do?
• What is his most recent work or project?

Project 4

Do Internet or library research on a famine in history. Research these questions:

• How did the famine occur?
• Under what government did the famine take place?
• How long did the famine last, and why did it end?
• How could the famine have been avoided, according to Amartya Sen's economic theories?

Project 5

Do Internet or library research to find the statistics for Gross Domestic Product (GDP) or average income, educational level, life expectancy, and adult literacy in any five countries. (**Hint:** Try the website for the Human Development Report.) Research these questions:

• What do you notice about the statistics for the five countries? Compare and analyze them.
• Do countries with a high GDP usually have better statistics in the other areas?
• How do you think adult literacy affects the other areas?

Speaking Strategy

Negotiating Responsibilities for a Group Presentation

When you need to give a group presentation in class, prepare for it by dividing the tasks. Each person should do what he or she does best and feels most comfortable with. For example, one person might be in charge of doing the Internet research. Another might do library research and find articles, books, and visuals.

Example: **A:** Who would like to do the Internet research?
B: I have a computer, so I can do that.
C: When you have the information, I can help you organize it.
A: I don't have a computer, but I could do some research at the library.

Together, decide who will present which information. At this point, each person becomes responsible for putting his or her information in note form onto note cards and practicing it.

STEP 2

After choosing a project, do your Internet or library research. Look for answers to the questions listed for your project. (To review how to choose key words for an Internet search, see Chapter 1, page 30.) Negotiate who will do what. Take notes.

Speaking Strategy

Taking Turns

When you collaborate in a group, it's important to take turns talking. If you like to talk, make sure to give quieter group members a chance to speak. You can help them by asking them for their opinions.

Examples: Mario, what's your opinion about this information? Should we use it?
Pat, what is your answer to this question?

If you don't like to talk, force yourself to make at least one comment. If you are shy, sometimes it helps to write down your ideas first, and then say them.

STEP 3

In your group, go over the notes and organize the information. Take turns speaking and make sure everyone participates in the discussion. Decide who will give each part of the presentation.

Practice giving your presentation without looking at your notes. Don't read from your notes. Time your presentation to make sure it's not too long. Think of ways to make it interesting: Would visuals (pictures and graphics) help? Would a map, table, or graph make something clearer? If so, make visuals a part of your presentation.

STEP 4

Give your group presentation. Be sure to:
• use your notes; don't read
• make eye contact with your audience
• ask for questions from the audience when you are finished

As you listen to each presentation, write down any questions to ask later. Be prepared to ask a question or tell the speakers what was interesting in the presentation.

CHAPTER 4

The Global Economy

Discuss these questions:
- What's the woman doing?
- What might her country sell to other countries?
- What products do you buy that come from other countries?

PART 1 INTRODUCTION Responding to the Needs of Developing Nations

A remote village in Nepal

Deforestation in the Amazon

A. THINKING AHEAD In small groups, discuss these questions.

1. What makes some countries poor and others rich?

2. What challenges do countries with little fuel, water, and other natural resources have? What are some possible solutions to these challenges?

3. What modern technologies might be appropriate in **developing nations** (nations with a low level of industry, productivity, and technology)? Why might they be appropriate?

B. VOCABULARY PREPARATION: INTERNET TERMS In the next reading, there are some terms related to Internet technology. In small groups, share what you know about the terms in the box. Then write the correct letters on the lines.

a. be connected	**c. connectivity**	**e. virtual whiteboard**
b. connect virtually	**d. digital divide**	**f. wireless networking**

_____ **1.** connecting to communication systems without the use of wires

_____ **2.** a computer application that allows people in different locations to share ideas by writing on and making changes to the same computerized board at the same time

_____ **3.** the condition of being connected to others by means of computers and/or the Internet

_____ **4.** the gap between people who have access to technology and people who do not

_____ **5.** communicate with other people by computer and/or over the Internet; that is, not face-to-face

_____ **6.** be able to communicate with other computers and/or other computer users

C. READING Read about technologies in developing nations. As you read, think about this question:
• How is modern technology solving problems in resource-poor nations?

Solar Ovens

For all of his working life, John Roche was a research engineer with a passion for solar technology. When he retired, he thought about where in the world solar
5 energy could be used most effectively. The answer seemed clear: developing nations with a scarcity of wood and an abundance of
10 sunlight. So Roche and two partners founded the Solar Oven Society in Minneapolis, MN. Solar ovens use
15 sunlight to heat and cook food.

Limenih, a native of Ethiopia, had been coming to the Solar
20 Oven Society for several months. Limenih belongs to an organization of Ethiopian immigrants who are trying to transfer U.S. technology to
25 Ethiopia. He dreams that the widespread use of solar ovens could help alleviate droughts.

A Cambodian family with their new solar oven

At first, Limenih was skeptical about solar ovens—that is, he says, "until I ate the rice out of it, and chicken. And it even baked our bread. I tasted it, then I started believing."

In Ethiopia, so many trees have been cut down that the climate has changed and droughts are more frequent, a problem Limenih has seen first-hand. In fact, he has seen rivers dry up and forests disappear in his own lifetime.

Now Limenih's organization is sending Solar Oven Society cookers home to Ethiopia.

Since it first started producing them, the Solar Oven Society has sent over 700 cookers to 25 developing countries. However, cost and other obstacles currently stand in the way of their widespread use.

But Solar Oven Society co-founder Mike Port believes those obstacles will someday be overcome. Says Port: "I like to remind people that it took the paper clip 17 years to be accepted."

Source: "Solar Oven Society Hopes to Make a Difference" (Losure)

Wireless in South Africa

In South Africa, students and teachers in five schools across the country "talk" to each other using virtual whiteboards, microphones, and the World Wide Web, thanks to the Ulwazi e-learning project.

Using just some basic wireless networking equipment and computers, the set-up is cost effective and simple for teachers and students, according to those behind the project.

The project is just one example of how wireless technology is helping bridge the digital divide, giving people in less affluent or more remote areas a cheaper, more efficient and just as effective way to connect virtually.

The growing use of wireless—and the relatively low expense of setting up such a system compared to building fiber-based networks like those used in the United States and other affluent areas—has made it more possible to set up communication systems in previously hard-to-reach places.

And cutting the need to build complex, expensive infrastructure means skipping a big step that had long divided developed and less developed areas, says Dennis Stipati, the director of International Markets for Motorola's Canopy Wireless Broadband group.

"This allows people to stay connected and be involved around the world, and I think that it means a lot to each country to have [widespread Internet connectivity]," said Stipati. "It is really bringing the whole world closer together, and [wireless technology] is becoming a basic service."

"To do these types of things allows students everywhere to get a good education, and to be competitive in the modern world," said Stipati. "We're enabling these different parts of the world to be connected."

Source: "Wireless Third World" (Botelho)

A South African student uses a virtual whiteboard to answer his instructor who is miles away.

Fab Labs

95   Remember the *Star Trek* Replicator machine? It made a copy of all the molecules of any given object and stored them in what would have to be the universe's biggest database. Whenever

100 Captain Kirk or his crew needed anything, the Replicator would cheerfully spit out a shiny new copy of the desired object.

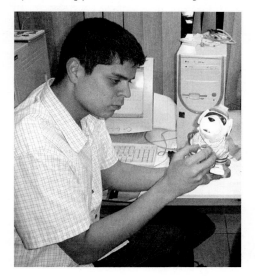

At a Fab Lab in Costa Rica, a student designs an electronic toy to be manufactured locally.

    We'll probably need to wait a couple of centuries for someone to come up with a

105 real world machine that's as capable as the Replicator. Meanwhile, MIT's Center for Bits and Atoms "Fab Labs" may be the next best thing.

    The Fab Lab, first built in 2002, is a

110 hands-on laboratory that provides the technology needed to build just about anything from inexpensive and locally available materials.

    Fab Labs have opened up all around

115 the world, from Boston's South End to far above the Arctic Circle. Recently, a team from the MIT center set up a Fab Lab on the campus of the Takoradi Technical Institute in southwestern Ghana.

120   Like other Fab Labs, the Ghana lab has about $20,000 dollars worth of equipment . . . along with associated computers, software, small electronics tools, and component parts.

125   The Ghana lab is working on practical projects, including antennas and radios for wireless Internet networks and solar-powered machinery for cooking, cooling, and cutting. Fab Lab staff developed

130 activities with local users to address unmet needs.

    A Fab Lab that opened in August, 2002, near Pabal in the western part of Maharashtra, India, has focused on

135 developing agricultural instruments. Interests there include testing milk for quality and safety, and tuning diesel engines to run more efficiently.

    Another Fab Lab, in Bithoor in the

140 Indian state of Uttar Pradesh, is developing 3-D scanning and printing systems for rural artisans to produce the wooden blocks used in local embroidery.

Source: "Ghana Gets a Fab Lab" (Delio)

D. VOCABULARY CHECK Look back at the reading on pages 99–101. Find words or phrases to match the definitions below. Write the correct words and phrases on the lines.

Solar Ovens

1. a strong interest in (1–5) _____

2. a shortage (5–10) _____

3. a great deal of (5–10) _____

4. lessen the effects of (25–30) _____

5. barriers (45–50) _____

Wireless in South Africa

6. using the Internet to learn (55–60) _____

7. inexpensive (55–60) _____

8. rich (70–75) _____

9. physical support systems such as roads and wires (75–80) _____

Fab Labs

10. produce (idiom) (100–105) _____

11. provide necessary items or services (phrasal verb) (100–105) _____

12. craft persons; artists who create useful objects (140–145) _____

E. DISCUSSION In small groups, discuss these questions.

1. How does each of the three technologies described in the reading solve problems in developing nations?

2. What other countries might benefit from these technologies?

3. What other technologies might be useful in developing nations?

F. RESPONSE WRITING Choose *one* of the topics below. Write about it for 15 minutes. Don't worry about grammar and don't use a dictionary. Just write as many ideas as you can.
• Which article and use of technology is the most interesting to you? Why?
• In your opinion, is modern technology always a positive change in developing nations? Explain your answer.
• What are some of your own ideas for solutions to the problems that developing nations face?

PART ② SOCIAL LANGUAGE Summer Jobs

BEFORE LISTENING

A. THINKING AHEAD You are going to hear Brandon, Jennifer, and Tanya talk about jobs. In small groups, discuss these questions.

1. What career are you considering? What are you doing to prepare for it?

2. Some students work after school or during school vacations. Do you ever work while going to school? Why or why not? If you work during school vacations, what kind of work do you do?

3. Some students also work during school vacations to get experience in the field they are preparing for. These jobs are sometimes called internships. Have you ever had an internship or any job that was related to your career plans? Explain.

B. PREDICTING In the conversation, Brandon, Jennifer, and Tanya discuss companies that hire workers overseas instead of using workers at home. With a partner, discuss this question:
• What is one possible reason that companies hire overseas workers?

C. VOCABULARY PREPARATION Read the sentences below. The words and phrases in orange are from the conversation. Match the definitions in the box with the words and phrases in orange. Write the correct letters on the lines.

a. and everything; and things like that	d. I have to leave right away.
b. because	e. That sounds great!
c. boring; unpleasant, unsatisfying	f. What bad luck!

_____ **1.** I don't want some **dumb** job this summer—I really want to do something interesting.

_____ **2.** I can't work this summer 'cause I have to go to school.

_____ **3.** When Bill told me that he got a job at Microsoft, I said, "Cool!"

_____ **4.** Tell me about your new job. Do you have your own office an' all?

_____ **5.** I heard you lost your job. What a drag!

_____ **6.** Class is starting in five minutes. I'm outta here!

LISTENING

A. LISTENING FOR THE MAIN IDEA Listen to the conversation. As you listen, think about this question:
• What is Brandon's career goal?

B. LISTENING FOR DETAILS Listen to the conversation again. Take *notes* to answer these questions.
Don't write complete sentences.

1. Why does Jennifer think Brandon is lucky?

_____

2. What kind of job did Brandon have last summer?

_____

3. Why is Brandon's company hiring programmers in Eastern Europe?

_____

4. How long has Brandon been working with computers?

_____

5. Why does Brandon say that he would hire cheap labor overseas?

_____

Now compare your answers with a partner's answers.

○ Making Inferences about Attitudes or Feelings

In Chapter 1 (page 9), you learned that inferences are guesses or assumptions about information that isn't given directly. Standardized tests often ask you to make inferences about conversations that you hear. These test questions may ask you to make an inference about the purpose of the conversation, the location of the conversation, or the attitudes or feelings of the speakers.

To answer questions about attitudes or feelings, listen to both the speakers' tone of voice and the things that they say. For example, if a speaker is speaking quickly or is hesitating and is requesting something from an authority figure (such as a professor), you might infer that the speaker is nervous.

Example: **Kevin:** Uh, um, Professor Jones?
         Professor Jones: Yes, Kevin?
         Kevin: Uh, I was wondering . . .
         Professor Jones: Go on.
         Kevin: Um, I was wondering if I could hand in my paper a day late since I've been sick.

C. MAKING INFERENCES ABOUT ATTITUDES OR FEELINGS Listen to parts of the conversation again and make inferences. Circle the correct answers.

1. How do you think Tanya feels about the possibility of getting a good job this summer?

   A. She's optimistic; she thinks she has a good chance.

   B. She's pessimistic; she doesn't think she has a good chance.

   C. She's indifferent; she doesn't care.

   D. She doesn't have any idea of her chances.

2. How do you think Brandon feels about computer programming as a career goal?

   A. He's excited about it.

   B. He doesn't really want to do it anymore.

   C. He thinks he's too good to do it.

   D. He doesn't have an opinion.

3. How does Brandon's career goal compare to the kind of work that he's been doing since he was 13?

   A. It's about the same.

   B. It requires less responsibility.

   C. It requires more responsibility.

   D. It's in a totally different field.

4. Why might Jennifer think that Brandon's plan to hire cheap labor overseas for his company is a bad idea?

   A. The company loses money.

   B. It's bad for the economy of the country where the workers live.

   C. It's bad for U.S. citizens who need jobs.

   D. It makes products cost more.

5. Why might some people think Brandon's plan to hire cheap labor overseas for his company is a good idea?

   A. People who don't have a lot of money can buy his products.

   B. U.S. workers will have more jobs.

   C. He can give jobs to people who need them.

   D. It will make his products available overseas.

AFTER LISTENING

A. VOCABULARY CHECK Read the sentences below. The words and phrases in orange are from the conversation. Guess from the context the meanings of the words and phrases in orange. Write your guesses on the lines. Then compare your answers with a partner's answers.

1. Datasoft offered Monica a summer job **writing code**, but she's tired of computer programming.

   Guess: _____

2. Ken is worried about losing his job because several people in his department were **let go** last month.

   Guess: _____

3. Datasoft thinks it can save money by **laying people off**.

   Guess: _____

4. I have a new business. In order to reduce costs and keep **overhead** low in the first few years, I'm not going to rent an office, buy a lot of equipment, or hire very many people.

   Guess: _____

5. My company has a talented **workforce**—it hires only people who are highly trained and have a lot of experience.

   Guess: _____

6. Instead of giving Chris a full-time, permanent job, the company is **contracting with** him for two months. When the project ends, he'll leave.

   Guess: _____

B. TAKING A SURVEY
Interview six classmates about international hiring. First, think about your own answers to the question below. Then ask six classmates. Write their answers in the chart.

• Many international companies **outsource**—contract out their work to workers in developing countries. Labor is often cheaper in developing countries. Do you think it is a good idea for companies in a country such as the United States to use cheap labor overseas? Why or why not?

Classmates	Yes, it's a good idea because . . .	No, it's a bad idea because . . .
Total	_____ students thought outsourcing was a good idea.	_____ students thought outsourcing was a bad idea.

C. DISCUSSING SURVEY RESULTS
In small groups, discuss the results of your survey. Answer these questions:

• Within your group, what is the total number of people interviewed? Count each person just once.
• How many people thought outsourcing was a good idea? A bad idea?
• What were the most common reasons given?

A Chinese seamstress making clothes for a U.S. company

PART ③ THE MECHANICS OF LISTENING AND SPEAKING

LANGUAGE FUNCTIONS

🎧 Asking for Confirmation

Sometimes we say something based on an **assumption**—information that we believe (or assume) is true. To be polite, we may ask the listener to **confirm** (or support) our assumption. To ask for confirmation, add a tag question to your statement or add a separate question.

Examples: Brandon always seems to get a career-related summer job, **doesn't he? (Tag question)**
You always get a career-related summer job, **don't you? (Tag question)**
You always get a career-related summer job, **huh? (Tag question)**
Brandon always seems to get a career-related summer job. **Isn't that so? (Separate question)**

Offering an Explanation

When someone makes an assumption about you, it may or may not be correct. If the speaker asks for confirmation, you can:
• express agreement
• express disagreement
• make a correction
• offer an explanation

Examples: **A**: You always have good luck finding a career-related summer job, don't you, Brandon?
B: Well, I was lucky last summer . . . **(Agreement)**
Not always. The summer before last I worked at the video store. **(Disagreement)**
I wouldn't call it luck . . . more like persistence. **(Correction)**
True, but I work pretty hard to find it. **(Explanation)**

🎧 **A. ASKING FOR CONFIRMATION AND OFFERING AN EXPLANATION** Listen to five assumptions. Then listen to different responses to the assumptions. In each conversation, decide if the response is agreement, disagreement, correction, or explanation. Check (✓) the correct answer.

Response	Agreement	Disagreement	Correction	Explanation
1				
2				
3				
4				
5				

INTONATION

🎧 Tag Question Intonation

The intonation for a tag question depends on whether or not you are sure that your assumption is correct and that the listener will agree with you. If you are sure, you use falling intonation.

Example: You always have good luck finding a summer job, don't you? (Sure)

If you are *not* sure of your assumption, you use rising intonation.

Example: You always have good luck finding a summer job, don't you? (Not sure)

🎧 **B. HEARING TAG QUESTION INTONATION** Listen to the following statements with tag questions. Decide whether the speaker is sure or not sure. Circle the correct answers.

1. Sure   Not Sure

2. Sure   Not Sure

3. Sure   Not Sure

4. Sure   Not Sure

5. Sure   Not Sure

6. Sure   Not Sure

7. Sure   Not Sure

8. Sure   Not Sure

👥 **C. USING TAG QUESTION INTONATION** Practice tag question intonation with a partner. Student A asks the questions below and chooses to be *sure* (using falling intonation) or *not sure* (using rising intonation). Student B listens and decides whether Student A is sure or not sure and circles the correct answer. After asking the eight questions, Student A checks the answers. Then exchange roles.

1.	Chrissy's smart, isn't she?	Sure	Not Sure
2.	Evan has a great job this summer, doesn't he?	Sure	Not Sure
3.	You always land on your feet, don't you?	Sure	Not Sure
4.	Brandon's lucky, isn't he?	Sure	Not Sure
5.	That video game is popular, isn't it?	Sure	Not Sure
6.	Using programmers in Asia isn't fair to U.S. workers, is it?	Sure	Not Sure
7.	You're not leaving now, are you?	Sure	Not Sure
8.	You worked in a video store last summer, didn't you?	Sure	Not Sure

PRONUNCIATION

Reduced Forms of Words: Tag Questions

As you learned in Chapters 1 and 3, in natural conversations, some words and combinations of sounds become reduced, or shortened. This type of reduction often happens with tag questions.

Examples:

Long Forms	Reduced Forms
You got a good job, **didn't you**?	You got a good job, **didncha**?
You didn't know that, **did you**?	You didn't know that, **didja**?
You always have good luck, **don't you**?	You always have good luck, **doncha**?
You're taking Econ 1, **aren't you**?	You're taking Econ 1, **arncha**?

D. REDUCED FORMS OF WORDS Listen to the questions and write the *long* forms of the reduced words you hear.

1. You got a great summer job, _____?

2. You didn't study last night, _____?

3. You're pretty lucky, _____?

4. You think you're pretty smart, _____?

5. You're working for a computer company, _____?

6. You didn't get an internship this summer, _____?

WORDS IN PHRASES

Interrupting Incorrect Assumptions

People sometimes make incorrect assumptions without asking for confirmation. When this happens, you may want to stop them before they go too far with the assumption. If you need to interrupt someone and correct him or her immediately, here are some phrases for doing so:

Let me stop you there.
Excuse me, but . . .
Wait a minute.
Hold on.
Not so fast.
Hang on just a sec*.
} *That's not true.* + Explanation

Example: **A:** You don't have to work; your parents pay for everything. (Incorrect assumption)
B: Wait a minute! That's not true. I pay for everything except rent and school fees. (Interruption and explanation)

*Sec. is an informal abbreviation for *second.*

Which phrases are formal? Which are informal?

PUT IT TOGETHER

A. MAKING ASSUMPTIONS Your teacher will select a partner for you. Using the questions below and the box of personal qualities and conditions, think of some assumptions about your partner.

1. What kind of student do you think your partner is?

2. Do you think your partner likes his or her teachers?

3. What assumptions could you make about your partner's summer plans?

smart	good summer job	good student
lucky	bad summer job	bad student
unlucky	fun vacation plans	doesn't study a lot
rich	no vacation plans	studies a lot
hard working	goes out most nights	doesn't like his/her teachers
well-traveled	stays home most nights	likes his/her teachers

Write three assumptions you are sure are true about your partner.

1. _____

2. _____

3. _____

Write three assumptions you are not sure are true about your partner.

1. _____

2. _____

3. _____

B. MAKING ASSUMPTIONS AND OFFERING EXPLANATIONS Now tell your partner your assumptions. Practice using both kinds of tag question intonation: falling if you're sure and rising if you're not sure. Your partner can decide how to answer: agreeing, disagreeing, interrupting you, correcting you, or giving more information. Then exchange roles.

Example: **A:** School is easy for you, isn't it?
　　　　　　　B: Hold on! I work just as hard as you do.

　　　　　　　A: You always have fun vacation plans, don't you?
　　　　　　　B: No, not always, but I did have a good vacation last summer.

　　　　　　　A: You study a lot, huh?
　　　　　　　B: Well, yes, actually I do.

BEFORE LISTENING

A. THINKING AHEAD You are going to hear a radio program about an American-style donut shop, Mister Donut, in Japan. In small groups, discuss these questions.

1. Do you think that a donut shop in Japan would be the same as a donut shop in the United States? Why or why not?

2. If you think the shops would be different, how might they be different? For example, do you think a donut shop in Japan would have the same kind of donuts as in the United States?

A Mister Donut shop in Tokyo, Japan

B. GUESSING THE MEANING FROM CONTEXT Read the sentences below. The words and phrases in orange are from the radio program. Guess their meanings from the context. Write your guesses on the lines.

1. People like the **gracious** service at the new restaurant. The servers are very polite and formal.

   Guess: _____

2. **Wax paper** is better than plastic wrap for food because food doesn't stick to it. You can easily pull wax paper off of food.

   Guess: _____

3. Briana serves the coffee so quickly that it **sloshes** out of the cup and spills on the table.

   Guess: _____

4. The tables and counters in this restaurant are **gleaming**! The servers must clean them very carefully.

   Guess: _____

5. A server in Japan might call guests "**honorable** customers." This is because the customers are important and respected.

   Guess: _____

6. Martin got a job as a **disk jockey** at a radio station in Japan. Listeners can't understand what he is saying, but they like the way that he announces the music.

Guess: _____

7. Martin plays only **goldie oldies**—rock 'n' roll music from the 1950s and 1960s.

Guess: _____

8. This drink is a strange **concoction**. It's a mixture of orange juice and carrot juice.

Guess: _____

Now compare your answers with a partner's answers.

C. VOCABULARY PREPARATION The phrases on the left are from the radio program. Match the definitions on the right with the phrases. Write the correct letters on the lines.

_____ **1.** dirt cheap	**a.** to claim something
_____ **2.** to get the better end of a bargain	**b.** to get the better result in an exchange
_____ **3.** to pour out of	**c.** to discuss
_____ **4.** to purport to be	**d.** to be very popular
_____ **5.** to take by storm	**e.** to exit a place quickly, with a lot of other people
_____ **6.** to talk over	**f.** very inexpensive

D. FINDING THE RIGHT WORD You'll hear the word *draw* in the radio program. One meaning of *draw* is "make pictures with a pen or pencil." In the box are two other meanings of *draw*. They are both nouns. Match each meaning to the context. Write the correct letters on the lines.

a. attraction	**b. a tie; not a win or a loss**

_____ **1.** I like the donuts at this store, but I like the service at the other store. I can't decide which I like better. It's a **draw**.

_____ **2.** Many people go to that restaurant. What's the **draw**? Can you tell me the reason for its success?

LISTENING

A. LISTENING FOR THE MAIN IDEA IN AN INTRODUCTION: Listen to the introduction of the radio program and answer this question:
• Is Mister Donut successful in Japan?

B. LISTENING FOR COMPARISONS: SECTION 1 How does Mister Donut in Japan compare with Mister Donut in the United States? Listen to Section 1 twice. Complete the T-chart with details about Mister Donut in Japan and Mister Donut in the United States. Think about service, cleanliness, and the quality of the food and the coffee.

Mister Donut in the U.S.	Mister Donut in Japan
server in greasy apron	server in white cap, bow tie

C. LISTENING FOR DETAILS: SECTION 2 Listen to Section 2. According to T. R. Reid, Mister Donut does something wrong. What is it?

_____

_____

D. JAPANESE WORDS AND PHRASES T. R. Reid uses some Japanese words and Japanese-sounding words. He tells you what they mean. Listen again for these words and their meanings. Then write the meanings on the lines.

1. *Missu Do*   Mister Donut _____

2. *lucky kaado*   _____

3. *kawari*   _____

4. *kakkoi*   _____

AFTER LISTENING

A. DISCUSSION In small groups, discuss these questions.

1. Would Mister Donut be successful in other countries? Explain your answer.

2. What American fast-food restaurants are popular outside the United States? Why do you think they are popular?

3. What are your favorite fast-food restaurants? How are they like Mister Donut? How are they different?

B. BRAINSTORMING Work with a partner. Think of a new fast-food restaurant to open near your school. You want your restaurant to draw students. Complete the chart with your ideas about possible names, the kind of food that your restaurant will serve, the design and interior, and any special draw.

Possible names	
Kind of food	
Design and interior (music, lighting, seating, decoration)	
Any special draw (such as free coffee refills)	

Share your restaurant description with the class.

PART 5 ACADEMIC ENGLISH Emerging Nations

BEFORE LISTENING

Critical Thinking Strategy

Realizing What You Already Know

As you learned in Chapter 1 (page 22), lectures often build on information that you have already studied. Other times, they present information that is entirely new to you. You usually know the topic of a lecture because it is indicated in your syllabus or related to material in your textbook. When you know the topic of a lecture, think about what you already know about the subject. This will also help you realize what you *don't* know about it. Doing this will help you mentally prepare for the information that you will hear and helps you focus your attention while you listen.

Example: **You know:** You are going to listen to a lecture with the title "American Fast-Food Restaurants in Japan: Successes and Failures." You heard a radio program about American-style donut shops in Japan, so you already know a little about one type of successful American-style restaurant in that country.

You don't know: You may not know about other types of restaurants—for example, ice cream shops—and you may not know about some of the failures of American-style restaurants in Japan. Therefore, as you listen to the lecture, you can focus on new examples.

A. REALIZING WHAT YOU ALREADY KNOW You will hear a lecture about the differences between two economic systems. To prepare, find out what you already know about socialism and market capitalism. Take the following true/false quiz. Circle *T* if the statement is true or *F* if the statement is false.

1. Under market capitalism, government planners decide how resources will be used.   **T**   **F**

2. Under market capitalism, workers usually work where the government tells them to work.   **T**   **F**

3. One of the pros (advantages) of socialism is an emphasis on free medical care for all.   **T**   **F**

4. One of the pros of socialism is the freedom to choose the job that you want.   **T**   **F**

5. One of the cons (disadvantages) of market capitalism is unemployment.   **T**   **F**

6. One of the cons of market capitalism is constant shortages.   **T**   **F**

7. Australia is a socialist country.   **T**   **F**

8. The current economic system of Russia is moving toward market capitalism.   **T**   **F**

9. China is an example of a country with a socialist economy.   **T**   **F**

10. The economic system of France is market capitalism.   **T**   **F**

👥 In small groups, compare your answers. Then look at the correct answers on page 127.

B. REALIZING WHAT YOU DON'T KNOW

B. REALIZING WHAT YOU DON'T KNOW Look at the note-taking outlines and graphic organizers on pages 120–124. What would you like to know about the economics of socialism and market capitalism? Write three questions on the lines.

Question 1: _____

_____

Question 2: _____

_____

Question 3: _____

_____

Now look over the questions in Activity A on pages 124–125. Are any of these similar to your own questions?

C. GUESSING THE MEANING FROM CONTEXT Read the sentences below. The words and phrases in orange are from the lecture. Guess their meanings from the context. Write your guesses on the lines.

1. The garden is large, but right now it's **sparsely** planted. There's a lot of empty space left for the fruit trees next summer.

Guess: _____

2. Paying taxes is **inherent in** being a citizen; you can't avoid it.

Guess: _____

3. We were impressed by the **magnitude** of Ms. Fuller's generosity. She gave the school well over a million dollars.

Guess: _____

4. I felt **constrained** by the strict rules at my high school, so I asked my parents to send me to one where there was more freedom.

Guess: _____

5. Evan gave a **plausible** excuse for why he was absent, so the teacher let him take a make-up exam.

Guess: _____

6. Maribel has no friends; she spends such an **inordinate** amount of time studying that she has no time left for social activities.

Guess: _____

7. Only the **elite** in Xenrovia—the wealthy and people who worked for the government—had access to foreign luxury products.

Guess: _____

8. Max and Sam's friendship is good because there is a lot of **give and take**. For example, Max drives Sam to work, but Sam buys the gas.

Guess: _____

Now compare your answers with a partner's answers.

D. TAKING NOTES: ABBREVIATIONS Write your own abbreviations for these words and phrases from the lecture.

1. central economic planning   _____

2. market economies   _____

3. resources   _____

4. economies   _____

5. government   _____

6. democratic   _____

7. undemocratic   _____

8. socialism   _____

9. consumers   _____

10. shortages   _____

LISTENING

A. LISTENING FOR THE MEANINGS OF NEW WORDS AND PHRASES Listen to sentences with these economics words and phrases from the lecture. Then match the terms on the left with the definitions on the right. Write the correct letters on the lines.

_____ **1.** a trade-off

_____ **2.** centralize

_____ **3.** cost

_____ **4.** decentralized

_____ **5.** technocrats

_____ **6.** the private sector

_____ **7.** scarcity

_____ **8.** strategic output

_____ **9.** fiscally sound

_____ **10.** privatize

a. economic planners in socialist government

b. the exchange of one thing for another

c. to put power or authority in a central organization

d. to give power or authority to private citizens

e. handling money in a smart way

f. not the government; private citizens

g. what is given up in order to get something else

h. materials or products that help a country defend itself

i. power distributed among several groups

j. shortage; lack of

Listening Strategy

Listening for the Main Points in an Introduction

You can often get the main points of a lecture from its introduction. Professors often list the main topics that they intend to cover at the beginning of a lecture. This helps you think ahead and plan your note-taking. Listen for phrases such as these:

Today, we're going to look at . . .
We'll also examine . . .
I'm going to cover . . .
I'll also touch on . . .

Example: Today, we're going to **look at** health care in Costa Rica, and **I'll also touch on** health care in Thailand.

B. LISTENING FOR THE MAIN POINTS IN AN INTRODUCTION Listen to the introduction of the lecture. In the box below, take notes on the main points of the lecture.

The lecture will cover:
1. economic issues that _____
2. two ways that _____
3. transition from _____

C. TAKING NOTES: USING A VARIETY OF GRAPHIC ORGANIZERS For this lecture, different graphic organizers are used for different sections of the lecture. The organizers reflect the type of information given in the different sections. You will listen to each section twice. Fill in as much as you can. Don't worry if you can't fill in everything. (You'll listen to the whole lecture again later.) Remember to use abbreviations. In this activity, you will listen to Sections 1–3. You will listen to Sections 4 and 5 in Activity D (page 122).

Emerging Nations in a Global Economy

Section 1
Economic Issues that Affect All Nations

Number of nations: _____

```
┌─────────────────────────────────────────────────────────────┐
│                  Ways in Which Nations Differ                 │
└─────────────────────────────────────────────────────────────┘
```

1. Age _____	2. _____	3. Wealth not measured by
Examples: _____	Sparse: _____	_____
_____	_____	Measured by _____
_____	Tightly packed: _____	_____

Some nations are rich in human resources, but poor in natural resources.	1. _____	2. Natural _____
Examples: _____	Examples: _____	Examples: _____
_____	_____	_____
	_____	_____
	_____	_____

Section 2
Trade-offs

1. All nations must confront _____

Scarcity of resources: _____

Cost: every choice involves _____

Ex: _____

2. Trade-offs: _____

Central Economic Planning	Market Capitalism

Section 3
Facts About Economic Planning Under Socialism

1. Technocrats developed plans for: _____

How _____

What _____

For whom _____

2. The plans were plausible because _____

_____

3. The central plan was not simple because _____

_____

4. Technocrats' priorities: _____

_____

5. How planners used the power of the state: _____

Ex: In the 1960s, one Soviet leader claimed they would "bury" the West, meaning _____

_____

Therefore, placed emphasis on _____

_____

Listening for Causes and Effects

Professors explain reasons and causes in many different ways. Often they will use cause and effect phrases such as *causes, results in, leads to, as a result, because,* and *because of.* Some lecturers may also pose a question and then answer it themselves.

Example: With more consumer-oriented goods sacrificed to produce strategic output, there were *persistent* shortages. **Why? Because consumer demand always exceeded the supply of things consumers wanted.**

You may also hear synonyms for terms such as *caused* and *resulted in.*

Example: So shortages not only **posed** a great hardship on consumers but also **encouraged** corruption and **perpetuated** inequalities in a political system that claimed to believe in fairness.

Another way to say this is: So shortages not only **resulted in** a great hardship on consumers but also **led to** corruption and inequalities in a political system that claimed to believe in fairness.

Here are some other words used to express causes and effects.

Examples: Labor costs around the world **have an impact on** local economies.
One **effect** of sending work overseas is lower costs for companies.
Low-cost labor overseas **impacts** the availability of employment for local workers.

D. TAKING NOTES: SECTIONS 4 AND 5 Listen to Sections 4 and 5 twice and take notes.

Section 4
Results of Socialism

1. Unemployment: _____

_____

_____

_____

2. Emphasis on strategic production: _____

_____

_____

_____

3. Wages, banks, and money: _____

_____

_____

_____

4. Other results: _____

_____

_____

_____

Shortages often occurred in the former Soviet Union

Present day Russia

Section 5
Transition to Market Capitalism

Socialism	Market Capitalism

Results of transition: _____

_____

Source: Adapted from a lecture by Ryszard D. C. Trainer, Ph.D.

E. CHECKING YOUR NOTES Listen to the whole lecture again. As you listen, review your notes and fill in any missing information.

AFTER LISTENING

A. COMPREHENSION CHECK Work with a partner. Use your notes to answer these questions.

1. How do we measure the wealth of a nation? _____

_____

_____

2. What economic reality must all nations face? _____

_____

_____

3. What is the "cost" of producing the things that people need? _____

_____

_____

4. In which two main ways have nations tried to deal with trade-offs? ____

_____

_____

5. How does central economic planning deal with trade-offs? _____

_____

_____

6. How does market capitalism deal with trade-offs? _____

_____

_____

7. How are socialism and capitalism different? _____

_____

_____

8. Who made economic decisions in a socialist economy? What usually were the priorities in socialist economies? _____

_____

_____

9. What were some positive results of socialism? What were some negative results?

_____

_____

_____

B. DISCUSSION The lecture focused mainly on socialism. In particular, it gave a lot of detail on the failures of socialist systems, but it didn't give the same kinds of details on market capitalism. In small groups, discuss these questions.

1. What are the positive aspects of market capitalism, in your opinion?

2. What are some of the negative aspects of market capitalism?

C. MAKING CONNECTIONS Think about the positive and negative aspects of market capitalism in terms of the reading in Part 1, the conversation you listened to in Part 2, the radio program in Part 4, and the lecture you just heard. In small groups, discuss these questions.

1. Who benefits when a wealthy nation such as the United States hires cheap labor overseas? Would this happen in a socialist economy? Why or why not?

2. Who benefits when a fast-food chain is imported to another country (such as Mister Donut in Japan)?

3. How might the market respond better to people's needs than a government can?

4. In what situations do you think the government response might be better than that of the market?

PUT IT ALL TOGETHER

Speaking Strategy

Choosing a Topic

Occasionally, you will have a choice of topics for a speaking assignment. However, you often don't have much time to make a choice, and you certainly don't have time to make a choice and then change your mind. Therefore, it's a good idea to have some strategies for making good, quick topic choices.

Here are some things to think about when you choose a topic for an assignment. You should be able to answer "yes" to at least two of these when you choose a topic:

- Are you curious about or interested in the topic?
- Do you already know something about it?
- Even if you don't know much about it, do you have a pretty good idea of how or where to get information on it?
- Do you have enough time to get all the necessary information and do a good job on it?

Example: You have to choose a speaking topic from a list. One topic is reasons for the success or failure of new restaurants. Your uncle owns a restaurant and you worked there for a few months the first year it was open. You have ideas based on your experience. This would be a good topic for you to choose.

RESEARCHING For this activity, you will do Internet or library research to find out about the success or failure of a product, business, or service when it was imported from another country. Then you will give a report on your findings to your classmates.

Step 1
Choose a topic to research. Ideas might include:

- food products such as soft drinks
- restaurants
- package delivery services

Write down your topic and the specific name of the product, business, or service.

_____

Step 2
Do a key word search on an Internet search engine. Try key word searches such as the following:

> [name of product, business, or service] + cultural differences
> [name of fast-food chain] + [name of country] + cultural differences

Step 3
Gather information about your topic. Organize your information to prepare for your presentation. What did you find out? What was interesting? For example, explain how the product, business, or service differs in another country and discuss whether this is a factor in its success or failure. Find out if it has affected the local culture or economy in any way and if so, explain what the effects are.

Giving a Presentation from Notes

When you give a presentation, it's a good idea to speak from notes, not to read complete sentences that you have written. To speak from notes, you need to prepare and practice. Here are some suggestions.

1. Make an outline of what you want to discuss.
2. Read your outline many times—try to memorize it.
3. Make a less detailed outline, with just the main points (for example, Roman numeral heads and capital letter heads).
4. Practice giving your presentation from this less detailed outline. See if you can remember the missing details.
5. Make an outline with only the Roman numeral heads.
6. When you can give your report by just glancing at these heads, you're ready to speak in front of the class. This way, you can make eye contact and be a more interesting speaker.

Below is an example of some notes for a report on foreign-style restaurants in Xenrovia:

I. Successful restaurants in Xenrovia
    A. South American
        1. Good service
        2. Xenrovians like grilled meat
    B. Sushi bar (Japanese)
        1. Many Japanese immigrants in Xenrovia
        2. People like to watch sushi chef work

Note that only general ideas appear in the outline. For example, for the first Roman numeral, the speaker will give specific examples of successful South American-style restaurants in Xenrovia and explain why they are successful.

Step 4

Organize your notes. Prepare for your presentation by following the steps in the box above. Think about including pictures, charts, or any other visual material that is relevant to your topic.

Step 5

Give a brief presentation to the class on what you have learned. When you give your presentation, make sure you just glance at your notes—don't read them.

Listen carefully to your classmates' reports. Try to think of a question to ask to show that you are paying attention and to learn more about the topic.

Answers for Activity A (page 116):

1. F	**6.** F
2. F	**7.** F
3. T	**8.** T
4. F	**9.** T
5. T	**10.** T

UNIT 2 VOCABULARY WORKSHOP

Review vocabulary items that you learned in Chapters 3 and 4.

A. MATCHING Match the words to the definitions. Write the correct letters on the lines.

Words

_____ **1.** affluent

_____ **2.** concoction

_____ **3.** drought

_____ **4.** enterprise

_____ **5.** infrastructure

_____ **6.** obstacle

_____ **7.** perseverance

_____ **8.** plausible

_____ **9.** scarcity

_____ **10.** starve

Definitions

a. long period with no rain in seasons that are usually rainy

b. believable, reasonable

c. die of hunger

d. business

e. basic facilities (such as roads, bridges, and dams) that a country needs in order to function

f. determination; not giving up

g. not enough of something

h. something that stands in your way and prevents progress

i. an unusual combination of ingredients in food or drink

j. rich

B. WORDS IN PHRASES Fill in the blanks with words from the box.

| dirt | do | garments | oldies | regime |
| disasters | end | off | over | storm |

1. I can't believe what a bargain this is! It's absolutely _____ **cheap**.

2. The Cleavers have problems, but lack of money isn't one of them. They're a **well-to-**_____ family.

3. This new style has **taken the country by** _____. Everyone is really excited about it.

4. The company has to **lay** _____ some of the workers because of the bad economy.

5. Who do you think **got the better** _____ of the bargain—the seller or the buyer?

6. Tim's company produces shirts, dresses, and other **ready-made** _____.

7. I love all those **goldie** _____ by the Beatles and Elvis Presley and other rock 'n' roll singers.

8. The **authoritarian** _____ in Xenrovia was corrupt and feared by the people of the country.

9. Mary and Becky get together at a donut shop after class to **talk** _____ what happened that day.

10. It's important to be prepared for hurricanes, earthquakes, floods, and other **natural** _____.

C. THE ACADEMIC WORD LIST In the boxes below are some of the most common academic words in English. Fill in the blanks with words from these boxes. When you finish, check your answers in the readings on page 70 (for items 1–5) and page 100 (for items 6–15). For more words, see the Academic Word List on pages 315–318.

community	credits	economic	global	impact

Fatimata Lonfo fled Cote d'Ivoire in October 2001. Now the proud owner of Windyla's Boutique and Hair Braiding Salon in Staten Island, New York, Fatimata

_____ her success to God, to perseverance, and to ACCION New York, a
1

non-profit microfinance organization that gave her first small business loan. Her business supports her and her three children, the oldest of whom started community college this past fall. She was

chosen as the winner of the New York contest of the _____
2

Microentrepreneur Awards due to the great _____ and social
3

_____ of her business on her family and _____.
4   5

| according | compared | equipment | relatively | technology |
| affluent | efficient | project | remote | virtually |

Using just some basic wireless networking _____ and computers, the
6

set-up is cost effective and simple for teachers and students, _____ to those
7

behind the _____.
8

The project is just one example of how wireless _____ is helping
9

bridge the digital divide, giving people in less affluent or more _____ areas
10

a cheaper, more _____, and just as effective way to connect
11

_____.
12

The growing use of wireless—and the _____ low expense of setting up
13

such a system _____ to building fiber-based networks like those used in the
14

United States and other _____ areas—has made it more possible to set up
15

communication systems in previously hard-to-reach places.

LITERATURE

Chapter 5
Poetry

Chapter 6
Heroes in Literature

Poetry

Discuss these questions:

- This is Maya Angelou, a famous American poet. Do you read poetry for pleasure? Who are your favorite poets?
- What poetry have you studied in school?
- Did you have to analyze the poems or memorize and recite them?

Gypsies in Granada, Spain (circa 1900). Although there are many **stereotypes** (overgeneralizations) about gypsies, most are not true. Gypsies are now referred to as Roma.

This popular **bumper sticker** tells people not to believe everything that they hear from people in a position of **authority** or power.

A. THINKING AHEAD You are going to read some poems. In small groups, discuss these questions.

1. What are some differences between **contemporary** (modern) poetry and poetry from the past? Make a list.

2. One of the poems you will read is about the language of teenagers in the U.S. Teenagers often use a word differently from its common usage. For example, when teenagers use words like *totally, like, whatever,* and *you know,* the words have almost no meaning. They are fillers—words used between thoughts. In your language, are there certain words that only teenagers use? If so, what are some? How are they used?

3. One of the poems refers to a popular bumper sticker that reads, "Question Authority." Why is it important to question authority?

Gypsies   by Alden Nowlan

Jessie, my cousin, remembers there were gypsies
every spring, cat-eyes in smoky faces,
hair like black butter on leather laces.
Mothers on the high wagons whose babes sucked
5 flesh on O'Brien Street, I'd be ashamed.
The men stole everything and damned if they didn't
shrug if you caught them—giving back a hen
filched from your own coop like a gift to a peasant.
The little girls danced, their red skirts winking,
10 their legs were lovely, greasy as drumsticks.
And they kidnapped children. Oh, every child
hoped secretly to be stolen by gypsies.

laces = strings used to tie shoes

shrug = move the shoulders to mean "I don't care"   **filched** = stolen   **coop** = house for chickens   **drumsticks** = the leg of a cooked chicken or turkey

Source: "Gypsies" (Nowlan)

Totally like whatever, you know?   by Taylor Mali

In case you hadn't noticed,
it has somehow become uncool
to sound like you know what you're talking about?
Or believe strongly in what you're saying?
5 Invisible question marks and parenthetical (you know?)'s
have been attaching themselves to the ends of our sentences?
Even when those sentences aren't, like, questions? You know?

Declarative sentences—so-called
because they used to, like, DECLARE things to be true
10 as opposed to other things which were, like, not—
have been infected by a totally hip
and tragically cool interrogative tone? You know?
Like, don't think I'm uncool just because I've noticed this;
this is just like the word on the street, you know?
15 It's like what I've heard?
I have nothing personally invested in my own opinions, okay?
I'm just inviting you to join me in my uncertainty?

What has happened to our conviction?
Where are the limbs out on which we once walked?
20 Have they been, like, chopped down
with the rest of the rain forest?
Or do we have, like, nothing to say?
Has society become so, like, totally...
I mean absolutely... You know?
25 That we've just gotten to the point where it's just, like...
whatever!

declare = say strongly   **as opposed to** = in contrast to   **hip** = cool   **interrogative** = question   **the word on the street** = what people are talking about

conviction = certainty that something is true   **limb** = tree branch   **go out on a limb** = have the courage to express unpopular beliefs

And so actually our disarticulation... ness
is just a clever sort of... thing
to disguise the fact that we've become
30 the most aggressively inarticulate generation
to come along since...
you know, a long, long time ago!

I entreat you, I implore you, I exhort you,
I challenge you: To speak with conviction.
35 To say what you believe in a manner that bespeaks
the determination with which you believe it.
Because contrary to the wisdom of the bumper sticker,
it is not enough these days to simply QUESTION AUTHORITY.
You have to speak with it, too.

Source: "Totally like whatever, you know" (Mali)

disarticulation = state of not being articulate, not able to express clearly
-ness = a suffix meaning "state of"
disguise = hide
inarticulate = unable to express ideas clearly
entreat, implore, exhort = beg; request strongly
bespeaks = indicates
determination = firm belief and decisiveness

Thinking Twice in the Laundromat   by Harley Elliott

1. *Bird Dance*

Seeing you
in the laundromat
a beautiful African
5 form   certain and terse
as dark wood

I began my little
bird dance of hope
        afraid I may say something
10   small town   and inane
                    like
            "welcome to america"

small town (adj.) = unsophisticated
inane = stupid; foolish

Your arm
loading clothes in an arc
15   into the shining chrome circle
is alive

        as something that should
        point over plains
            (the other hand shading
20   your eyes)

plains = wide spaces of flat land

I am there
among mimosa trees

I release green birds toward you
I approach you
25   and my arms are full of long
            rare feathers

I will buy you soap

I will help you fold

your gleaming sheets.

30 *2. Pink Blues*

Shyly   after you left
coasting on the memory of your
deep skin
I found the brown wool sock
35   sprawled outside your dryer

In my hand

knowing the foot it holds
more than I should
exploring him   (he is
40 solemn he
wears glasses)

and remembering your pink lips

and my pink lips

perhaps it could be
45 someday   the way I'd like
seeing you in a supermarket
I would want
to say
meet me in the laundromat
50   I have your
husband's sock
O la,   o   la.

gleaming = shining brightly

sprawled = lying on the floor

solemn = very serious

Source: "Thinking Twice in the Laundromat" (Elliott)

C. FINDING THE MAIN IDEA Match each poem with the correct main idea or **theme**. Write the correct letters on the lines.

_____ **1.** "Gypsies"

_____ **2.** "Totally like whatever, you know?"

_____ **3.** "Thinking Twice in the Laundromat"

a. a man's fascination with a beautiful woman

b. a stereotype of a group of people whom one hasn't met

c. the importance of believing strongly in something and speaking clearly and directly about it

"Gypsies"

1. From whom did the speaker of the poem learn about gypsies?

2. What are some of the stereotypes of gypsies in this poem? For example, according to the poem, what did gypsies use to wear?

3. What did children hope secretly for?

"Totally like whatever, you know?"

4. Look back at the poem and make a list of words and expressions that American teenagers frequently use.

5. These days, American teenagers tend to use question intonation at the end of many sentences that are not really questions. Find examples of this in the poem. (In other words, which question marks should really be periods, instead?) Which questions in the poem are true questions?

"Thinking Twice in the Laundromat"

6. Where does the speaker imagine that the beautiful woman is from? What makes you think this? Does he really know where she's from?

7. What words does the speaker use to make the Laundromat sound more beautiful than it really is?

8. The speaker has two fantasies about the woman and himself—one in "Bird Dance" and one in "Pink Blues." What are these fantasies?

Critical Thinking Strategy

Analyzing Poetry: A Poetry Primer

Most good poems can be understood on several different levels. However, a poem must be read several times to understand the different levels of meaning. It also helps to hear the poem read aloud as you read silently.

An important tool for students is the ability to **analyze** a piece of literature, such as a poem. When you analyze, you look at the different parts in order to better understand the whole. By using logic and understanding the poem's context, you can figure out much of the meaning. Analysis is a skill you will need in many types of classes, not just in English or literature classes.

When you analyze a poem, look for these elements and think about how they are used in the poem.

Elements	Explanations
Theme	This is either the topic or the main idea of the poem. Sometimes the main idea is clearly stated. More often, you need to infer it.
Speaker	Sometimes the speaker is the poet, but often the poet writes in the voice of another person.

Symbolism	A symbol is a material thing that represents another thing or idea.
	Example: A road is symbolic of a person's life.
	A flag represents a country.
Metaphor and Simile	A metaphor is a type of symbol. It describes something by comparing it to something else (without using *like* or *as*).
	Example: His hand was a knife stabbing the air.
	A simile is a metaphor that includes the word *like* or *as*.
	Example: His hand was **like** a knife stabbing the air.
Imagery	Images in poetry are mental pictures in words. There are five types of images: sound, sight, touch, smell, and taste.
	Example: . . . the first day of summer: the stickiness of peach juice running down my chin; the warmth of sand on bare feet; the prickliness of sun drying ocean salt on my skin.
Juxtaposition	Good poems often have a bit of juxtaposition—something surprising, such as two ideas or words that you don't expect to see side by side.
	Example: . . . and so I waited and worked and prepared, month after month, year after year, until the day arrived that I finally stood before the door and then—turned aside and walked away.
Ambiguity	Sometimes part of a poem is ambiguous. In other words, you can't completely understand it, or it's possible to interpret it in different ways. If *too* much is ambiguous, you can't understand the poem.
	Example: Wordless, she stood each day and watched the children in the playground.
	The reader wonders, why did she watch them? Why didn't she speak? If something in the poem doesn't make this clear, it is ambiguous.

E. ANALYZING POETRY In small groups, discuss these questions to analyze the poems on a deeper level.

"Gypsies"

1. What are the similes in this poem?

2. Line 11 says, "And they kidnapped children. Oh, every child . . ." What do you *expect* the next line to say? What does line 12 say? Which element of poetry is the poet using here?

3. Do you think that the speaker believes these stereotypes? Explain your answer.

"Totally like whatever, you know?"

4. In which stanza (part, similar to a paragraph) does the poet use only the language of an educated adult? How do you know? Which stanzas have a combination—some lines in the language of teenagers and some in the language of adults?

5. What is the metaphor in the third stanza?

6. The theme of this poem is clearly stated. In which lines can you find it?

7. Read the lines below. Which element is this an example of?

> I approach you
> > and my arms are full of long
> > rare feathers
>
> I will buy you soap
>
> > I will help you fold
>
> your gleaming sheets.

8. What is a simile from the first stanza?

9. Most of this poem is in the imagination of the speaker. What are the facts in the poem? In other words, what is the reality and what is the speaker's fantasy?

F. RESPONSE WRITING Choose *one* of these topics. Write about it for 15 minutes. Don't worry about grammar and don't use a dictionary. Just write as many ideas as you can.

- Which poem did you like the best? What did you like about it? How did it make you feel? Can you relate it to your own life?
- Describe a person from a part of the world that seems very **exotic** (strange, mysterious, and wonderful) to you.
- Can you think of a time when you were fascinated by a stranger? Describe the situation and the stranger.
- What is a fantasy of yours? What is the difference between it and the present reality?

PART ② SOCIAL LANGUAGE Surviving Poetry

BEFORE LISTENING

THINKING AHEAD You are going to listen to a conversation. In the conversation, Victor is having difficulty in his American literature class. In small groups, discuss these questions.

1. What can a student do if he or she is having trouble in class? List the possibilities.

2. Do you prefer **prose** (fiction and nonfiction written in paragraph form) or poetry? Why? Is it possible for a poem to tell a story?

3. In conversation, students often use abbreviations for the names of their classes. What do you think the abbreviations below mean? Do you know any other abbreviations?

anthro	Brit lit	contemp lit	poli sci
biochem	chem	econ	psych

LISTENING

🎧 **A. LISTENING FOR THE MAIN IDEA** Listen to the conversation. As you listen, think about this question:
• What two things especially worry Victor about the poetry unit?

🎧 **B. LISTENING FOR INFERENCES** Listen to part of the conversation again. Listen to it twice. As you
listen, answer the following questions by making inferences. Circle the correct letters.

1. Who is Pam?

   A. a friend of Victor's

   B. a professor in the English department

   C. Victor's American literature professor

   D. Dr. Sears' T.A. (teaching assistant)

2. If students are afraid that they might fail a class, what can they do?

   A. find a tutor to help them

   B. drop the class at any time

   C. drop the class before a certain deadline (the latest time to do something)

   D. drop the class before the final exam

3. What can you infer about Robert Frost and Maya Angelou?

   A. They are modern poets who write conversational poems.

   B. They are traditional poets who write poems with rhyme and rhythm.

   C. They write short stories and other prose.

   D. They are professors of literature.

C. GUESSING THE MEANING FROM CONTEXT Listen to part of the conversation again. Guess the meanings of the words and phrases in orange from the context. Then complete the sentences.

1. Two examples of **conventions** in poetry are _____

2. Writing that is **concise** has _____

D. LISTENING FOR IMPORTANT DETAILS Listen to part of the conversation again. Listen for information to complete these sentences.

1. Older or more traditional poetry has _____ and

_____. Most contemporary poetry doesn't.

2. Much contemporary poetry is even _____, similar to

_____, in some ways.

3. Contemporary poetry may seem difficult because it's more _____ than traditional poetry.

E. LISTENING TO POETRY Listen to these two poems. What images come to you as you listen?

A Sunday Morning After a Saturday Night   by LoVerne Brown

She's so happy, this girl,
she's sending out sparks like a brush fire,
so lit with life
her eyes could beam airplanes through fog,
5 so warm with his loving
we could blacken our toast
on her forehead.

The phone rings
and she whispers to it
10 "I love you."
The cord uncoils
and leaps to tell him
she said it,
the receiver melts in her hand
15 as if done by Dali,
the whole room crackles

and we at the breakfast table
smile
but at a safe distance
20 having learned by living
that love so without insulation
can immolate more than the toast.

"The Persistance of Memory" by Salvador Dali, whose paintings often depict melting objects

Source: "A Sunday Morning After a Saturday Night" (Brown)

Without Stopping by Cherry Jean Vasconcellos

In the dream
I can't stop crying.
Neighbors drop in.
They whisper while I
5   straighten pillows
on the couch,
my face wet
and silent as porcelain.
Later, my picture shows up
10 in supermarkets
nationwide: *Woman*
Never Quits Weeping.

In the real world,
he's gone two years
15 and I hardly *ever* cry.
Crude and shameless,
life has filled in the spaces
as it does with everyone.
Now, for example, I remember
20 how he touched me,
but I don't feel his hand
cup my hip the way I used to
in the first, bitter
euphoria after his death
25 when he rose up around me
like incense burning.

Source: "Without Stopping" (Vasconcellos)

AFTER LISTENING

A. COMPREHENSION CHECK Write your answers to these questions on the lines.

1. Which poem from pages 142 and 143 is about new love? _____

2. Which poem is about lost love? _____

3. Are these two poems traditional or contemporary? Explain your answer. _____

_____

_____

_____

Compare your answers with a partner's answers.

B. GUESSING THE MEANING FROM CONTEXT Look back at the two poems on pages 142 and 143 to find words for these definitions. Write the words on the lines.

"A Sunday Morning After a Saturday Night"

1. particles of fire thrown off by burning wood = _____

2. makes many small, sudden, sharp noises = _____

3. something that protects one from heat = _____

4. destroy by fire = _____

"Without Stopping"

5. the thin, shiny material of fine quality cups and plates = _____

6. curve one's hand in a rounded shape (verb) = _____

7. feeling of joy, great happiness = _____

8. something that smells sweet when it is burned (often for religious reasons) = _____

C. ANALYZING POETRY In small groups, analyze the poems and discuss these questions.

"A Sunday Morning After a Saturday Night"

1. The central image of this poem seems to be heat. What are five examples from the poem that support this?

2. How old do you think the person in love is? Why?

3. Who are "we" (in line 17)? What is their attitude toward "this girl"?

"Without Stopping"

4. What is the main difference between the woman in the dream (stanza 1) and the woman in the real world (stanza 2)?

5. How do you know that this poem is about her lover or husband who has died—not about another person (such as a child, friend, or parent) whom she loves?

6. Why did she feel "euphoria" (line 24)? Why was the euphoria "bitter"?

INTONATION

🎧 Questions and Statements

Generally, the voice goes up at the end of *yes/no* questions and down at the end of *wh-* questions.

Examples: *Yes/No* Questions

Do you have a few minutes?

Could I make an appointment?

Would it be possible on another day?

Wh- Questions

When would you like to come in?

What's giving you problems?

How can I help?

In conversation, people often change a statement into a *yes/no* question simply by making their voice go up at the end.

Example: You don't have anything earlier. (Statement)

You don't have anything earlier? (Question)

Even single-word statements can be changed into questions. The exact meaning depends on the context.

Examples: Statements

Yes. = That's correct.

Oh. = I heard what you said.

Questions

Yes? = Really? OR May I help you?

Oh? = Really? OR Is that true?

A. QUESTIONS AND STATEMENTS
Listen to each sentence or word. Is it a question or a statement? Circle the correct answer.

1. Question   Statement
2. Question   Statement
3. Question   Statement
4. Question   Statement

5. Question   Statement
6. Question   Statement
7. Question   Statement
8. Question   Statement

Questions with *Or*

The word *or* can be used in two types of questions: *yes/no* questions and *either/or* questions. Both types of questions can have the exact same words but different intonation. The intonation determines what kind of answer is expected.

If the speaker's voice goes up at the end of the sentence, then he or she is asking a *yes/no* question.

Example: A: Would you like to come in on Monday or Tuesday?
         B: Yes.

If the speaker's voice goes up and then down at the end of the sentence, he or she is asking an *either/or* question.

Example: A: Would you like to come in on Monday or Tuesday?
         B: Monday.

B. HEARING QUESTIONS WITH OR
Listen to each question. Circle the letter of the correct answer. After a pause, you will hear the answer.

1. **A.** Yes.
   B. Short stories.

2. **A.** No.
   B. Chapter 6.

3. **A.** No.
   B. Frost.

4. **A.** Yes, please.
   B. The term paper.

5. **A.** Yes.
   B. Saturday.

6. **A.** No, I'm not.
   B. World literature.

7. **A.** Sure.
   B. Thursday

8. **A.** No, not yet.
   B. The T.A.

C. SAYING QUESTIONS WITH *OR* Repeat the following questions and statements after the speaker.

1. *Yes/No* **Questions**

Do you have a few minutes?

Will it be too late?

Would it be possible another day?

2. *Wh-* **Questions**

What's giving you problems?

When would you like to come in?

What do you think?

3. **Statements**   **Questions**

Oh.   →   Oh?

I can't.   →   I can't?

It's not possible.   →   It's not possible?

4. *Yes/No* **Questions**   *Either/Or* **Questions**

Do you like poetry or novels?   →   Do you like poetry or novels?

Can you come in on Monday or Tuesday? →   Can you come in on Monday or Tuesday?

Have you studied poetry or drama?   →   Have you studied poetry or drama?

D. USING QUESTIONS WITH *OR* IN CONVERSATION Work with a partner. Student A reads each of the following questions using either *yes/no* intonation or *either/or* intonation. Student B draws arrows to show the intonation he or she hears. Then Student A checks to make sure the arrows are correct.

1. Do you like poetry or novels?

2. Are you free Saturday or Sunday?

3. Did you talk with the professor or the T.A.?

4. Can you come in on Monday or Tuesday?

5. Have you studied poetry or drama?

Exchange roles. Student B asks the questions, and Student A draws arrows. Student B checks the arrows.

WORDS IN PHRASES

Responding to Negative Questions: Agreeing

In most languages, when people agree with a negative question, they say "yes" because they're thinking: "Yes. That's true." However, in English, the answer is "no." In the example below, Speaker A is trying to make an appointment.

Example: A: You don't have anything earlier?
       B: No. (= No, I don't have anything earlier.)

After this "no," it's possible to add either a short answer or the correct information.

Example: A: You don't have anything earlier?
       B: | No, I don't.
           | No, I'm afraid I don't.
           | No, I'm sorry. I don't.
           | No. That's the only opening I have.

E. RESPONDING TO NEGATIVE QUESTIONS: AGREEING Work with a partner. Student A will ask the negative questions in the box below using rising intonation at the end. Student B will agree and add a short answer, as in the example in the box above.

Student A

1. Learning English in a week isn't possible?

2. You haven't studied American lit?

3. You can't help me with my homework?

4. The test last week wasn't hard?

5. You didn't understand yesterday's lecture?

6. It wasn't too late to drop the class?

7. There isn't any class on Saturday?

8. The teacher won't be here tomorrow?

Then exchange roles. Student B will ask the negative questions in the box below. Student A will answer.

Student B

1. You've never studied poetry before?

2. We don't have homework tonight?

3. Analyzing poetry isn't difficult for you?

4. You don't like studying after 10:00 PM?

5. You haven't ever been to Alaska?

6. Our teacher can't speak Swedish?

7. There isn't any class on Tuesday?

8. They won't offer this class next term?

WORDS IN PHRASES

🎧 Responding to Negative Questions: Disagreeing

People use negative questions to confirm what they know. In other words, they *expect* the answer to be "no," but they're checking the assumption, just to make sure. However, sometimes the assumption is incorrect, so the other person disagrees. In such a case, the response is "yes." It's important to use emphasis in the voice. Notice the intonation in these sentences.

Examples: **A**: You don't have any appointments earlier than 11:00?
B: *Yes, we **do**.*

A: You haven't read it yet?
B: *Yes, I **have**.*

A: We won't have to do a term paper?
B: *Yes, we **will**.*

It's also possible, after the "yes," to add the correct information.

Example: **A**: You don't have any appointments earlier than 11:00?
B: *Yes, we **do**. Actually, we have an opening at 10:00.*

👥 **F. RESPONDING TO NEGATIVE QUESTIONS: DISAGREEING** Go back to page 148 and do Activity E again. This time, disagree (say "yes") and add a short answer.

Example: **A**: You don't have anything earlier?
B: *Yes, we do.*
Yes, actually we do.

PRONUNCIATION

◌ The Medial *T*

The medial *t,* or the /t/ sound in the middle of many words, sometimes actually sounds like a *t,* but frequently it doesn't. This is how you might expect these words to be pronounced:

Group 1: butter later Saturday literature

Group 2: written mountain button appointment

Listen to the groups of words again. This time the medial *t* is pronounced as a North American native speaker would. Notice that the *t* in Group 1 sounds similar to a *d.* The *t* in Group 2 sounds similar to an *n.*

You might choose to pronounce them the first way, but *it's important to understand native speakers* who pronounce them the second way.

◌ **G. THE MEDIAL *T*** Listen and write the words that you hear.

1. _____

2. _____

3. _____

4. _____

5. _____

6. _____

7. _____

8. _____

9. _____

10. _____

LANGUAGE FUNCTION

Making Appointments and Negotiating Time

When you make an appointment, it's often necessary to negotiate for a time different from the one first offered. Here is a typical phone conversation to make an appointment and negotiate a time.

A: Could I make an appointment for next week?
B: We have an opening at 3:00 on Tuesday.
A: Hmm. You don't have anything earlier?
B: No, I'm afraid not.
A: Um, well, I have classes Tuesday afternoon. Would another day be possible?
B: Sure. How's 10:00 on Friday?
A: Great.
B: O.K. See you then.
A: Thanks a lot. Bye.

To make an appointment, there are several things you might say:

Could I make an appointment for next week?
I'd like to make an appointment, please.
Is it possible to make an appointment with the doctor for next week?

There are several ways to negotiate time:

I have classes in the afternoon. Is there any opening in the morning?
That's a difficult time for me. Would it be possible at 10:00?
Are there any appointments available in the morning?
I'm afraid I can't make it at that time. Do you have something earlier?

PUT IT TOGETHER

MAKING APPOINTMENTS AND NEGOTIATING TIME With a partner, role-play the situations in the boxes. First, Student A wants to make an appointment, and Student B is the receptionist. Negotiate the time of the appointment. Use the intonation, phrases, and pronunciation that you've learned in Part 3 together with some of the structures in the box on page 148. Then exchange roles.

Student A	Student B
Make an appointment with…	Make an appointment with…
your dentist	your doctor
your teacher	your T.A.
your hairstylist or barber	your career counselor
your car mechanic	your lawyer

BEFORE LISTENING

Maya Angelou

👥 **A. THINKING AHEAD** You're going to hear part of a radio program with Maya Angelou, a writer of poetry and prose. In the program, she talks about an extraordinary incident that happened when she was seven, growing up in the African-American section of a town in the southern United States. In small groups, discuss these questions.

1. Sometimes a child **stands out from the crowd**—is special or different in some way. What might be some reasons for this? Is it good or bad to stand out?

2. Some people have unhappy childhoods due to poverty, serious illness, lack of love, loss of parents, or other reasons. However, most are able to survive, and many become healthy, happy, successful adults. What are some possible reasons for this? In other words, how are they able to rise above tragedy?

3. The interviewer says, "Words *do* have enormous power." Has someone ever said something that made a big change in your life? If so, was it a good change or a bad change?

B. VOCABULARY PREPARATION Read the sentences below. The words and phrases in orange are from the radio program. Match the definitions in the box with the words and phrases in orange. Write the correct letters on the lines.

a. ability to live through a bad situation
b. actively attracted
c. after that
d. appropriate
e. believed to be the result of
f. move on hands and knees
g. outsider; person thrown out of society
h. prejudice; treatment against a person or group of people
i. a serious test or trial
j. sexually attacked

_____ **1.** Alexa was very different from the others in the group. They didn't include her in their activities, so she began to feel like a **pariah**.

_____ **2.** In many countries, people of minority racial or religious groups suffer from **discrimination** from the rest of society.

_____ **3.** Martin's success can be **credited to** his education.

_____ **4.** The woman was **raped** by a man in the neighborhood. She was so traumatized by this that she refused to name the man. Finally, she decided she had to tell the police who the man was.

_____ **5.** Allen committed a crime. **Subsequently**, the police found him and arrested him.

_____ **6.** Years and years of reading is **apt** preparation for someone who wants to become a writer.

_____ **7.** When José saw hatred and injustice all around him, he had to stop himself—with difficulty—from committing violence. This was a terrible **crucible** for him.

_____ **8.** When I was a child, I used to put a blanket over the kitchen table and then **crawl** under the table. It was great—like a cave, my own secret place.

_____ **9.** With a bit of food, I **lured** the frightened cat from its hiding place.

_____ **10.** People in the village depended on each other for their **survival** during the long war.

LISTENING

Listening Strategy

🎧 Listening for Rhyme and Rhythm

Rhyme and *rhythm* are two conventions in poetry. Rhyme refers to the sound of two or more words when stressed vowels (*a, e, i, o, u*) and the consonants after them are the same.

Examples: cost lost pain stain

Rhythm is the order of stressed and unstressed syllables. In some poems, it is regular and predictable; in others, it is not. The rhythm of a poem can be shown with stress marks (′) over stressed syllables and rounded marks (˘) over unstressed syllables.

Example: Thĕ breézĕs táste

Ŏf ápplĕ peél.

Thĕ aír ĭs fúll

Ŏf smélls tŏ feél.

—John Updike, "September"

A. LISTENING FOR RHYME AND RHYTHM Before listening to the interview with Maya Angelou, listen to one of her poems as you read along. Listen for the poem's rhyme and rhythm.

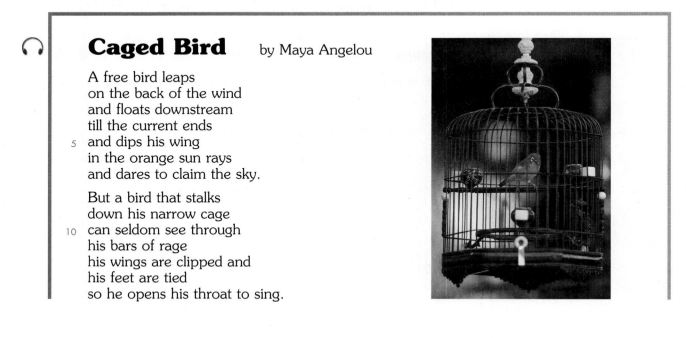

🎧 **Caged Bird** by Maya Angelou

A free bird leaps
on the back of the wind
and floats downstream
till the current ends
5 and dips his wing
in the orange sun rays
and dares to claim the sky.

But a bird that stalks
down his narrow cage
10 can seldom see through
his bars of rage
his wings are clipped and
his feet are tied
so he opens his throat to sing.

15 The caged bird sings
with a fearful trill
of things unknown
but longed for still
and his tune is heard
20 on the distant hill
for the caged bird
sings of freedom.

The free bird thinks of another breeze
and the trade winds soft through the sighing trees
25 and the fat worms waiting on a dawn-bright lawn
and he names the sky his own.

But a caged bird stands on the grave of dreams
his shadow shouts on a nightmare scream
his wings are clipped and his feet are tied
30 so he opens his throat to sing.

The caged bird sings
with a fearful trill
of things unknown
but longed for still
35 and his tune is heard
on the distant hill
for the caged bird
sings of freedom.

Source: *Shaker, Why Don't You Sing?* (Angelou)

With a partner, underline the words that rhyme in the poem. Then read the second stanza aloud. Mark the syllables that are stressed.

Test-Taking Strategy

Taking Notes While Listening

In the listening sections of some standardized tests, you can take notes as you listen to a selection. Sometimes you will read the questions before you listen; other times, you will listen and then hear the questions. Taking notes while listening will help you answer the test questions afterwards. When listening to a short lecture or interview, take notes on the main ideas, key points, and important names, dates, and places. Use abbreviations to save time.

B. LISTENING FOR MAIN IDEAS Listen to the radio program. In the program, Stephen Banker interviews Maya Angelou. As you listen, think about the questions below. Take notes.
• Why did Maya Angelou stop speaking?
• How did this indirectly lead to her becoming a poet?

Understanding the Passive Voice

The passive voice is used for a variety of reasons.

1. The speaker doesn't know who did an action.

    Example: Someone hurt Catherine. **(Active voice)**
                    Catherine **was hurt**. **(Passive voice)**

2. The speaker knows who did an action but doesn't want to say who it was.

    Example: My brother committed a crime. **(Active voice)**
                    A crime **was committed**. **(Passive voice)**

3. It isn't important for the listener to know who did an action.

    Example: Several people encouraged Rosa to read. **(Active voice)**
                    Rosa **was encouraged** to read. **(Passive voice)**

4. Less common is the use of passive gerunds. Like gerunds, which are used as nouns, passive gerunds are used as noun phrases.

    Examples: **Being introduced** to poetry changed Britney's entire life.
                    (= Britney was introduced to poetry, and this changed her entire life.)

                    Kevin's parents were upset about his **being expelled** from school.
                    (= Kevin was expelled from school, and his parents were upset about this.)

🎧 **C. UNDERSTANDING THE PASSIVE VOICE** Listen again to the central part of Angelou's story. As you listen, write the passive voice verbs on the lines.

    Well, um, I—at seven and a half, I _____, and, uh, I said so. I mean,
                                                    1

I, after pressure from my brother, who I loved a lot, I named the man. Um, the man

_____ subsequently _____, I mean, almost
               2   2

immediately. And, uh, I believed that because I had spoken, ah, the man was dead. And it

_____ that he _____ to death. Um, I thought that
               3   4

my saying his name caused directly his _____, and I guess it is so.
                                              5

👥 Compare your answers with a partner's answers. Then discuss this question:
  • In your opinion, why is Angelou careful to use the passive voice five times in this short passage?

D. LISTENING FOR INFERENCES Listen to a section of the program. This time, listen for names. Fill in the blanks with the names you hear. Write your answers on the lines.

Angelou: Well, that same Mrs. Flowers, um, used to read to me, and she read poetry, and I had memorized by then large sections of _____ 1 , Paul Lawrence Dunbar, Countee Cullen, Langston Hughes. Uh, I had memorized portions of _____ 2 because I had nothing else to do, and I loved to memorize things. Uh, and Mrs. Flowers told me that poetry was music written for the human voice and that I must speak it. To really understand it, I must put it on my tongue and use my lips to form the words.

Banker: So they weren't your words.

Angelou: No, they weren't mine, but I loved them, and I began, um, under the bed—we had a high country bed, you know—and I used to crawl under the bed and sit way back against the wall and read Poe—and I loved Edgar Allen Poe. My brother and I called him "Eap." And, uh, so I, I, started reading _____ 3 aloud and _____ 4 aloud. And then I would try with my brother, and finally, it was poetry alone that, um, that lured my voice out of its hidden place.

Compare your answers with a partner's answers. Then discuss this question:
• What can you infer about the people whose names you wrote down?

AFTER LISTENING

A. DISCUSSION In small groups, discuss these questions.

1. What two things "almost directly" helped Angelou to survive a difficult childhood?
2. What can you infer about society in Angelou's "little town"?
3. What is a "volunteer mute"?
4. Why did Angelou become a volunteer mute?
5. Why wasn't she afraid to speak to her brother?
6. Why did Mrs. Flowers say Angelou "must speak" poetry—read it aloud?
7. How did Angelou begin to speak again?

B. MAKING CONNECTIONS What were the events or steps that led to Maya Angelou becoming a poet? In a strange and terrible way, it appears that her rape as a child was, indirectly, the first step toward "finding her voice" as a poet. What were the other steps? Fill them in on this graphic organizer.

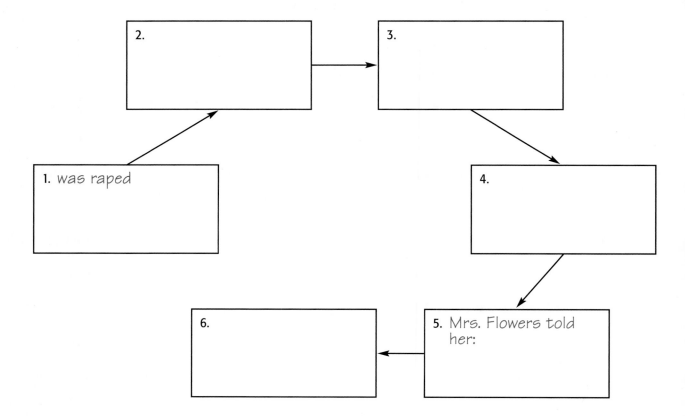

PART ⑤ ACADEMIC ENGLISH American Poets

BEFORE LISTENING

A. THINKING AHEAD You're going to hear a lecture about American poets. Before you listen, discuss these questions in small groups.

1. It often takes many years for a poet to find his or her **voice**—a specific, unique style of expression. What poets in your native language have a unique voice? How would you describe the poet's voice or style of expression?

2. The lecturer explains three of the **creative impulses** in American poetry—three reasons that people write poetry. In your opinion, why do people write poetry? Brainstorm possible impulses that lead people to create poetry.

B. GUESSING THE MEANING FROM CONTEXT Read the sentences below. The words in orange are from the lecture. Guess their meanings from the context. Write your guesses on the lines.

1. I can't give you an example of a "typical" American poet because these poets are a very **diverse** group.

   Guess: _____

2. Although Ethan now writes mostly prose—both fiction and nonfiction—he began by writing **verse**.

   Guess: _____

3. Nobody knew much about Emily Dickinson because she had withdrawn from society and become a **recluse**. She led a solitary life for many years.

   Guess: _____

4. William Saroyan's short stories have an **idiosyncratic** use of punctuation. For example, he never uses quotation marks at all. This is highly unusual, and Saroyan is the only writer I know who does this.

   Guess: _____

5. Even if you don't understand the language, you can identify Saroyan's poems at a **glance** because of the way they look on the page.

   Guess: _____

6. Since the **advent** of the Internet, people have had far greater access to information that was difficult to find before.

   Guess: _____

7. Olivia had very strong **convictions** about the importance of freedom and **egalitarianism**. It was her belief that people couldn't really be free if they didn't also have equality with everyone else in society.

   Guess (convictions): _____

   Guess (egalitarianism): _____

8. In Langston Hughes' poetry, he **incorporated** the rhythms of jazz, gospel music, and the blues.

   Guess: _____

9. For many years, David went through **psychoanalysis**. His therapist helped him to **grapple** with his personal psychological demons, but it was a long, hard struggle.

   Guess (psychoanalysis): _____

   Guess (grapple): _____

Now compare your answers with a partner's answers.

C. TAKING NOTES: ABBREVIATIONS Write your own abbreviations for these words from the lecture.

1. American _____

2. poetry _____

3. impulse _____

4. conviction _____

5. rhythm _____

LISTENING

A. RECOGNIZING NAMES Listen to the pronunciation of these names of poets mentioned in the lecture. Notice the spelling so that you'll be able to take notes more easily. Write the initials for each name. You can use initials as your abbreviations.

1. John Berryman _J.B._

2. e.e. cummings _____

3. Emily Dickinson _____

4. Langston Hughes _____

5. Anne Sexton _____

6. Walt Whitman _____

B. VOCABULARY PREPARATION Listen to one part of the lecture. What does the lecturer mean by the term *wordplay*?

Wordplay means _____

_____

Listening Strategy

Listening for the Main Ideas in a Lecture

A well-organized professor often makes the main ideas clear by repeating them, in somewhat different words, several times during a lecture: in the introduction, at the end of each major section, and again in the conclusion. Read these examples from the lecture you are about to hear.

Example: You hear in the introduction: The second creative impulse is the desire to represent the **common dramas of a multi-racial, multi-ethnic society**.

You hear at the end of a section: These two poets, Walt Whitman and Langston Hughes, are examples of American poets whose creative impulses led them to portray the **culture, the society**.

C. TAKING NOTES: USING AN OUTLINE Listen to the lecture. It's in four sections. You will listen to each section twice. Fill in as much of the outline as you can. Don't worry if you can't fill in everything. You'll listen to the whole lecture again later.

There are three main ideas. You'll hear each one three times—once in the introduction, once in the middle, and again in the conclusion.

American Poets

Section I

I. Introduction: Three Impulses that Create Voice in American Poetry

    A. _____

    B. _____

    C. _____

Section 2

II. Creative Impulse: _____

    A. Poet: _____

        1. Background info. abt. her:

           a. woman, 19th century, recluse

           b. _____

        2. Use of punctuation

           a. _____

           b. _____

Emily Dickinson

    B. Poet: _____

        1. Background info. abt. him:

           a. _____

           b. _____

        2. Use of punctuation (possible because of the typewriter)

           a. _____

           b. squeezed, stretched, separated words, phrases, and lines in the manner

             of a _____

III. Creative Impulse: _____

    A. Poet: _____

        1. Background info. abt. him:

            a. _____

            b. _____

            c. _____

        2. Wanted his poems to voice _____

            _____

        3. Masterpiece: "Song of Myself"

            a. _____

            b. _____

            c. _____

    B. Poet: _____

        1. Background info. abt. him:

            a. Mem. of the Harlem Renaissance (a literary movement), which celebrated _____

            _____

            b. _____

        2. Created _____

        3. In his poems, you can hear _____

            _____

Walt Whitman

Langston Hughes

IV. Creative Impulse: _____

    A. Poet: _____

        1. Background info. abt. him:

            a. _____

            b. _____

        2. His poetry

            a. Wrote in the voice of "Henry"

            b. Book *Dream Song*—an attempt to help him with _____

            _____

B. Poet: _____

   1. Reason for writing poetry: _____

   2. Her poetry: _____

   _____

Section 5

V. Conclusion

   A. Primary creative impulse

   B. But _____

   _____

Source: Adapted from a lecture by Jill Hanifan, Ph.D.

D. CHECKING YOUR NOTES Listen to the whole lecture again. As you listen, review your notes and fill in any missing information.

AFTER LISTENING

A. USING YOUR NOTES With a partner, use your notes to answer these questions.

1. Which two poets wrote for highly personal and psychological reasons?

2. Which two poets are known for their unique and challenging use of punctuation?

3. Which two poets represented the diversity of American society?

B. MAKING CONNECTIONS Look back at the three poems in Part 1, pages 135–137. In small groups, discuss these questions.

1. Which two poems make use of wordplay?

_____

2. Which two poems represent ethnic diversity in the society?

_____

3. How are all three poems also personal expressions?

_____

C. DISCUSSION In small groups, discuss these questions.

1. Is there one poem in this chapter that you especially like? If so, what do you like about it?

2. In the poem, are there any specific lines that you like? If so, why do you like them?

PUT IT ALL TOGETHER

Speaking Strategy

Giving a Speech

You will occasionally need to give a speech in front of the class. These suggestions will help you give an effective speech.

• Prepare, prepare, prepare. Organize your ideas and write your speech as you would organize an essay.

• Don't memorize what you are going to say. If necessary, though, you might memorize short pieces. For example, you might memorize a quotation or a few lines of a poem.

• Put just notes on 3 x 5 index cards. These notes might be the first few words of each section of your speech, or they might be phrases that you are afraid you will forget.

• Practice your speech several times at home. Present your speech to a friend or family member or even to your bathroom mirror.

• During your speech, glance at your index cards whenever you need help remembering something. Always look up while speaking.

• As you're speaking, have eye contact with the people in your audience, the people to whom you're speaking. If it makes you nervous to have eye contact, look at people's foreheads instead of their eyes.

• Don't forget to breathe.

GIVING A SPEECH You are going to prepare and give a speech.

STEP 1

Choose *one* of the following projects.

Project 1
Analyze one poem written in English.

Project 2
Tell about a person or event that changed your life.

STEP 2

Follow these steps for the project you have chosen.

Project 1
Choose *one* poem from this chapter to analyze. Prepare a short speech about your poem. In preparing your analysis, include your ideas about:
• how the poet's background is reflected in the poem
• the poet's use of wordplay, social conviction, and/or personal emotion
• the images or symbols in the poem
• the meaning of the poem

Project 2
Tell about a person or event that changed your life. To help you begin, think of the radio program in Part 4. Maya Angelou related the story of one person, Mrs. Flowers, who changed Angelou's life by encouraging her to read poetry aloud.

Now think back over your life. Think about the people who have influenced you and the events that have shaped your life. Choose *one* person or event. Here are some suggestions:

People	Events
a family member	a very difficult situation
a friend	a funny event
a teacher	a small incident that gave you a big idea
a person you've read about who has influenced you	

STEP 3

Give a short speech about your topic. Follow the guidelines in the box on page 164 to practice and give your speech.

Listening Strategy

Being an Active Listener

Be an active listener when a classmate is giving a speech! Remember how difficult it is for most people to stand in front of the class. Try to make it as comfortable as possible for the speaker. You can do this by paying attention and occasionally nodding or smiling at an appropriate moment. Have a pencil and a piece of paper on your desk. **Jot down** (write quickly) any question that comes to mind during the speech or anything that you especially like. Save your questions and comments for after the speech.

STEP 4

As you listen to each speech, take brief notes. Be prepared to ask a question or tell the speaker what you enjoyed about the presentation.

CHAPTER 6

Heroes in Literature

Discuss these questions:
- What do you see in the photo?
- In what way is this character a hero?
- Name some heroes in literature. What makes them heroic?

"One day, it is said, a farmer saw a buffalo wandering in
his rice field."

A. THINKING AHEAD You are going to read a folktale from Thailand. **Folktales**, oral stories passed down through generations, reflect the values of the culture they are a part of. Usually the author is anonymous; in fact, most folktales have many authors—the storytellers who tell the tales through the years.

In small groups, discuss these questions.

1. In your culture, do people enjoy telling folktales? If so, when and in what situations? Can anyone tell these stories, or are they told only by certain people?

2. What are some folktales you know? How old do you think the oldest one is?

3. Many folktales from around the world have common themes. For example, one theme is the **unlikely** (not expected) **hero**, such as a fool, who does something very brave or good. Other folktales may explain things in nature, for example why certain geological formations (mountains, rivers, and such) exist or why animals are the way they are. What are some other common themes in the folktales from your culture?

B. READING Read the folktale from Thailand. As you read, think about this question:
• What did the farmer do to confuse the lorikeet?

Why the Parrot Repeats

In ancient times it was not the parrot that was kept in the house by man and taught to speak, but the lorikeet. For people had found that this small bird was a very intelligent creature, and he needed very little teaching. If he heard a word, he could repeat it easily. Not only that, he often spoke his own thoughts to man instead of
5 merely imitating the sounds he heard around him.

But it happened one time that all this changed.

One day, it is said, a farmer saw a buffalo wandering in his rice field. It was his neighbor's animal, but the farmer took the buffalo, killed it, cut up the meat, cooked some and ate it, and the remainder he hid. Part of the meat the man hid on the top of
10 the rice house. The rest he hid in the rice bin[1].

The next day the neighbor came looking for his animal, saying to the farmer, "Have you seen my lost buffalo?"

The farmer replied, "No, I have seen no lost buffalo."

But just then the farmer's lorikeet spoke up. "My master killed it. He ate some and
15 hid some. Part he hid in the rice bin and part he hid over the rice house."

When the neighbor heard this, he looked in the places the bird had mentioned, and there he found the buffalo meat.

But the farmer said, "Yes, this is where I always keep meat. But I did not see your buffalo. This is the meat of another animal."

20 The lorikeet called out again: "He killed it. Part he hid in the rice bin and part he hid over the rice house."

The neighbor was perplexed. He didn't know whether to take the word of the man or the bird. And so he took the matter to court. The trial was set for the following day.

The farmer who had stolen the meat said to himself. "Why should the word of a
25 lorikeet be taken, rather than my word?"

That night he took the bird from its cage and placed it in a large brass pot. He covered the pot with a cloth, so that it was dark inside. Outside, the night was clear and bright. The moon was full. But inside the pot, the lorikeet could see nothing of this. The man began to beat on the pot, softly at first, then more loudly, until it
30 sounded like thunder. He took a dipper of water, dripping a little of it on the cloth now and then so that it sounded like rain. All night long he pounded on the pot and dripped water, and he stopped only when dawn[2] came. Then he took the lorikeet and put it back in its cage.

When it was time for the trial, the farmer took his bird and went to court. The
35 neighbor who had lost the buffalo told how the lorikeet had instructed him where to find the stolen meat. The judge asked the lorikeet for his testimony. The bird repeated what he had said before:

"He killed the buffalo. Part he hid in the rice bin and part he hid over the rice house."

[1]**bin:** a large container for storing things
[2]**dawn:** time of day when sunlight first appears

The man who had stolen the buffalo spoke, saying "The meat that was in the rice bin and over the rice house was that of another animal. How can it be that you give more weight to the words of this stupid bird than to my words?"

"The lorikeet is indeed intelligent," the judge said.

"He speaks more often with nonsense than with sense," the farmer replied. "Ask him another question. Ask him what kind of a night we had last night."

So the judge asked the lorikeet, which replied, "Last night was dark and stormy. The wind blew, the rain poured down, and the thunder roared."

"If you remember," the farmer said, "last night was calm and clear, and the moon shone with all its brightness. Can you now condemn me for a crime on the testimony of this bird?"

The people were convinced, and the judge was convinced. They said:

"No, you are innocent, and your life was endangered by the foolish testimony of the lorikeet. Henceforth we will not keep this bird in our houses and care for him as though he were one of us."

So the man who stole the buffalo was freed, and the lorikeet was expelled and sent back into the forest. The lorikeet lived as he had before he had known man, fending for himself and caring for his own needs. But one day the lorikeet saw a new bird in the forest, larger than himself and covered with brilliant red and green feathers. He spoke to the new bird, asking him who he was.

"I am the parrot," the bird answered. "I have come from the South, and now I am going to live in this country. I speak the language of man."

Then the lorikeet said, "Welcome to the country. As you are a stranger here, accept my advice and warning. I too speak the language of man. For many years I was kept in man's house and cared for. I saw with my eyes and heard with my ears. I spoke not only words that man spoke, but what was in my own mind as well. But when I said what was in my own mind, it displeased man, and I was driven away. This is my warning: When man learns that you can speak his language, he will capture you and bring you into his house. Say nothing but what he teaches you. Repeat his words and nothing more. For man loves to hear only his own thoughts repeated. He is not interested in truth or wisdom from any other source."

The parrot listened to the lorikeet and thanked him. And it came about as the lorikeet had predicted. Man learned of the arrival of the talking parrot, and the parrot was captured and brought to man's house. He was fed and cared for, as once the lorikeet had been cared for, and he was taught the things that man wanted him to say.

But fearful of *ever* saying his true thoughts lest man resent them, the parrot only echoes the words that he hears from man's lips.

Source: *Ride with the Sun* (Courlander)

C. VOCABULARY CHECK

Look back at the reading on pages 169–170. Find words or phrases to match the following definitions. Write the correct words and phrases on the lines. Line numbers are given in parentheses.

1. confused (20–25) _____

2. statements usually made in court (35–40) _____

3. believe (a phrase) (40–45) _____

4. give severe punishment to a criminal (45–50) _____

5. from this time on (formal) (50–55) _____

6. forced to leave (55–60) _____

7. taking care of oneself without assistance (55–60) _____

8. for fear that (formal) (80–82) _____

D. ANALYZING THE STORY

With a partner, analyze the story by discussing these questions.

1. What is the theme of the story?

2. Who is the hero in this story? Describe the hero's personality.

3. What does the hero do that is brave or good?

4. Does the hero learn a lesson? If yes, what is it?

5. What does the folktale explain about the behavior of parrots and lorikeets?

E. RESPONSE WRITING

Choose *one* of these topics. Write about it for 15 minutes. Try to use new vocabulary but don't use a dictionary. Just write as many ideas as you can.

• What is your reaction to "Why the Parrot Repeats"? Did you like the story? Why or why not?
• Describe your favorite folktale. What is your favorite part of the story?
• Who is your favorite folktale hero? Why?
• What folktale do you know that explains something in nature? What is the story about?

PART ② SOCIAL LANGUAGE Movie Heroes

BEFORE LISTENING

The Magnificent Seven, directed by John Sturges (1960)   *The Seven Samurai,* directed by Akira Kurosawa (1954)

A. BRAINSTORMING As a class, brainstorm names of **westerns** (movies about the so-called American Wild West) and film stars from these westerns. Write as many as you can think of. Then brainstorm names of recent **blockbuster** movies—expensively produced and widely popular films—and their stars.

B. THINKING AHEAD In most movies, there is a **protagonist**—a central character who is usually a hero*. In some movies, this character is an **antihero**—not a "bad guy" necessarily, but rather a protagonist who lacks some of the moral qualities of a typical hero. In small groups, discuss these questions and fill in the box.

1. Which well-known actors* have often played a hero? What characteristics do you associate with a hero?

2. Which well-known actors have played antiheroes? What characteristics do you associate with antiheroes? List them.

	Actors	Characteristics
Heroes		
Antiheroes		

*Nowadays, the words *hero* and *actor* can be used to refer to either male or female. Some people also use *heroine* and *actress* to refer to a female.

C. VOCABULARY PREPARATION. Read the sentences below. The words and phrases in orange are from the conversation. Match the definitions in the box with the words and phrases in orange. Write the correct letters on the lines.

a. made possible

b. movies about the American Wild West that were made by Italians and/or filmed in Italy

c. people who help or support

d. person who chooses to spend a lot of time alone

e. punishment for criminals that causes them to suffer as much as their victims suffered

f. unclear; understood in more than one way

_____ **1.** In *The Magnificent Seven*, the hero has six **allies** with him when he rides into town.

_____ **2.** The ending to the movie is **ambiguous**, so we argued for a long time about what it meant.

_____ **3.** The Japanese film *The Seven Samurai* **paved the way for** the American film *The Magnificent Seven*, which was filmed several years later.

_____ **4.** In many westerns, there's an **eye-for-an-eye sort of justice**.

_____ **5.** When the stranger first came to town, we were all very curious about him. He didn't talk much and seemed to be a **loner**.

_____ **6.** My favorite movies are the **spaghetti westerns** with background music by Ennio Morricone.

LISTENING

A. LISTENING FOR THE MAIN IDEA Listen to the conversation. As you listen, think about this question:
• Why do Ashley and Rachel decide to watch an old Clint Eastwood movie?

B. LISTENING FOR DETAILS Listen to the conversation again. Write short answers to these questions.

1. What kind of character does Clint Eastwood play in *A Fistful of Dollars*? _____

_____

2. What film is *A Fistful of Dollars* based on? _____

_____

3. What characters in movies from the 1980s and 1990s did Eastwood's character influence?

_____

_____

_____

C. MAKING INFERENCES Listen to part of the conversation. You'll hear it twice. As you listen, make inferences to answer these questions.

1. How does Ashley feel about Rachel's suggestion? _____

_____

2. How does Rachel feel about her own suggestion? _____

_____

AFTER LISTENING

A. TAKING A SURVEY Interview three classmates about their favorite movies. First, think about your own answers to the questions in the chart below. Then ask three classmates the questions and write their answers in the chart.

Questions	Classmate 1	Classmate 2	Classmate 3
1. What is your favorite movie?			
2. In what culture or country does the movie take place?			
3. What qualities does the movie's hero have?			
4. Is there any connection between the hero's qualities and the culture or country in which the movie takes place?			

B. DISCUSSING SURVEY RESULTS Form small groups. Try not to be in a group with someone that you interviewed. Discuss the results of your survey by answering these questions.

1. What type(s) of movies were most people's favorites?

2. What were the similarities and/or differences among the heroes that people described?

3. Did you find many connections between the qualities of the heroes and the countries or cultures that they came from? Give examples.

PART ③ THE MECHANICS OF LISTENING AND SPEAKING

WORDS IN PHRASES

Starting a Conversation

There are several ways to start a conversation with someone you know. One way is to ask a question about what the person has been doing lately.

Examples: **What have you been doing lately?**
What have you guys* been up to lately?
So what's new?
How was your weekend?

* *Guys* is used informally to refer to a small group of people. It can be used to refer to both men and women.

LANGUAGE FUNCTION

Keeping a Conversation Going

When an **acquaintance**—someone you know, but not very well—starts a conversation with a question such as one in the box above, you probably do not need to give a detailed answer. Usually you return the question.

Examples: **A:** What have you been doing lately?
B: Oh, not much. How about you?

A: How was your weekend?
B: Pretty good, but too short. How about yours?

When a closer friend starts a conversation by asking the same question, you usually give a more specific, honest answer. This answer usually leads to more conversation.

Example: **A:** What have you been doing lately?
B: I was at the library all weekend. I have a big exam next week.
Well, I saw a great movie last night.
Um, I went to the beach on Sunday.

Either person can continue the conversation by asking another question.

Examples: **A:** What have you been doing lately?
B: Well, I saw a great movie last night.
A: Oh, really? What did you see?

👥 **KEEPING A CONVERSATION GOING** Work with a partner. Practice keeping a conversation going. Student A asks: "What have you been doing lately?" Student B gives a general, short answer or a more specific answer. Then Student A or Student B tries to keep the conversation going by asking a question. Then exchange roles.

Examples: **A:** What have you been doing lately?
                 B: Not much. How about you? (Short answer; question keeps the conversation going)

                 A: What have you been doing lately?
                 B: Well, I went to the beach last weekend. (Specific answer)
                 A: Great! How was it? (Question keeps the conversation going)

INTONATION

🎧 Question Intonation

In Chapter 5 (page 145), you learned that your voice goes up at the end of *yes/no* questions and down at the end of *wh-* questions.

Examples: Did you do anything interesting this weekend? ↗

                 What did you do this weekend? ↘

When you hear a *yes/no* question, the speaker expects an answer beginning with *yes* or *no*. When you hear a *wh-*question, the speaker expects a longer, more informative answer.

In casual conversation, sometimes a statement is said with a *yes/no* question intonation. In using this structure, the speaker is asking for confirmation—a *yes* or *no* answer—of what he or she already thinks is true.

Examples: You went to the beach this weekend? ↗

                 You were busy this weekend? ↗

🎧 **A. HEARING QUESTION INTONATION** Listen to the questions. Does the speaker expect a *yes/no* answer or an information answer? Circle the correct answer.

1. Yes/No   Information   **4.** Yes/No   Information

2. Yes/No   Information   **5.** Yes/No   Information

3. Yes/No   Information   **6.** Yes/No   Information

👥 **B. STARTING A CONVERSATION** Work with a partner. Student A asks Student B the questions below using the correct question intonation. Student B answers the questions. Then exchange roles.

1. What did you do this weekend?   **4.** You saw a Clint Eastwood movie?

2. How was your weekend?   **5.** What have you been doing lately?

3. Did you see a movie last night?   **6.** You're going to the library tonight?

PRONUNCIATION

🎧 Reduced Forms of Words: *Wh-* Questions

When people speak naturally, some words (and combinations of sounds) become reduced, or shortened. This often happens when you ask a *wh-* question with an auxiliary verb (*do, did, have,* etc.).

Examples:	Long Forms	→	Reduced Forms
	What did you do this weekend?	→	Whadja do this weekend?
	How did your weekend go?	→	Howdjer weekend go?
	Whom did you go with?	→	Whoodja go with?
	When did you go?	→	Whendja go?
	Where did you go last weekend?	→	Wheredja go last weekend?
	How have you been?	→	Howveya been?
	What have you been up to?	→	Whadaya been up to?

Notice that the *y* (as in *you*) sounds like *j* when it follows the /d/ sound. It is pronounced as /dʒ/.

Examples:	Long Forms	→	Reduced Forms
	did you	→	didja
	could you	→	couldja
	would you	→	wouldja

🎧 **C. REDUCED FORMS OF WORDS** Listen to the conversation. Write on the lines the *long* forms of the reduced words you hear.

David: Hi, Sarah. _____

do this weekend?   1

Sarah: Hi, David. I went to the beach.

David: _____ go?
2

Sarah: On Sunday.

David: _____ go?
3

Sarah: To Mariner Point. It was great.

David: Wow. _____ go with?
4

Sarah: Jeff.

David: _____ go surfing?
5

Sarah: No, it was too cold to go in the water, so we just sat on the sand and talked.

PRONUNCIATION

⌒ The Voiced *th*: /ð/

The voiced *th*—/ð/—may sound like /d/ or /z/, but all three sounds are pronounced differently. Listen to these contrasts.

/ð/	/d/	/z/
then	den	Zen
breathing	breeding	breezing
bathe	bade	bays

Note: The IPA (International Phonetic Alphabet) symbol for the voiced *th* sound is /ð/.

⌒ **D. HEARING** /ð/ In each pair of words, circle the word that you hear.

1. then	Zen		**6.** worthy	wordy
2. breathing	breeding		**7.** clothing	closing
3. bathe	bays		**8.** though	dough
4. than	Dan		**9.** they've	Dave
5. they	day		**10.** loathe	load

⌒ **E. PRONOUNCING** /ð/ Look again at the box above. Repeat the words that you hear.

⌒ **F. PRONOUNCING** /ð/ **IN SENTENCES** Read along as you listen to these short conversations. Then listen again and repeat each sentence after the speaker.

1. **A:** So there's a problem with my essay?
   B: Well, it's a little wordy. It wouldn't be hard to shorten it, though.

2. **A:** Those guys say Professor Day loathes us!
   B: They're right! He loads us with assignments every week.

3. **A:** I just heard that my favorite clothing store is closing for good!
   B: You mean Then Zen is going out of business? Good! Their clothes were always much too expensive. I never dared to go there.

👥 Now practice the conversations with a partner.

PUT IT TOGETHER

STARTING A CONVERSATION AND KEEPING IT GOING Work with a partner. Use the questions in the box below. Student A starts a conversation by asking a question about what Student B has been doing lately. After Student B answers, Student A asks a related question to keep the conversation going. Be sure to use correct question intonation. Try to use reduced forms. Then exchange roles.

Example: **A:** What did you do this weekend?
B: I saw a movie.
A: What did you see?
B: That new horror movie at the Grand.
A: Oh, how was it?
B: It was great. Really scary!

Starting a Conversation

What have you been doing lately?
How was your weekend?
What's new?
What's new with you?
How have you been?
Did you do anything interesting this/last* weekend?
What have you been up to?

Keeping It Going

How was it?
Where did you go?
Who did you see?
Who did you go with?
What did you see?
What did you think of it?

*You can say "this weekend" during the weekend or shortly after the weekend—for example, on Monday. After Monday, say "last weekend."

Luke Skywalker, Princess Leia, and Han Solo—characters in the *Star Wars* series

BEFORE LISTENING

A. BRAINSTORMING You're going to hear a radio program about the original *Star Wars* movies. Have you seen any of the movies in this series? If so, tell your group what you remember about the **plot** (the story) and the characters.

B. VOCABULARY PREPARATION Read the sentences on page 182. The words and phrases in orange are from the radio program. Match the definitions in the box with the words and phrases in orange. Write the correct letters on the lines.

a. brave

b. die

c. a formal, ritualized introduction into an organization

d. had outdated beliefs

e. having a negative or disrespectful attitude

f. inaction

g. inheritance

h. nonreligious

i. orphan; someone without parents

j. problems

k. search; a trip taken to find something of value

l. taken care of by someone other than one's parents

m. trustworthy, faithful companion

_____ 1. When we first meet Luke Skywalker, he's a **foundling** living with his aunt and uncle.

_____ 2. Luke is **fostered** by his aunt and uncle because his parents are dead.

_____ 3. Yoda, a Jedi master, prepares Luke for his **initiation** into the Jedi knights.

_____ 4. Princess Leia is a strong character. She's a **plucky** hero who helps fight against the Empire.

_____ 5. Even though Han Solo is a **cynical** character, he also has heroic qualities.

_____ 6. In fact, Han is willing to **lay down his life** to help Luke and Princess Leia.

_____ 7. In many myths and folktales, the hero goes on a **quest** to find something valuable.

_____ 8. In some myths and folktales, the hero's **patrimony** is stolen, and he or she goes on a journey to have his or her family property returned.

_____ 9. Another feature of many stories is that the hero often has a period of **quiescence**, a quiet time before a great event occurs.

_____ 10. Myths and folktales help simplify the complicated moral **dilemmas** that people in all cultures face.

_____ 11. The old western movies **carried** a lot of **ideological baggage**, such as the idea that the European pioneers were superior to Native Americans.

_____ 12. Some say that George Lucas, the creator of the _Star Wars_ series, has been influenced by both **secular** ideas, such as samurai culture, and religious ideas, such as the story of Mohammed or Christ.

_____ 13. In many myths and legends, the hero has a **sidekick** who helps him or her on the journey.

LISTENING

Test-Taking Strategy

Listening for the Main Idea

On standardized tests, you listen to a passage and answer questions about it. You often have the chance to listen to a passage more than once. When you know that you will listen more than once, don't try to answer the questions during the first listening. Just listen for the main idea. Then listen for the answers to the questions during the second or third listenings.

For example, you see the following test item:

Listen to the lecture about William Saroyan and answer the question that follows. You will hear the lecture twice.

Question: Where did Saroyan get many of the ideas for his stories?

In this case, just listen to the entire lecture the first time. Don't try to answer the question during the first listening. Then, the second time that you hear the lecture, jot down ideas that will help you to answer the question.

A. LISTENING FOR THE MAIN IDEA: SECTION 1 Listen to Section 1 of the radio program. Listen to the section twice. As you listen, think about this question:
• Where might George Lucas have gotten some of the ideas for *Star Wars*?

B. LISTENING FOR DETAILS: SECTION 2 Listen to Section 2. In this section, Slotkin, a mythology expert, discusses the "hero's journey." The "hero's journey" is a theme found in many myths and folktales. Listen to the Section 2 twice. Listen for the characteristics of the hero's journey and complete the graphic organizer below.

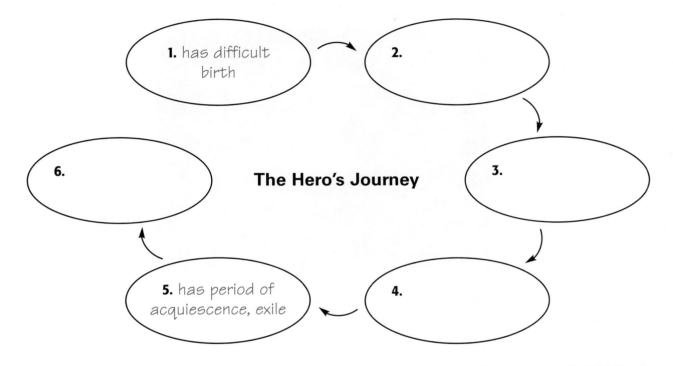

1. has difficult birth

2.

3.

4.

5. has period of acquiescence, exile

6.

The Hero's Journey

Listening Strategy

Listening for Influences

Speakers use certain words and phrases to describe how a creative work or artist is influenced by other works or other artists. Some of these words and phrases include:

incorporates elements of/from
echoes
has influences (from)
is influenced by
borrows (from)
resembles
is similar to

Examples: The American Western *The Magnificent Seven* **was influenced by** the Japanese movie *The Seven Samurai.*

The plot of *A Fistful of Dollars* **echoes** *Yojimbo.*

C. LISTENING FOR INFLUENCES: SECTION 3 Listen to Section 3 twice. Write the influences that you hear.

George Lucas was influenced by _____

_____

_____

Actor Hayden Christensen on the set with *Star Wars* creator George Lucas

D. LISTENING FOR INFLUENCES: SECTION 4 Listen to Section 4 twice. As you listen, think about the answers to these questions:
- What parts of society did westerns ignore?
- What is positive about *Star Wars*, according to Slotkin?

AFTER LISTENING

Critical Thinking Strategy

Analyzing a Story

One way to analyze a literary piece is to compare it to a **framework**, a set of criteria or characteristics that have been established by someone else. Many frameworks for analyzing literature come from other disciplines, such as anthropology, psychology, and political theory.

The hero's journey is one example of a framework. Joseph Campbell (mentioned in the radio program) developed the idea of the hero's journey after studying myths, legends, folktales, and religious stories from many cultures. This framework provides one way to analyze a story.

A. ANALYZING A STORY Work with a partner. Think of another example of the hero's journey. It can be a myth, a folktale, a children's story, or the plot of a movie or novel. It can be from your culture or another culture.

Analyze it according to the characteristics of the hero's journey. Write your notes in the chart below. Your story may not have all of the typical characteristics of a hero's journey.

Title, Source, or Type of Story: _____

Hero: _____

Characteristics	Examples from Story
Difficult birth	
Loses patrimony	
Is fostered	
Has a period of quiescence	
Goes on a quest	
Has one or more "sidekicks"	
Finally finds the thing of value that he or she was looking for	

Now share your chart with the class. Discuss the similarities and/or differences among all the stories that you analyzed.

B. EXTENSION As a class, brainstorm a list of recent movies. Then, in small groups, discuss these questions:
- Do any of them have influences from other older movies? If so, what are they?
- Do they have any influences from literature, myths, or older stories? If so, what are they?

PART ⑤ ACADEMIC ENGLISH Folk Heroes

BEFORE LISTENING

A. THINKING AHEAD You're going to hear a lecture about the characteristics of the hero in folktales. Before you listen, discuss these questions in small groups.

1. What are the characteristics of the hero in the hero's journey story? (This type of hero is also called the **archetypal hero**, a hero who is a model for all heroes.)

2. Who are some heroes in the folklore of your culture? Why are these heroes important in your culture? In other words, what do they represent or explain about your culture?

3. Make a prediction: Is the hero in a folktale similar to or different from the hero in the hero's journey-type story?

B. BACKGROUND READING Before listening to the lecture, read these two folktales. One is the American tale of "Pecos Bill," and the other is the Japanese folktale "Momotaro, or The Peach Boy." Read for the main idea—you don't need to understand every word. As you read, think about these questions:
• What is the theme of each story?
• What are the characteristics of the heroes?

Pecos Bill

Any creature living near the Pecos River can tell you that the best cowboy who ever lived was Pecos Bill.

When Bill was a little baby, he was already as tough as nails. His family was living on their ranch in east Texas when another family moved in 50 miles away. Well, Bill's
5 pa decided that the neighborhood was getting just *too* crowded, so the whole family packed up and started moving west.

One day, while the family was crossing the wide desert of west Texas, little Bill fell out of the back of the wagon. Nobody noticed he wasn't there until it was too late. Bill was sitting there in the dirt when a coyote came along. This creature decided that Bill must be a lost little
10 coyote, so she picked him up by the scruff of his neck[1] and took him back to her den[2].

So it was that Pecos Bill grew up among coyotes. He learned the ways of nature, and he learned to talk with the creatures. It was a fine life. Then one day, 17 years later, a cowboy was riding through the desert when he saw Pecos Bill. It's hard to say who was more surprised.

15   "Who are you?" the cowboy asked.

"Coyote," said Bill.

"No you ain't[3]," said the cowboy. "You're a cowboy, just like me."

[1] **scruff of his neck:** skin at the back of his neck
[2] **den:** home of a coyote
[3] **ain't:** nonstandard form of *am/is/are not*

186   UNIT 3 Literature

Pecos Bill considered this. He had sometimes suspected that he was a little different from the other coyotes. Maybe this was the reason.

20   Sadly, he said goodbye to his coyote family and friends and rode off to be with the cowboys. He had to learn how to wear clothes, take an occasional bath, and be a regular cowboy. Bill learned most things very quickly. It was certainly easier than learning to be a coyote—except for the baths.

One night he heard some of the cowboys talking about a dangerous gang of outlaws[4],
25   the Hell's Gate Gang, which was creating all sorts of trouble in west Texas. Pecos Bill decided to do something about this. He jumped on his horse and set out to find them. He figured he could tame[5] these outlaws the same way he tamed a wild horse.

On his way to find the outlaws, his horse broke her ankle, so Bill had to sling the poor creature around his shoulders and carry her. After walking a few hundred miles,
30   he ran into a deadly rattlesnake. It was at least 50 feet long, and it wanted to have Bill for dinner. It wrapped itself around Bill and squeezed and squeezed. But Bill just squeezed back even harder until all the poison was squeezed right out of that rattler. Then he made a neat coil[6] of the rattlesnake and put it over his arm. So it was that Pecos Bill invented the first *lariat*—the rope that became as important to all cowboys
35   as their horse or gun.

After a few hundred more miles of walking, Pecos Bill neared the camp of the Hell's Gate Gang. Now, the outlaws didn't even notice him at first because they were staring at something else that was coming their way—*fast*—the biggest, meanest tornado that had ever hit Texas. Well, Pecos Bill looked up into the sky and saw this terrible black
40   funnel cloud. He took the rattlesnake, made a careful loop with it, and began to swing it in huge circles over his head. Yelling the loudest war whoop[7] that anyone had ever heard, he swung that lariat and grabbed the tornado. The tornado pulled him up into the
45   sky, but he held on and rode it just like a wild horse. He rode and rode and pulled the lariat tighter and tighter until all the rain was squeezed out. That day it rained over Texas, Oklahoma, New Mexico, and Arizona. They
50   sure did need that rain—it hadn't rained a drop of water in years. Finally, the tornado was all tired out. Pecos Bill slipped off the tornado over California. He fell so hard that the ground level sank and created Death
55   Valley, which, as everyone knows, is 200 feet below sea level.

The outlaws were astonished. They decided right then that Pecos Bill would be their boss and that they would give up the outlaw life. They learned from him how to swing a rope to capture wild longhorn cattle, and that was the beginning of cattle ranches.

60   But Pecos Bill's coyote family missed him terribly. To this day, whenever you hear a coyote howling at the moon, you know that it's calling sadly for Bill to return.

[4]**outlaws:** criminals hiding from authorities
[5]**tame:** to train to be gentle, harmless
[6]**coil:** something wound up into a round shape
[7]**whoop:** a loud shout

Momotaro, or The Peach Boy

If you'll believe me, there was a time when the fairies[1] were not as shy as they are now. That was the time when beasts talked to men, when there were spells[2] and enchantments and magic every day, when there was hidden treasure to be dug up and adventures for the asking.

5 At that time, you must know, an old man and an old woman lived alone by themselves. They were good and they were poor and they had no children at all.

On one fine day, the old woman asks, "What are you doing this morning, good man?"

"Oh," says the old man, "I'm off to the mountains to gather sticks for our fire. And what are you doing, good wife?"

10 "Oh," says the old woman, "I'm off to the stream to wash clothes. It's my washing day," she adds.

So the old man went to the mountains, and the old woman went to the stream.

Now, while she was washing the clothes, what should she see but a fine ripe peach that came floating down the stream. The peach was big and rosy red on both sides.

15 "I'm in luck this morning," says the old woman, and she pulls the peach to shore with a bamboo stick.

By and by, when her husband came home from the hills, she set the peach before him. "Eat, good man," she said. "This is a lucky peach I found in the stream and brought home for you."

20 But the old man never got a taste of the peach. And why did he not?

All of a sudden the peach burst in two, and there was no pit to it, but a fine baby boy where the pit should have been.

"Mercy me!" says the old woman.

"Mercy me!" says the old man.

25 The baby boy first ate up one half of the peach, and then he ate up the other half. After he had done this he was finer and stronger than ever. "Momotaro! Momotaro!" cries the old man. "The eldest son of the peach."

30 "That is true," says the old woman. "He was born in a peach."

Both of them took such good care of Momotaro that soon he was the biggest and bravest boy in the countryside. He made his

35 parents proud, you may believe. The neighbors nodded their heads and they said, "Momotaro is a fine young man!"

"Mother," says Momotaro one day to the old woman, "make me a good store of *kimi-dango*" (which is what that they call millet dumplings[3] in those parts).

40 "Why do you want *kimi-dango*?" says his mother.

[1]**fairies:** small imaginary creatures with magic powers and wings
[2]**spells:** magic words said to make something happen
[3]**dumplings:** small balls of dough cooked and eaten with soup or meat

"Why," says Momotaro, "I'm going on a journey, or as you may say, an adventure, and I shall be needing the *kimi-dango* on the way."

"Where are you going, Momotaro?" says his mother.

"I'm off to the Ogres' Island,[4]" says Momotaro, "to get their treasure, and I would appreciate it if you'd let me have the *kimi-dango* as soon as possible," he says.

So his mother made him the *kimi-dango,* and he put them in a pouch[5], and he tied it to his belt and off he went.

"*Sayonora,* and good luck to you, Momotaro!" cried the old man and the old woman.

"*Sayonora*! *Sayonora*!" cried Momotaro.

He hadn't gone far when he met a monkey.

"Kia! Kia!" says the monkey. "Where are you going, Momotaro?"

Says Momotaro, "I'm off to the Ogres' Island for an adventure."

"What do you have in the pouch hanging on your belt?"

Says Momotaro, "I've some of the best *kimi-dango* in all Japan."

"Give me one," says the monkey, "and I will go with you."

So Momotaro gave a *kimi-dango* to the monkey, and the two them jogged on together. They hadn't gone far when they met a pheasant[6].

"Ken! Ken!" said the pheasant. "Where are you off to, Momotaro?"

Says Momotaro, "I'm off to the Ogres' Island for an adventure."

"What do you have in the pouch hanging on your belt, Momotaro?"

"I've got some of the best *kimi-dango* in all Japan."

"Give me one," says the pheasant, "and I will go with you."

So Momotaro gave a *kimi-dango* to the pheasant, and the three of them walked on together. They hadn't gone far when they met a dog.

"Bow! Wow! Wow!" says the dog. "Where are you going, Momotaro?"

Says Momotaro, "I'm off to the Ogres' Island."

"What have you got in your pouch, Momotaro?"

"I've got some of the best *kimi-dango* in all Japan."

"Give me one," says the dog, "and I will go with you."

So Momotaro gave a *kimi-dango* to the dog, and the four of them walked on together. Soon they came to the Ogres' Island.

"Now, brothers," says Momotaro, "listen to my plan. The pheasant must fly over the castle gate and peck[7] the Ogres. The monkey must climb over the castle wall and pinch the Ogres. The dog and I will break the gate's bolts and bars. He will bite the Ogres, and I will fight the Ogres."

Then there was a great battle.

The pheasant flew over the castle gate: "Ken! Ken! Ken!"

[4]**Ogres' Island:** an island of cruel monsters
[5]**pouch:** small purse
[6]**pheasant:** a large bird with a long tail
[7]**peck:** hit or bite with the beak

Momotaro broke the bolts and bars, and the dog leaped into the castle courtyard.
80 "Bow! Wow! Wow!"

The brave companions fought till sundown and overcame the Ogres. Those that were left alive they took prisoner and bound with cords—a wicked lot[8] they were.

"Now, brothers," says Momotaro, "bring out the Ogres' treasure."

So they did.

85 The treasure was worth having, indeed. There were magic jewels there, and capes and coats to make you invisible. There was gold and silver, and jade and coral, and amber and tortoise-shell and mother-of-pearl.

"Here's riches for all," says Momotaro. "Choose, brothers, and take your fill."

"Kia! Kia!" says the monkey. "Thanks, my Lord Momotaro."

90 "Ken! Ken!" says the pheasant. "Thanks, my Lord Momotaro."

"Bow! Wow! Wow!" says the dog. "Thanks, my dear Lord Momotaro."

Source: *Japanese Fairy Tales* (Hearn)

[8]**wicked lot:** a group of morally wrong and bad people

C. GUESSING THE MEANING FROM CONTEXT Read the sentences below. The words and phrases in orange are from the lecture. Guess their meanings from the context. Write your guesses on the lines.

1. The archetypal hero does not represent a real person; rather, it is an **idealized** human with special powers.

Guess: _____

2. In many Greek legends, the hero gets **supernatural** help from a god or goddess.

Guess: _____

3. In some stories, a male hero **seeks revenge for** his father; for example, he might try to kill his father's murderer.

Guess: _____

4. In *Star Wars,* Luke has to **prove himself**. He needs to show that he can become a Jedi warrior.

Guess: _____

5. At the end of some stories, the hero is rewarded **spiritually**, but at the end of "Momotaro, or The Peach Boy," the hero is rewarded with great riches.

Guess: _____

6. Momotaro's quest ends in **prosperity** for him and for all his helpers. We imagine that the treasure they win allows them all to live happily ever after.

Guess: _____

7. Studying folklore lets you **tap into** the concerns of all humans. It gives you a picture of the wishes and desires of humanity as a whole.

Guess: _____

8. Campbell's analysis of the archetypal hero is **compelling**. Most folklorists find it very persuasive.

Guess: _____

Now compare your answers with a partner's answers.

D. HAVING QUESTIONS IN MIND Look at the outline for the lecture on pages 193–194 and think about the two folktales you read. What would you like to know about folk heroes? On a separate piece of paper, write three questions.

E. TAKING NOTES: ABBREVIATIONS Write your own abbreviations for these words and phrases from the lecture.

1. hero(es) _____

2. mythology _____

3. religion _____

4. collective unconscious _____

5. archetypal hero _____

6. characteristics _____

7. universal _____

8. folktales _____

9. geological formations _____

10. symbol _____

11. symbolizes _____

12. technological _____

In small groups, compare your abbreviations.

LISTENING

A. GUESSING THE MEANING FROM CONTEXT Listen to the following words and phrases in the context of sentences. Then match the words and phrases with the definitions on the right. Write the correct letters on the lines.

_____ **1.** collective unconscious   **a.** a long adventure story with a hero

_____ **2.** saga   **b.** monsters

_____ **3.** prowess   **c.** upsetting

_____ **4.** traumatic   **d.** kind

_____ **5.** humble   **e.** uses his intelligence

_____ **6.** simpleton   **f.** superior skills; also, personal power

_____ **7.** uses his wits   **g.** plain; simple; ordinary

_____ **8.** benevolent   **h.** unconscious thoughts that all people share

_____ **9.** ogres   **i.** a person who isn't very smart

Listening Strategy

Listening for Topic Signals

Professors often use topic signals in lectures. These words and phrases can help you to organize your notes because they often signal when the speaker is going to introduce the next subtopic of the lecture.

Examples: Let's take a look at the reasons for . . .
Let's turn our attention to why . . .
This brings us to the topic of . . .

When you hear a topic signal, prepare for a transition to the next subtopic or important point in a lecture.

B. TAKING NOTES: LISTENING FOR TOPIC SIGNALS Listen to the lecture. It's in five sections. Listen to each section twice. Notice that the note-taking organizer is much less structured than in previous chapters. There are only a few headings and notes given for each section, such as the section topics and a few key terms. Use them as a guide but remember to take notes on all the important information in the lecture. In addition, listen carefully for topic signals. You'll hear a few of them in this lecture.

Characteristics of the Folk Hero

Section 1: Definition of "Hero"

Archetypal hero: _____

_____

_____

Folk hero: _____

_____

_____

Section 2: The Archetypal Hero

Campbell's characteristics: _____

_____

_____

_____

_____

How folk heroes differ: _____

_____

_____

What they give us: _____

_____

_____

Section 3: The Folk Hero

Folk heroes: _____

_____

Characteristics: _____

_____

_____

_____

_____

_____

What the folk hero reflects: _____

_____

Section 4: Two Folk Heroes: Pecos Bill & Momotaro

What Pecos Bill represents/reflects: _____

_____

_____

What the story explains: _____

_____

_____

What Momotaro symbolizes: _____

_____

_____

What the other characters symbolize: _____

_____

_____

_____

_____

Section 5: Conclusion

What folk heroes help us understand: _____

_____

_____

_____

Source: Adapted from a lecture by Alf H. Walle, Ph.D.

Understanding a Summary in the Conclusion to a Lecture

A well-organized speaker often gives students a summary of the speech or lecture in its conclusion. In other words, the lecturer uses the conclusion to restate, or to review, the main ideas. This gives you the opportunity to hear the main points again, in slightly different words.

For example, you are listening to a lecture that compares the hero in folktales from two different cultures. At the end of the lecture, the speaker summarizes by saying: "As you have seen, the heroes in these two stories share many of the same characteristics, even though they come from vastly different cultures." When you hear this, you are reminded of the main idea of the lecture.

C. UNDERSTANDING A SUMMARY IN THE CONCLUSION TO A LECTURE Review the notes you took on the conclusion on page 194. Listen again to Section 5 and add to your notes if necessary.

D. CHECKING YOUR NOTES Listen to the whole lecture again. As you listen, review your notes and fill in any missing information.

AFTER LISTENING

Listening Strategy

Comparing Lecture Notes

Most students find it helpful to form a study group with classmates. With a study group, you can compare your lecture notes with those of your classmates, fill in any information that you missed, and correct anything that you misunderstood.

Example: Student A wrote these notes about Section 3:

Characteristics
unusual birth circumstances
????
sometimes an animal with human characteristics
accomplishes a heroic deed
????

Student B has these notes:

Characteristics
unusual birth circumstances
animal companions
sometimes an animal with human characteristics
?????
gains riches or wisdom

By comparing notes, Students A and B can fill in the missing characteristics of the folk hero.

A. COMPARING LECTURE NOTES In small groups, compare your notes. Ask questions to check your notes and to fill in any missing information. Revise your notes as needed.

B. USING YOUR NOTES With a partner, use your notes to discuss these questions about the lecture.

1. What is an archetypal hero?

2. What do Campbell's ideas about the archetypal hero explain?

3. In what ways is the folk hero different from the archetypal hero?

4. What can the folk hero tell us about a culture?

5. What is the significance of the Pecos Bill story?

6. What is the significance of the Momotaro story?

7. Why have folktales been with us for thousands of years?

C. DISCUSSION Discuss these questions in small groups:
• Do you agree with the lecturer's analysis of "Pecos Bill"?
• Do you agree with his analysis of "Momotaro, or The Peach Boy"? Explain your answers.

D. MAKING CONNECTIONS Think about the folktales you read in Parts 1 and 5. Analyze them according to the characteristics you learned about in the lecture. Complete the chart on page 197 with check marks (✓) to indicate which characteristics are included in each story.

The hero . . .	"Why the Parrot Repeats"	"Pecos Bill"	"Momotaro, or The Peach Boy"
has unusual birth circumstances.			
has animal companions or helpers.			
is an animal with human characteristics.			
leaves family and goes on a journey.			
accomplishes a heroic deed (such as killing a monster).			
gains riches or wisdom.			
is responsible for something in nature (e.g., a geological formation or for the nature or condition of an animal).			
uses wits to get out of a bad situation.			

PUT IT ALL TOGETHER

GIVING A GROUP PRESENTATION In small groups, you are going to prepare and give a short presentation about a folktale. In your presentation, you will retell the folktale and give a brief analysis.

STEP 1
As a group, choose a folktale from the list below, or choose a different folktale.

- "The Lucky Table" (Costa Rican)
- "Paul Bunyan" (American)
- "The Monkey King" (Chinese)
- "Li Chi Slays the Serpent" (Chinese)
- "Getting Common Sense" (Jamaican)
- "Anansi" (African/African American/Caribbean)
- "Brer Rabbit" (American/African American)
- "The Hodja and the Cauldron" (Turkish)
- "The Monkey and the Crocodile" (Indian)

STEP 2

As a group, make a list of what needs to be done for the presentation. Negotiate who will do which tasks. Review "Negotiating Responsibilities for a Group Presentation" on page 95 in Chapter 3. Make sure that everyone in the group has a turn to contribute and participate in your group discussions.

STEP 3

Do Internet or library research to find the story. Remember that there are many versions of the same folktale because there is not just one author. You can find many folktales on the Internet.

If you do Internet research, do a key word search using a search engine. Try the following key words:

- folktales + [country]; for example: folktales Mexican
- [name of folktale] + folktale; for example: Momotaro folktale

---

Speaking Strategy

Telling a Story

When you tell a story, you want to make it interesting to your listeners. Here are some tips for telling a folktale.

1. Start with an orientation expression, an expression that sets the story in a time and/or a place.

Examples: Once upon at time, . . .
A long time ago in a far away land, . . .
Back in the days of the wild west, . . .

2. Use the past tense to tell the folktale.

Examples: An old man and an old woman **lived** alone by themselves.
She **pulled** the peach to the shore.

(**Note**: Storytellers sometimes use the present tense in informal situations, if the story is recent, or if the storyteller wants to make the listener feel that the story is very real or present, as though it is happening now.)

3. Include descriptive details that help the listener "see" the important events in the story. Include details that relate to the five senses: sight, sound, touch, taste, and smell.

Example: All things went wrong on their little farm. Their **little patch of corn** dried up, so they had no corn with which to make tortillas. Their stomachs **ached** with hunger. The beans were **dry and brown, dying on the vines**. The ground was so dry that their footsteps made a **crunching noise that hurt their ears**. At night they dreamed of the **taste of sweet water** and the **smell of black beans cooking with rice**.

4. Use reported speech. Sometimes when you tell a story, you quote or "act out" the characters' speech. However, when you have less time and are summarizing a story, you need to report what the characters said.

Example: Quoted speech: The boy said, "I'll trade my table for the cow."
Reported speech: The boy said that he would trade his table for the cow.

(**Note**: In reported speech, verb tenses shift back in time—for example, *will trade* becomes *would trade*.)

STEP 4

Follow these steps to prepare for your group presentation.

1. Think through the entire story.

2. Put key actions or points of the story on index cards, in note form. Do not write out the whole story. Remember: Your presentation is only a few minutes long, so you will need to summarize the story.

3. Look up any words that you need but don't already know in English.

4. Include in your notes any explanations that your audience might need. For example, in the story about Momotaro, the listeners might need to know that a "millet dumpling" is something to eat.

5. Now make notes of analysis of your folktale. In other words, prepare to tell your listeners what this story expresses about the culture or country it comes from.

6. Decide who in the group will tell or explain each part of your presentation. Make sure everyone has something to say.

STEP 5

Follow these steps as your group gives its presentation.

1. As you're telling your folktale, don't read from your notes. Instead, just glance at them occasionally if you need to jog your memory. Try to relax and enjoy telling the story.

2. After you've told your folktale, pause for a few seconds before giving the analysis, to signal the end of the story.

3. Keep the analysis short and focused. Your analysis shouldn't attempt to include the entire history or social structure of a culture.

4. At the end, ask your listeners if they have any questions.

STEP 6

As you listen to each presentation, write down any questions or comments you have. Be prepared, in case there is time to do so, either to ask a question or to tell the speakers what you enjoyed about the presentation.

UNIT ③ VOCABULARY WORKSHOP

Review vocabulary items that you learned in Chapters 5 and 6.

A. MATCHING Match the words to the definitions. Write the correct letters on the lines.

Words	Definitions
_____ **1.** advent	**a.** after that
_____ **2.** ambiguous	**b.** strong belief
_____ **3.** concise	**c.** varied; different
_____ **4.** conviction	**d.** long, dramatic story
_____ **5.** diverse	**e.** not probable; not expected
_____ **6.** perplexed	**f.** confused
_____ **7.** saga	**g.** idea that is overgeneralized about a group of people
_____ **8.** stereotype	**h.** with few (but well-chosen) words
_____ **9.** subsequently	**i.** not clearly explained; possible to interpret in different ways
_____ **10.** unlikely	**j.** beginning; invention

B. WORDS IN PHRASES Fill in the blanks with words from the box.

baggage	herself	way	wits
crowd	life	weight	word

1. Because John was small and weak, he had to **use his** _____ in order to survive.

2. Sasha's new job was important to her, and she wanted to make a good impression. She knew that she had to **prove** _____.

3. Gary wasn't sure that he wanted to marry Janet because she had a big family filled with strange people, but he realized that he **carried a lot of** _____, too.

4. You don't have to **take my** _____ for it. You can ask anyone. They'll tell you the same thing.

5. From an early age, Cathy had an amazing ability to play the piano. For this reason, she **stood out from the** _____.

6. I don't **give a lot of** _____ to what TV commercials say. The advertisers want us to buy their product, so they'll say almost anything to persuade us.

7. Simon deeply loves his family. He would **lay down his** _____ for them.

8. The Japanese film *The Seven Samurai* **paved the** _____ for the American film that came later, *The Magnificent Seven*.

C. TRUE OR FALSE? Read the statements below. Circle *T* if the sentence is true. Circle *F* if the sentence is false.

1. A person who gives **testimony** is usually in court.   T   F

2. A **recluse** is sociable and enjoys being with other people.   T   F

3. You put a **bumper sticker** in the front window of your house.   T   F

4. If Adam wants **an eye-for-an-eye** sort of justice, he wants to forgive the person who hurt his sister.   T   F

5. An **idiosyncratic** writer has a unique or unusual style.   T   F

6. Someone who is **plucky** might be small and weak but is also unafraid.   T   F

7. Reading extensively and memorizing good poetry is probably **apt** preparation for a writer.   T   F

8. The **sidekick** is the star of a western movie.   T   F

9. The church is a **secular** institution.   T   F

10. A heavy blanket provides good **insulation** against cold.   T   F

D. THE ACADEMIC WORD LIST In the boxes below are some of the most common academic words in English. Fill in the blanks with words from these boxes. You will use one word twice. When you finish, check your answers in the Critical Thinking Strategy boxes on page 138 (for items 1–5) and page 184 (for items 6–13). For more words, see the Academic Word List on pages 315–318.

analysis	analyze	context	elements	logic

Most good poems can be understood on several different levels. However, a poem must be read

several times to understand the different levels of meaning. It also helps to hear the poem read aloud

as you read silently.

An important tool for students is the ability to _____ a piece of
1

literature, such as a poem. When you analyze, you look at the different parts in order to better

understand the whole. By using _____ 2 _____ and understanding the poem's

_____ 3 _____, you can figure out much of the meaning.

_____ 4 _____ is a skill you will need in many types of classes, not just in English

or literature classes.

When you analyze a poem, look for these _____ 5 _____ and think about how

they are used in the poem.

| criteria | framework | mentioned | psychology |
| cultures | literary | myths | theory |

One way to analyze a _____ 6 _____ piece is to compare it to a

_____ 7 _____, a set of _____ 8 _____ or characteristics that have

been established by someone else. Many frameworks for analyzing literature come from other

disciplines such as anthropology, _____ 9 _____, and political

_____ 10 _____.

The hero's journey is one example of a framework. Joseph Campbell,

(_____ 11 _____ in the radio program) developed the idea of the hero's journey after

studying _____ 12 _____, legends, folktales, and religious stories from many

_____ 13 _____. This framework provides one way to analyze a story.

ECOLOGY

CHAPTER 7

Endangered Species

Discuss these questions:
- Where might this tiger live?
- What are some reasons tigers and other animals are in danger of extinction?
- What can people and governments do to save endangered animals?

Thirty years ago, the **tree kangaroo** had disappeared from its natural habitat **in the wild** in Papua New Guinea. Now, after **breeding** them **in captivity** in zoos, the Tree Kangaroo Conservation Program is returning them to the wild. **Indigenous** (native) landowners in Papua New Guinea have set aside more than 80,000 acres of rain forest—land on which not only the tree kangaroo but also many other species will be protected.

Papua New Guinea and surrounding areas

A. BRAINSTORMING In small groups, brainstorm as many **endangered** animals as you can think of. In other words, which animals might become **extinct** (no longer living) in the near future? Where does each animal live? Write a list on a separate piece of paper.

1. Read this list of reasons why so many species are endangered. What might be the reason for the endangerment of the animals that you listed in Activity A (page 206)?
   - pollution
   - **habitat loss**—destruction of the environment in which the animals live
   - new species* that come into the environment (usually brought by humans)
   - hunting by humans (for sport, food, animal parts)
   - low rates of reproduction

2. Of these reasons, which one do you think is the main cause of animal endangerment today? Why do you think this?

3. What do four of these reasons listed above have in common? Make an inference.

4. What do you know about kangaroos? Have you ever heard of tree kangaroos?

*Species refers to a group of animals or plants of the same kind that can breed with each other. The word species is both singular and plural.

C. READING Read about zoos. As you read, think about this question:
- What is Lisa Dabek doing to help tree kangaroos?

Zoos Unite to Keep Animals in the Wild

Bushwack, an orangey-brown and black Matschie's tree kangaroo, ambles down the tree to nibble on the bamboo leaves that Lisa Dabek holds.

5 This endangered three-foot-long animal is found only on the Huon Peninsula of Papua New Guinea and in certain zoos, such as this one, the Roger Williams Park Zoo in Providence, Rhode Island. Ms. Dabek is the zoo's conservation and research director.

Most people have never heard of these cuddly,
10 docile kangaroos, but Dabek has spent much of her life trying to protect them. She is doing this quite successfully, thanks to a zoo conservation program, the Species Survival Plan (SSP).

Every year, Dabek spends two or three months in
15 Papua New Guinea studying the tree kangaroo and working with villagers.

After visiting universities and nonprofit organizations and meeting with local experts, Dabek realized how little was known about tree kangaroos.
20 She devised a three-step plan involving research, conservation, and education to save them.

Lisa Dabek and a tree kangaroo at a zoo

Research hasn't been easy. "The animals are quite shy and well camouflaged," Dabek says. Their orangey fur is the same color as the moss that hangs in the trees of New Guinea. "You look up and think you are seeing tree kangaroos, but it is really moss—and vice versa."

Educating local hunters helps

Dabek's group plans to capture animals and put radio collars on them. Then they can follow kangaroos at a distance. "Now that we have areas that are protected," she says, "we are seeing more animals. Maybe they aren't feeling as shy now that they aren't being hunted as much."

Dabek's conservation goal is a 150,000-acre (84,633-hectare) wildlife-management area. So far, local people have pledged 80,000 acres (51,376 hectares) of land to protect the kangaroos.

Lisa Dabek and Yawan villagers in Papua New Guinea

"Papua New Guinea is unique in that 95 percent of the land belongs to the indigenous people," Dabek says. "They have control over their own forests." For the past eight years, Dabek has taught people there about the importance of saving tree kangaroos. She asked them to set aside part of their hunting land for this purpose. The people know that if they don't act today, the tree kangaroo may disappear forever.

Tree kangaroos give birth to only one offspring every one or two years. That makes them more susceptible to hunting than animals that reproduce more often and have several offspring at a time. "I tell hunters that tree kangaroos are vulnerable because of their slow reproductive rate and suggest that they focus on other animals."

One reason for Dabek's success is that she hasn't asked people to change their culture. "We aren't asking the people not to hunt tree kangaroos," she says. "But we are suggesting that if they let the tree kangaroos breed in this managed, safe area, the offspring will move into areas where they can hunt."

But perhaps the biggest impact of Dabek's program has been on the lives of the people she reaches through education. "We are doing so much more than just protecting a population of an animal," she says. "We're helping the people, too."

Dabek uses some of her grant money to give local schools much-needed pencils, paper, scissors, and other supplies. "Schools are poorly equipped," she says, "and we realized that we needed to support the schools and the community if we were going to do this type of work."

Facts about Tree Kangaroos

- Tree kangaroos are marsupials, which means they carry their young in pouches. They live in the rain forests of Australia and Papua New Guinea.

- They are nocturnal (active at night) herbivores (plant eaters). They feed mostly on leaves but have been known to eat more than 90 kinds of plants, including ferns, fruits, and orchids.

- Ten species of tree kangaroo are known: two in Australia and eight in Papua New Guinea. More may exist. A new species was discovered in 1995.

- Tree kangaroos are very territorial and tend to stay in a small area. They are very good at hiding. Researchers had trouble spotting tree kangaroos in trees with sparse foliage even when signals from the animals' radio collars indicated where they were.

'Growing' more local biologists

Dabek even organized a scholarship for local students who want to go to college
70 and learn to teach. "We help fund their education," she says, "and in return they make
a commitment to come back and teach for at least 10 years."

She also trains local people and students from the University of Papua New Guinea
for her research team. "My goal is to get some of the New Guinea students into
graduate school," Dabek says. "They are going to be the world's future biologists, and
75 we need them."

Source: "Zoos Unite to Keep Animals in the Wild" (Toupin)

D. COMPREHENSION CHECK Discuss these questions with a partner.

1. What are two reasons for the endangerment of tree kangaroos?

2. What are the two main steps that are being taken to save the species?

E. VOCABULARY CHECK Look back at the reading on pages 207–209. Find words and phrases in the reading that match the meanings below. Write the correct words and phrases on the lines. Line numbers are given in parentheses.

1. moves slowly, in an easy way (1–5) _____

2. eat delicately, in small bites (1–5) _____

3. hidden by the use of coloring (20–25) _____

4. the other way around, also (25–30) _____

5. native or original (people) (35–40) _____

6. young (noun) (40–45) _____

7. vulnerable; easily affected (40–45) _____

F. DISCUSSION In small groups, discuss these questions.

1. What is necessary if this project—to reintroduce tree kangaroos to the wild—is going to be successful?

2. Why might this project be more successful than others to reintroduce other animals to their habitats?

3. This reading mentioned one habitat—the rain forest. What other habitats can you think of?

G. RESPONSE WRITING Choose *one* of these topics. Write about it for 15 minutes. Try to use new vocabulary but don't use a dictionary. Just write as many ideas as you can.

• What is your opinion about Dabek's plan for saving tree kangaroos?
• Do you think her approach can be used for other animals as well? Why or why not?
• What is another endangered species that you know about? What is being done to preserve it?

PART ② SOCIAL LANGUAGE Counting Jaguars

BEFORE LISTENING

A. THINKING AHEAD You are going to listen to Evan, Victor, and Chrissy talk about one way to spend summer vacation. In small groups, discuss these questions.

1. What are some reasons for doing volunteer work or community service during the summer or during your free time?

2. What are some possible volunteer jobs that help preserve endangered species? Where might these jobs be? Have you ever done any such work? If so, share your experiences with your group members.

B. VOCABULARY PREPARATION Read the sentences below. The idioms in orange are from the conversation. Match the definitions in the box with the idioms in orange. Write the correct letters on the lines.

a. can't participate	e. wait
b. a hidden difficulty or cost	f. we were just talking about you/him/her
c. to say it simply	g. yes
d. a unique opportunity	

_____ **1.** You want me to write that down? O.K., but **hold on**—I have to find a pen first.

_____ **2.** Do I want a fun summer job? **Yep**, of course I do!

_____ **3.** **Speak of the devil** . . . Victor just walked in. I'll put him on the phone.

_____ **4.** My summer job is . . . **in one word**—perfect!

_____ **5.** There's got to be **a catch**. You don't get something for nothing.

_____ **6.** Well, **I'm out**. I can't afford that kind of trip. You guys go ahead without me.

_____ **7.** This is the **chance of a lifetime**. You'll probably never again be able to see tigers in their natural habitat.

LISTENING

A. LISTENING FOR THE MAIN IDEA Listen to the conversation. As you listen, think about this question:
• What is "the catch" to Victor's idea?

B. LISTENING FOR DETAILS Listen to part of the conversation again. Listen for information that answers these questions. Write your short answers on the lines.

1. What kind of research does the organization sponsor?

_____

2. What can you do in the Mexican forest?

_____

3. Do you have to be an expert to work for the organization?

_____

4. How much does it cost to count jaguars?

_____

Compare your answers with a partner's answers.

C. LISTENING FOR INFERENCES Listen to part of the conversation again. You'll hear it twice. As you listen, make inferences to answer the questions. Circle the letter of the best answer.

1. How does Victor feel about his idea for the summer?

    A. bored

    B. excited

    C. worried

2. When Chrissy hears Victor say "exotic locations," how does she react?

    A. She becomes interested.

    B. She feels disappointed.

    C. She doesn't believe Victor.

3. What does Evan think about the opportunity to volunteer in Hawaii?

    A. He doesn't understand.

    B. He's skeptical.

    C. He thinks it's a good job.

4. What does Chrissy think when Victor says that you don't have to be an expert?

    A. She believes him.

    B. She's confused.

    C. She doesn't want to do it.

5. What is Evan doing when he says that Victor is on his way to count jaguars?

    A. He's telling the truth.

    B. He's making a joke.

    C. He's lying.

AFTER LISTENING

A. INFORMATION GAP: WHERE IN THE WORLD? With a partner, find out about current endangered species: their names, habitats, and reasons for endangerment. To do this, you both will ask and answer questions and complete a chart.

Student A

Use the chart on page 265. Ask your partner for the missing information and write the answers in your chart. Take turns asking and answering questions. Do not look at your partner's chart.

Example: **A:** What endangered species lives in the mountain forests of China?

   B: The giant panda.

Student B

Use the chart on page 266. Ask your partner for the missing information and write the answers in your chart. Take turns asking and answering questions. Do not look at your partner's chart.

Example: **B:** I have one reason for the endangerment of the giant panda: loss of habitat. What other reasons do you have?

   A: The other reasons are a slow rate of reproduction and China's warming climate.

B. DISCUSSION In small groups, discuss these questions.

1. Were you surprised by any of the information that you learned from Activity A (above)? What surprised you? Why?

2. What is the most common reason for endangerment for the endangered species in Activity A?

3. What endangered species are native to the region that you were born in? What endangered species are native to the region that you live in now?

PART ③ THE MECHANICS OF LISTENING AND SPEAKING

WORDS IN PHRASES

○ Answering the Phone and Taking a Message

1. You can answer your home or cell phone simply by saying "Hello."

Examples: **A:** Hello?

B: Hi. May I speak with Ethan?
Hi. Could I speak with Ethan?
Hi. Is Ethan there?

A: Speaking.
This is Ethan.
This is he.

B: Hi, Ethan. This is Sue. I'm calling to see if you want to study together tomorrow.

2. If the caller asks to speak with another person who is there, it's often a good idea to find out who is calling before you pass the phone to him or her.

Examples: **A:** Hello?

B: Hi. May I speak with Tom?
Hi. Is Tom there?

A: May I ask who's calling?
Can I tell him who's calling?
May I tell him who's calling?

B: Sure. This is Maria.

A: O.K. Hold on a minute while I get him.

3. If the caller asks to speak with another person who isn't there, offer to take a message.

Examples: **A:** Hello?

B: Hi. May I speak with Tom?
Hi. Is Tom there?

A: He's not here right now. Would you like me to give him a message?
He's just stepped out. May I take a message?
He isn't available right now. May I give him a message?

○ A. TAKING A MESSAGE

Listen to these phone calls and fill in the information on the message notes on page 215.

1.

Telephone Message
To _____
Here is a Message for You
_____   _____   _____   From _____   Phone No. _____ Ext. _____   ☐ Telephoned ☐ Will Call Again   ☐ Returned Your Call ☐ Wants to See You   ☐ Call ☐ Urgent
Taken by _____
Date _____ Time _____

3.

Telephone Message
To _____
Here is a Message for You
_____   _____   _____   From _____   Phone No. _____ Ext. _____   ☐ Telephoned ☐ Will Call Again   ☐ Returned Your Call ☐ Wants to See You   ☐ Call ☐ Urgent
Taken by _____
Date _____ Time _____

2.

Telephone Message
To _____
Here is a Message for You
_____   _____   _____   From _____   Phone No. _____ Ext. _____   ☐ Telephoned ☐ Will Call Again   ☐ Returned Your Call ☐ Wants to See You   ☐ Call ☐ Urgent
Taken by _____
Date _____ Time _____

4.

Telephone Message
To _____
Here is a Message for You
_____   _____   _____   From _____   Phone No. _____ Ext. _____   ☐ Telephoned ☐ Will Call Again   ☐ Returned Your Call ☐ Wants to See You   ☐ Call ☐ Urgent
Taken by _____
Date _____ Time _____

LANGUAGE FUNCTION

🎧 Clarifying Information on the Phone

When you take a message over the phone, you don't always hear clearly, so it's important to be able to ask for clarification. There are several ways to do this.

Examples: Excuse me?
What was that again?
How do you spell that?
Can you say that again, please?
Could you please repeat that?

Some letters sound the same as others over the phone. For this reason it helps to give a common word or name beginning with those letters when you spell out a name or word.

Example: A: Hi. May I speak with Tom?
B: He's not here right now. May I take a message?
A: Yes. Please tell him that Vinh called.
B: O.K. How do you spell your name?
A: It's Vinh. *V* as in Victor; *I*; *N* as in Nancy; *H*.
B: Thanks, Vinh. I'll tell him you called.

B. CLARIFYING INFORMATION ON THE PHONE Work with a partner. Student A asks Student B how to spell his or her first and last name. Student B spells out his or her first and last name using common words or names for some of the letters. Student A writes down the correct spelling. Student B checks the spelling. Exchange roles.

Example: A: How do you spell your first and last name?
B: My first name is Sara: *S* as in Sam; *A-R-A*. My last name is Lopez: *L-O-P* as in Peter, *E-Z* as in zebra.

🎧 **C. LISTENING FOR CLARIFICATION** Listen to these parts of phone conversations in which one person asks for clarification and another clarifies information. Write notes on what you hear.

1. _____

2. _____

3. _____

4. _____

Compare your answers with a partner's answers.

PRONUNCIATION

🎧 *Can* vs. *Can't*

In some cases, the words *can* and *can't* might sound the same because you can't always hear the /t/ in *can't*. This is especially true when a word beginning with /t/ or /d/ follows these words.

Examples: I **can discuss** this now.
  I **can't discuss** this now.

  I **can talk** with you later.
  I **can't talk** with you later.

1. Use the context to help you understand whether the person has said *can* or *can't*.

  Example: **I'm sorry, but I can't talk right now. I'll call you back.**

2. Ask for clarification.

  Example: **Did you say *can* or *can't*?**

3. Listen for stress and the vowel sound: Is it the full /æ/ sound in *can't* or the reduced /ə/ sound in *can*? Don't worry about the /t/ at the end.

  Examples: I **can** go with you. **(Reduced /ə/ sound)**
  I **can't** go with you. **(Full /æ/ sound)**

🎧 **D. *CAN* VS. *CAN'T*** Listen to the pronunciation of *can* and *can't* in these sentences. Then listen again and repeat each statement after the speaker.

1. a. I can help you.
  b. I can't help you.

2. a. Cathy can drive.
  b. Cathy can't drive.

3. a. Dylan can do it later.
  b. Dylan can't do it later.

4. a. Jill can take a message.
  b. Jill can't take a message.

5. a. You can leave a message.
  b. You can't leave a message.

6. a. We can tell him tomorrow.
  b. We can't tell him tomorrow.

🎧 **E. HEARING THE DIFFERENCE BETWEEN *CAN* AND *CAN'T*** Listen to each sentence. Does the speaker say *can* or *can't*? Circle the word that you hear.

1. can	can't	**5.** can	can't	**9.** can	can't
2. can	can't	**6.** can	can't	**10.** can	can't
3. can	can't	**7.** can	can't	**11.** can	can't
4. can	can't	**8.** can	can't	**12.** can	can't

LANGUAGE FUNCTION

🎧 Understanding Outgoing Messages

If you have voicemail or an answering machine, you'll need to record an outgoing message. This message should be short and clear. Depending on who is likely to call you, and the reasons for their calls, your message can be informal or formal. If your message is formal, give your full name and/or your phone number. If your message is informal, give only your first name and/or phone number. If you use your phone only for personal calls, an informal message is adequate.

Examples: Hi. This is Jason Thomas. I can't come to the phone right now, so leave a message.

Hi. This is Kim. You know the drill. Leave a message at the beep.

You've reached my cell phone. Leave me a message and I'll call you back as soon as I can.

If you use your phone for business, you might want a more formal message.

Example: Hello. You have reached 924-555-1234. Please leave a message, and we'll get back to you as soon as we can.

🎧 **F. UNDERSTANDING OUTGOING MESSAGES** Listen to the outgoing messages. Is each message formal or informal? Circle *Formal* or *Informal*.

1. Formal   Informal   **4.** Formal   Informal

2. Formal   Informal   **5.** Formal   Informal

3. Formal   Informal

G. COMPOSING AN OUTGOING MESSAGE Write down an outgoing message that you could use on your voicemail or answering machine.

In small groups, read your outgoing message. Make sure you speak clearly. Listen to your classmates' messages. Discuss the similarities and differences among the outgoing messages.

PUT IT TOGETHER

ANSWERING THE PHONE, TAKING A PHONE MESSAGE, AND ASKING FOR CLARIFICATION With a partner, practice answering the phone, taking a message, and asking for clarification. Follow the steps in the box below. Use the expressions you learned in Part 3. Then exchange roles.

A: Answer the phone.

B: Ask to speak with John.

A: Say that he isn't home (or available) and offer to take a message.

B: Leave a message with your name, phone number, and a good time to call you back.

A: Write down the message as you hear it. Ask for clarification on two pieces of information:
   • the spelling of the person's name
   • the phone number

B: Clarify the spelling of your name by using a common word for one of the letters in your name. Repeat your phone number slowly.

A: Say that you'll give John the message.

B: Thank the person.

A: End the conversation.

PART ④ BROADCAST ENGLISH Gifts from the Rain Forest

BEFORE LISTENING

A. THINKING AHEAD You're going to hear part of a radio program about life in the rain forest. To prepare, think about what you already know as you take this quiz. Circle the letter of the best answer.

1. How much rain is there annually in tropical rain forests?

   A. 20–50 inches (about 50 cm–127 cm)

   B. 50–200 inches (about 127 cm–508 cm)

   C. 80–400 inches (about 203 cm–1016 cm)

2. How much of the world's oxygen is produced in the Amazonian rain forest?

   A. 5 percent

   B. 10 percent

   C. more than 20 percent

People sleep in **hammocks** in a typical Amazonian village. Huts are **thatched** with palm leaves.

3. There are approximately ten million species of plants, animals, and insects in the world. How many live in tropical rain forests?

   A. more than 10 percent

   B. more than 20 percent

   C. more than 50 percent

4. Rain forests used to cover 14 percent of the earth's land surface. Today they cover only 6 percent. Why?

   A. climate change

   B. plant diseases

   C. deforestation (people cutting down the forests)

5. What is the main reason for deforestation?

   A. the building of towns and cities

   B. the search for gold and silver

   C. the timber (wood) industry, farming, and cattle ranching

In small groups, compare your answers. Then turn to page 234 for the correct answers.

B. VOCABULARY PREPARATION Read the sentences below. The words and phrases in orange are from the radio program. Match the definitions in the box with the words in orange. Write the correct letters on the lines.

a. cause disorder in	e. an interrelated system of people, plants, and animals
b. cause of great suffering	
c. in the most advanced position; leading a battle	f. placed; released into
	g. surprising fact
d. inland region	h. young trees

_____ **1.** The people of the Amazon rain forest often use saplings to build their houses because this wood is very flexible and easy to work with.

_____ **2.** Many people worry that tourism and technology will disrupt the traditions in the rain forest and change forever the way people live.

_____ **3.** Early explorers started at the coast, and it took them many days to travel to the interior of the country.

_____ **4.** The radio program was a real revelation for me: I didn't realize that there were so many useful plants in the rain forest.

_____ **5.** River blindness has always been the **scourge** of tropical climates, but a new drug may rid those areas of that disease forever.

_____ **6.** The World Health Organization is on the **frontline** of solving health problems in developing countries.

_____ **7.** The people of the rain forest know how to use the plants of their **ecosystem**. They make medicines, food, and other useful items from the plants that live there.

_____ **8.** If you were **turned loose** in the rain forest without any information, you probably wouldn't survive.

LISTENING

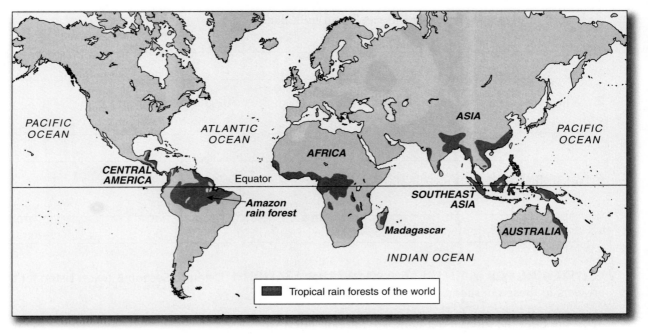

Tropical rain forests are found just north and south of the equator; they have been called the "lungs of the planet." What do you think this means?

A. LISTENING FOR MAIN IDEAS: SECTION 1 This radio program is about Mark Plotkin, an ethnobotanist who spent a long time in South America in the Amazon rain forest. He studied tribal people and how they made use of the forest. (**Note:** Plotkin speaks fast, so be prepared!) Listen to Section 1 twice. As you listen, think about these questions. Then write the answers on the lines.

1. What makes life in the rain forest possible?

_____

2. What is the relationship of the people with the forest around them?

_____

Listening Strategy

Listening for Details: Anecdotes

As you learned in Chapter 1 (page 13), an anecdote is a story or description of an incident. It supports the main idea of what the speaker is discussing and gives the listener a clear picture of it. Paying attention to the descriptive details in an anecdote helps you understand what you are listening to. Descriptive details often include adjectives that describe how people and things look and behave.

B. LISTENING FOR DETAILS: SECTION 2 Listen to Section 2 twice. Listen for an anecdote. You'll listen twice. As you listen, write answers to these questions on the lines.

1. Why was Plotkin surprised when he met Fritz van Troen? (In other words, what did the man's name lead Plotkin to expect? What did van Troen look like?)

   _____

   _____

2. Where did Fritz van Troen's ancestors come from in the 17th and 18th centuries?

   _____

   _____

3. What did van Troen know about?

   _____

   _____

C. LISTENING FOR MAIN IDEAS AND DETAILS: SECTION 3 Listen to Section 3 twice. Listen for the answers to these questions. Circle the correct letters.

1. What does the interviewer compare the rain forest to?

   A. a beautiful park

   B. paradise

   C. a drugstore

2. What seems to be Plotkin's attitude toward the indigenous and semi-indigenous people of the rain forest?

   A. He feels better educated than they are.

   B. He respects them.

   C. He doesn't understand them.

3. Why does Plotkin say that malaria is "the greatest scourge in human history"?

   A. because a cure hasn't been found

   B. because it has killed more people than any other two diseases combined

   C. because there isn't enough of the drug that cures it

4. What is quinine?

   A. a rain forest disease

   B. the frontline drug for malaria

   C. a combination of two diseases

5. Who discovered quinine?

   A. South American Indians

   B. Mark Plotkin

   C. Europeans

Listening Strategy

Listening to Fast English

Some people speak very fast. If you have trouble understanding someone in a conversation, you can ask that person to slow down. If you're listening to a fast speaker on an audio program, try listening more than once or listening to shorter sections. After listening several times, it will seem as if the person is speaking more slowly, and you will begin to hear things that you didn't understand the first time.

D. LISTENING TO FAST ENGLISH
Listen to parts of the radio program again. Listen for ways in which the people of the rain forest use the plants of their ecosystem. You will hear these parts twice. As you listen, fill in the chart.

Plants	Uses
palm thatch	
forest saplings	
cassava	
forest trees of the fig family	
vines	

AFTER LISTENING

A. DISCUSSION In small groups, discuss these questions.

1. What does Plotkin mean when he says that plants make life in the rain forest possible?

2. How would you describe the relationship of the people of the rain forest to their ecosystem? Give examples that support your explanation.

3. Describe the ecosystem that you live in. What plants, animals, and insects are indigenous to your area? How do you interact with them? How do you use them? How do they use you?

B. MAKING INFERENCES In small groups, discuss these questions about the quotation in the box below.

In the interview, Plotkin says:

"The great tragedy is these introduced diseases for which they often have no cure. Now you give these guys another 20,000 years, and maybe they can find a cure for the common cold, but they haven't had 20,000 years to find plants against it, only 500 years since it's been introduced."

1. What does Plotkin mean by "introduced diseases"? What might be some diseases introduced to the people of the Amazon? By whom were they introduced?

2. Who does he mean by "these guys"?

3. How long has the common cold been a sickness among the indigenous people of South America?

BEFORE LISTENING

Flamingos at the Jersey Wildlife Preservation Trust on the Island of Jersey, United Kingdom

A. THINKING AHEAD In small groups, discuss these questions.

1. What are the purposes of zoos?

2. What zoos have you visited? Describe them. If you have never been to a zoo, which animal would you be most interested in seeing?

3. Zoos vary in their quality. How do old-fashioned zoos compare to modern, state-of-the art ones? Give some examples of the two types.

4. Gerald Durrell has been called a "modern Noah." Who was Noah? What was he known for? What does the comparison to Noah suggest about Durrell?

B. HAVING QUESTIONS IN MIND Look over the main headings of the lecture outline on pages 227–229. What questions do you expect (or want) the professor to answer? Is there anything that you're curious about? What would you like to know about Durrell's life? Write your questions on the lines.

Question 1: _____

Question 2: _____

Question 3: _____

C. GUESSING THE MEANING FROM CONTEXT Read the sentences below. The words and phrases in orange are from the lecture. Guess their meanings from the context. Write your guesses on the lines.

1. In the past, animals that survived the trip from their natural habitat to zoos in Europe usually **perished** within a few months of their arrival.

   Guess: _____

2. Durrell wanted to be certain that the animals he collected would be well taken care of, so to **ensure** their safety, he paid his hunters more than other collectors did.

   Guess: _____

3. Durrell captured animals **humanely**. He was careful not to injure or stress them.

   Guess: _____

4. First and foremost, Durrell was a **keen** observer of wildlife. He noticed things about animal behavior that most other scientists didn't.

   Guess: _____

5. Jason wanted to understand the **plight** of the gorillas. He wanted to learn why their numbers had dropped so dramatically in recent years and why they may soon become extinct. He spent a month in the Republic of the Congo, studying and volunteering with primatologists there.

   Guess: _____

6. In Africa, many game preserves have been established as **safe havens** for endangered species. In these places, animals are safe from hunters and poachers.

   Guess: _____

7. The zoo's board of directors' decision was **unanimous**. Everyone agreed that the zoo should be redesigned in order to provide a better environment for the animals.

   Guess: _____

8. Jean spent all of her money to start a new business; the result is that she can't pay her bills and is now **bankrupt**.

   Guess: _____

9. Dr. Hanson left much more than money when he died; his **legacy** includes important research that changed the way scientists do research on endangered species.

   Guess: _____

Now compare your answers with a partner's answers.

LISTENING

🎧 **A. TAKING NOTES: USING AN OUTLINE** Listen to the entire lecture without stopping. This lecture is very similar to a university-level lecture. Fill in as much of the outline as you can. Don't worry if you can't fill in everything. (You'll listen to the whole lecture again later.)

Gerald Durrell: Designer of the Modern Zoo

I. Introduction

    A. Zoos before Durrell: _____

    B. Zoos after Durrell: _____

II. Durrell's Early Years

    A. Birth: _____

    B. Childhood: _____

        _____

    C. Job as a zookeeper: _____

        _____

III. Zoo Professionals

    A. Other zoo professionals

        1. _____

            a. _____

            b. _____

        2. _____

Gerald Durrell **founded** (started) the Jersey Wildlife Preservation Trust. A "trust" is a non-profit organization.

B. Durrell's approach

　1. _____

　2. _____

C. Durrell's qualities

　1. _____

　2. _____

　3. _____

IV. Durrell's Dream

　A. How he solved the money problems: _____

　B. Traditional zoos

　　1. _____

　　2. _____

　　3. _____

　　4. _____

　　5. _____

C. The problem of extinction

   1. causes (from human activity)

      a. _____

      b. _____

   2. how zoos can help to solve the problem

      a. _____

      b. _____

D. Durrell's plan (four principles)

   1. _____

   2. _____

   3. _____

   4. _____

E. The modern zoo

   1. _____

     _____

   2. _____

   3. _____

   4. _____

   5. _____

F. What others thought: _____

V. Jersey Wildlife Preservation Trust

A. What Durrell did: _____

   _____

B. The first years: _____

   _____

C. How he maintained the trust: _____

   _____

VI. Durrell's Legacy

A. Died: _____

B. His greatest legacy

   1. _____

   2. _____

Source: Adapted from a lecture by Jeff Schaefer, Ph.D.

Test-Taking Strategy

Listening for Signals

Professors often use signals to help students follow and pay attention to a lecture. Listening to these signals will help you take better notes and know what is important. During the listening portion of a standardized test, listening for signals will help you notice what is important. Signals can also help you predict what questions may be asked about a lecture.

1. One kind of signal indicates when the professor is starting a new topic or moving on to the next subtopic of the lecture.

> **New Topic Signals**
> (Now) Let's take a look at . . .
> Let's turn our attention to . . .
> This brings us to the topic of . . .

2. Professors sometimes use signals to get your attention in order to make you more interested in their topic. One signal is to ask a rhetorical question—a question to which the speaker does not expect an answer.

   Example: Why was Durrell so interested in the problem of extinction?

3. Another signal is to suggest a question that the audience may have.

   Example: You may very well wonder how Durrell funded his dream.

4. Professors also use topic cues when they list items. These can be ordinal numbers or simply ordering signals.

Ordinal Signals	**Ordering Signals**
First,	Next,
Second,	Then
Third,	Finally,/Lastly,/Last, but not least,

B. LISTENING FOR SIGNALS This lecture is longer than the previous ones, but it is easier to understand because it deals with a person's life and accomplishments. Therefore, the formal outline for this lecture is less detailed. The main topics are indicated with Roman numerals (I, II, III), and cues for the main subtopics are given after capital letters. However, some supporting details are missing.

Listen to the whole lecture again and fill in any information missing from your outline. Let the various signals help you.

AFTER LISTENING

A. USING YOUR NOTES With a partner, use your notes to discuss these questions about the lecture.

1. What was Durrell's approach to capturing animals successfully?

2. What special qualities made Durrell good at what he did?

3. How did Durrell earn money to start his zoo?

4. What were zoos like before Durrell founded his own?

5. What should the modern zoo be like, according to Durrell's vision?

6. What is Durrell's legacy?

B. DISCUSSION In small groups, discuss these questions.

1. According to Durrell, what should the main purpose of zoos be?

2. How well do most zoos today care for animal welfare?

3. Do you enjoy going to zoos? Why or why not?

4. What are some other ways to observe animals? How do these ways compare with zoos?

C. MAKING CONNECTIONS Think about the article in Part 1, the radio program in Part 4, and the lecture you just heard. In small groups, discuss these questions. Write your answers in the T-charts.

1. What are advantages and disadvantages of leaving animals in their natural habitat?

Advantages of the Natural Habitat	Disadvantages of the Natural Habitat

2. What are advantages and disadvantages of bringing animals to zoos?

Advantages of Zoos	Disadvantages of Zoos

PUT IT ALL TOGETHER

Critical Thinking Strategy

Using a Variety of Sources

It is important to use a variety of sources when you research information for a presentation. Here are some suggestions.

1. Don't rely on only one source because the information may be limited, it may have only one perspective, it may be outdated, or it may simply be wrong.

2. Read several sources and take notes on each one. Then prepare your presentation by combining all of the information in your notes in a short summary.

3. As you do your research and organize your information, eliminate contradictory information or information that is not on the topic.

4. Remember: The more you read, the better your understanding of a topic will be.

PRESENTING RESEARCH FINDINGS In small groups, you are going to research a topic and then present your findings to the class. Read the following project assignment and the list of possible sources. Write a check (✓) next to each source that you think would be good to consult for the assignment.

Assignment: Do research on the Jersey Wildlife Preservation Trust. How is it doing? Is it prospering? Is it popular? What are the attendance figures? Is it still run according to Durrell's principles?

Possible Sources
• a website on Gerald Durrell
• a website on the Jersey Wildlife Preservation Trust
• an encyclopedia entry on Gerald Durrell
• an encyclopedia entry on the Jersey Wildlife Preservation Trust
• a book about zoos written in the 1930s
• a book about zoos written after 2000
• a recent book about Durrell
• an article from a British publication about the Jersey Wildlife Preservation Trust

In small groups, compare your answers. Explain why you think each possible source is or is not a good source.

STEP 1

As a group, choose one of these projects to research.

Project 1

Choose an endangered species—animal, plant, or insect—that interests you. Do Internet or library research to find out as much as you can about the species, its habitat, reasons for its endangerment, and any attempts to save it. Present your information to the class. Bring photos of your species.

Project 2

Find out what individuals can do to help preserve endangered species. Research conservation organizations, publications, eco-volunteer opportunities, and activities in which people can participate in their everyday lives. Evaluate the various opportunities. Decide which efforts seem to be the most effective and why. Present your findings to the class.

Project 3

Research two zoos; they can be zoos located anywhere in the world. Try to find one that is old-fashioned and one that is managed according to Durrell's principles. Compare them. Present your findings to the class. Bring photos, if possible.

Project 4

Research the modern zoo. Find an example of a modern zoo that reflects Durrell's ideas. Alternatively, visit a nearby zoo and evaluate it according to Durrell's principles. Present your findings to the class. Bring photos, if possible.

Speaking Strategy

Using Visuals During a Presentation

A presentation is much more interesting if visuals—photos, illustrations, charts, and computer graphics—can be used. As you plan a presentation, look for ways to integrate visuals into your information.

Here are some useful ways to introduce a visual to your audience:

As you can see in this graph, . . .
This poster shows . . .
This illustration is interesting because . . .
If you compare these two photographs, . . .

Examples: **As you can see in this chart,** the area of rainforests in the Amazon has decreased.
This graph shows the rate of change in the average temperature of the water.
This photograph is interesting because it shows Durrell as a young man on a collecting trip in Africa.
If you look at these two photos, you can see many differences between the two zoos.

Be sure to practice introducing and using your visuals before you give your presentation. Remember not to look at your visuals during your presentation. If you are looking at your visuals, your back is toward your audience. Also, remember to stand to the side so that your audience can see the visual.

STEP 2

In your group, divide up the tasks to research and prepare for your group presentation. Think about including pictures, charts, or any other visual material that is relevant to your topic.

STEP 3

Do the Internet or library research to prepare for your presentation. As a group, review the information collected and plan what to include in the presentation. Make sure you use a variety of sources.

STEP 4

Practice giving your group presentation. Decide who will give each part of the presentation. Practice speaking from note cards and practice giving the entire presentation several times. Time your presentation and make sure your report is not too long. Discuss how your presentation can be improved.

STEP 5

Give a presentation to the class on what you have learned. When you give your presentation, make sure you just glance at your notes; don't read them. Also, remember to make eye contact with your audience. Finally, listen carefully to your classmates' presentations. Try to think of a question to ask to show that you are paying attention.

Answers to Activity A on pages 219–220: The correct answer to every question is C.

CHAPTER 8

Environmental Health

Discuss these questions:
- What do you think is happening in the picture?
- How is what they're doing helping to improve the environment?
- What do you do to help improve the environment?

Volunteers clean trash from a pond in Scotland.

A river town in India

A. THINKING AHEAD With a partner, look at the photos and discuss these questions.

1. What might be the cause of the situation in each photo?

2. What are some of the risks to the people in these situations?

3. What are some solutions to these problems?

4. What has been the effect of environmental problems on you, your community, or your country?

B. READING Read about solutions to waste problems in developing nations. As you read, think about these questions:

• What can result from poor sanitation in developing nations?
• What might be some low-cost solutions to the problem?

Success Story: Handling Waste

Waste is a life and death issue in many parts of the world. Poor sanitation and garbage collection, along with a poor water supply, play a big part in the deaths of some
5 1.8 million people, mostly children, who die from diarrhea each year. According to the World Health Organization, more than a third of these deaths could be avoided if sanitation was improved. Now professors at
10 Leeds University (United Kingdom) believe they have found a way to deliver low-cost solutions.

For Leeds civil engineering professors Ed Stentiford and Duncan Mara, this is
15 their life's work. And this year they are working on European-Union-funded projects in Vietnam, Thailand, Bangladesh, Nepal, and Colombia helping to clean up towns and cities that do not have the
20 infrastructure of wealthier nations.

The key in these poorer economies is to use locally available technology and resources, processing waste safely and recycling it or turning it into compost and
25 producing irrigation water from sewage where possible.

According to Professor Mara, "Often engineers in developing countries want high-tech water treatment systems, but
30 these are high-cost, too. They depend on unreliable electricity and equipment that can break down, needing expensive spares. We try to convince them that they should make the most of the resources they have
35 on hand like cheap land, plentiful labor, and sunshine."

Human Waste

The concrete sewers carry away human waste in the cities of wealthy nations. They run under roads and require
40 large-scale construction, which is out of the question in many poorer countries. A less expensive solution is small diameter pipes that run through back yards of houses and carry away sewage that usually runs in
45 open ditches.

Human waste is treated by aerating it to help bacteria break it down. The Leeds team recommends a simple solution for developing nations: waste ponds. These are large ponds
50 where the sewage is allowed to collect and green algae carries out the aeration. The set-up costs are 10–30 percent of western treatment systems and when the waste water has been treated, it can be used for
55 irrigation or fish farming. "Land is cheap and there's plenty of sunshine, so the message is to capitalize on what they have plenty of," said Professor Mara.

Garbage

Garbage is the other half of the
60 equation. Even in the least developed countries each person produces half a kilogram (1.1 pounds) every day. Poor or inadequate collection results in dumping in streets, clogged sewers and drainage
65 systems, contamination of water sources, and a profusion of rats, insects, and disease.

Professor Stentiford advises on ways of handling the problem. These include changing popular attitudes, organizing
70 effective collection, and sorting of waste to enable recycling where possible. Before, garbage was thrown into the canal. With sorting, the city can get back 75 percent of the value of plastic.

75 In Ho Chi Minh City, Vietnam, these ideas have been put into practice. The city now has an efficient collection system, and recycling has been made easier and safer. Locally built tricycles carry away garbage
80 to a transfer station. Recyclers now have a safe and convenient area in which to sort through garbage.

Says Stentiford, "We've improved waste collection and removed the health risk.
85 They're handling waste better now and getting it out of the city."

According to the United Nation, one-in-six of the world's population lacks adequate safe water supplies, and another
90 2.4 billion do not have adequate sanitation. The Leeds team is making a small difference to some of those lives.

Waste pickers of Ho Chi Minh City, Vietnam

Source: "Success Story: Where there's muck there's hope" (*The Reporter*)

C. VOCABULARY CHECK Look back at the reading. Find words or phrases to match the following definitions. Write the correct words and phrases on the lines. Line numbers are given in parentheses.

1. maintaining clean, healthy conditions (1–5) _____

2. organic material that helps plants grow (20–25) _____

3. stop working (30–35) _____

4. use (30–35) _____

5. impossible (40–45) _____

6. putting air into (45–50) _____

7. one-celled plants that live in water (50–55) _____

8. benefit from (55–60) _____

9. the other part of the problem (55–60) _____

10. a lot of (65–70) _____

D. EXTENSION In small groups, discuss these questions.

1. The reading discusses solutions to environmental health problems in developing nations. What are some of the solutions to environmental problems in *developed* nations?

2. How do wealthy industrial nations contribute to worldwide pollution problems? What are some of the results of these problems?

3. What do you personally do to help reduce environmental problems?

4. Are you optimistic or pessimistic about the health of the environment and the health of people? State the reasons for your answer.

E. RESPONSE WRITING Choose *one* of the topics below. Write about it for 15 minutes. Try to use new vocabulary but don't use a dictionary. Just write as many ideas as you can.

• What is your reaction to the reading? How do these success stories make you feel? Do you have any other solutions for the countries or problems described in the reading?

• What are your predictions about the future health of the world and its people?

• What are some other solutions to environmental health problems?

PART ② SOCIAL LANGUAGE Environmental Health Hazards

BEFORE LISTENING

A. THINKING AHEAD You are going to listen to Chrissy interview people on the street. In small groups, make predictions about the interviews. Discuss these questions.

1. Chrissy is going to ask people if they are worried about the effects of environmental **hazards** (dangers) on their health. What kind of answers do you think that most people will give?

2. Do you think that most of the people interviewed are worried about environmental health problems? What health problem do most people worry about?

B. VOCABULARY PREPARATION Read the sentences below. The words and phrases in orange are from the conversation. Match the definitions in the box with the words and phrases in orange. Write the correct letters on the lines.

a. appearing	e. look at; investigate
b. cause a result (verb)	f. make an effort
c. do, perform	g. result (noun)
d. handle; cope with	h. a small, raised growth (usually brown in color)

_____ **1.** Evan, you don't have to **conduct** this interview. Chrissy will do it for you.

_____ **2.** I don't know if I can help you, but I'll **give it a try**.

_____ **3.** One **effect** of getting too much sun is melanoma, or skin cancer.

_____ **4.** Environmental hazards **affect** everyone. It's impossible to avoid them.

_____ **5.** The best way to **deal with** the sun is to always cover up when you go outside.

_____ **6.** I have a strange-looking **mole** on my face, so I'm going to have the doctor remove it.

_____ **7.** Josh has a bumpy red rash on his skin, so he's going to have the doctor **check** it **out**.

_____ **8.** A lot of health issues that we've never seen before are **coming up**.

LISTENING

🔊 **A. LISTENING FOR THE MAIN IDEA** Listen to the interviews. As you listen, think about this question:
🎧 • Do most of the people interviewed worry about environmental health hazards?

🔊 **B. LISTENING FOR DETAILS** Listen to the interviews again. Are the speakers worried about
🎧 environmental health hazards? Circle *Yes* or *No* in the chart below. If the speaker is worried, write what he
or she is worried about.

Speakers	Worried?		What is he or she worried about?
1	(Yes)	No	*quality of air and food*
2	Yes	No	
3	Yes	No	
4	Yes	No	
5	Yes	No	
6	Yes	No	
7	Yes	No	

🔊 **C. LISTENING FOR EMOTIONS** Listen to the interviews again. Try to determine each speaker's emotional
🎧 state by using cues such as the tone of voice, how fast the speaker talks, and laughter. If you are watching
the video, you can also look for cues in the speaker's facial expressions and body movements to determine
his or her emotions. In the chart on page 241, circle the emotion for each speaker or add your own word.

Speakers	Emotions				(Other)
1	Not Concerned	(Somewhat Concerned)	Concerned	Can't Tell	_____
2	(Not Concerned)	Somewhat Concerned	Concerned	Can't Tell	_____
3	Not Concerned	Somewhat Concerned	(Concerned)	Can't Tell	_____
4	Not Concerned	Somewhat Concerned	Concerned	(Can't Tell)	_____
5	Not Concerned	Somewhat Concerned	(Concerned)	Can't Tell	_____
6	Not Concerned	Somewhat Concerned	(Concerned)	Can't Tell	_____
7	(Not Concerned)	Somewhat Concerned	Concerned	Can't Tell	_____

AFTER LISTENING

A. TAKING A SURVEY You are going to interview your classmates about their concerns about environmental health hazards. First, think of your own answer to the survey question below. Then ask your classmates. Take notes in the chart below.

Survey: Environmental Health Hazards

Question: Are you worried about the effects of environmental hazards on your health? If so, what are you concerned about?

Classmates	Worried?		What is he or she concerned about?
hianome	Yes	(No)	
rashed	(Yes)	No	air puule
Teck	(Yes)	No	activity
Jethu	(Yes)	No	globe worm
mother	(Yes)	No	sound pollvees
	Yes	No	
	Yes	No	
	Yes	No	
	Yes	No	
	Yes	No	
Total number of people you surveyed: _____			
Total number of people who said that they are worried: _____			

B. DISCUSSING SURVEY RESULTS Discuss the results of your survey with a partner. Answer these questions:

• Were most of your classmates concerned or not concerned?
• Did any of the concerns surprise you?
• What was the most common concern?

PART ③ THE MECHANICS OF LISTENING AND SPEAKING

WORDS IN PHRASES

Expressing Concern

In conversations and during class discussions, people often express their concern about problems. There are several ways to express concern or worry.

Examples: **I'm concerned about** overpopulation.
I'm worried about overpopulation.
My main concern is that there are too many people in the world.
I'm afraid that because of overpopulation, we'll run out of resources.

Your tone of voice can remain **neutral** (not showing emotion) when you make statements of concern; in fact, in an academic setting, it's often a good idea not to sound emotional in discussions.

LANGUAGE FUNCTION

Intensifying Concern

When you want to state your feelings more strongly, you can add the adverbs *rather, quite, very, really,* or *extremely* to statements with *be* + adjective (*concerned, worried*). These words are called intensifiers; they intensify your concern—in other words, make it stronger.

Examples: I'm **really** concerned about overpopulation.   **Weaker**
I'm **rather** concerned about overpopulation.
I'm **quite** concerned about overpopulation.
I'm **very** concerned about overpopulation.
I'm **extremely** concerned about overpopulation.   **Stronger**

Your tone of voice can still be neutral, but the intensifier strengthens your statement.

A. LISTENING FOR INTENSITY Listen for intensity in these statements. If you hear a statement that doesn't sound intense, circle *Not intense*. If you hear a statement that sounds intense, circle *Intense*.

1. Not intense   Intense
2. Not intense   Intense
3. Not intense   Intense
4. Not intense   Intense

5. Not intense   Intense
6. Not intense   Intense
7. Not intense   Intense
8. Not intense   Intense

INTONATION

🎧 Expressing Emotional Intensity with Stress

You can intensify a concern by adding stress or emphasis to certain words. For example, you can stress the intensifier (*very, quite, extremely, really*).

Examples: I'm *very* concerned about bad drinking water.
I'm *extremely* worried about my grades.

When you intensify with stress, you reveal emotion. This is appropriate in many situations, such as in social conversations or when you want to motivate your listeners to act.

🎧 **B. LISTENING FOR EMOTIONAL INTENSITY WITH STRESS** Listen to the following statements of concern. Listen for their emotional intensity. Circle *Neutral* or *Emotional*.

1. (Neutral)   Emotional   5. Neutral   (Emotional)
2. Neutral   (Emotional)   6. (Neutral)   Emotional
3. Neutral   (Emotional)   7. (Neutral)   Emotional
4. (Neutral)   Emotional   8. Neutral   (Emotional)

👥 **C. EXPRESSING CONCERN** With a partner, practice expressing concern about each the following issues. If you feel intense concern about an issue, use an intensifier and/or stress to intensify it. If you *aren't* concerned, say so with a neutral tone of voice. Give reasons. Then exchange roles.

Example: **A:** I'm not concerned about air pollution. The air never bothers me.
B: Really? **I'm extremely worried** about air pollution. I think it's getting worse each year. Every winter, I get a very bad cough from the pollution.

Issues

1. air pollution
2. overpopulation
3. getting sick
4. HIV/AIDS
5. natural disasters

6. making enough money
7. your grades
8. having a career and a family
9. finding love
10. (your concern)

PRONUNCIATION

> ## 🎧 Comparing /ɛ/, /æ/, and /ʌ/
>
> The /ɛ/, /æ/, and /ʌ/ sounds sometimes seem similar and are hard to pronounce. It's important to be able to pronounce the distinctions though; otherwise, people may not understand you.
>
> **Examples:**
>
> | /ɛ/ | /æ/ | /ʌ/ |
> |-----|-----|-----|
> | bed | bad | bud |
> | bet | bat | but |
> | dead | dad | dud |
> | flesh | flash | flush |
> | leg | lag | lug |
> | send | sand | sunned |
> | ten | tan | ton |
> | The trek is long. | The track is long. | The truck is long. |
>
> 🌐 Notice the two ways of spelling the /ɛ/ and the /ʌ/ sounds.

🎧 **D. HEARING /ɛ/, /æ/, AND /ʌ/** In each set of words, circle the one that you hear.

1. send	sand	sunned		**7.** hem	ham	hum
2. leg	lag	lug		**8.** pen	pan	pun
3. trek	track	truck		**9.** kept	capped	cupped
4. flesh	flash	flush		**10.** mess	mass	muss
5. dead	dad	dud		**11.** beg	bag	bug
6. mesh	mash	mush		**12.** better	batter	butter

🎧 **E. HEARING /ɛ/, /æ/, AND /ʌ/ IN SENTENCES** For each set of sentences, circle the letter of the one that you hear.

1. **A.** That's a funny pen.
B. That's a funny pan.
C. That's a funny pun.

2. **A.** Is that better?
B. Is that batter?
C. Is that butter?

3. **A.** Do you have a ten?
B. Do you have a tan?
C. Do you have a ton?

4. **A.** It's just a short trek.
B. It's just a short track.
C. It's just a short truck.

5. **A.** I kept it.
B. I capped it.
C. I cupped it.

F. PRONOUNCING /ɛ/, /æ/, AND /ʌ/ Work with a partner. Look at the word groups below. For each group, say one of the words. Your partner will circle the word he or she hears. When you have finished all of the items, check the answers. Then exchange roles.

1. send	sand	sunned		**7.** leg	lag	lug
2. trek	track	truck		**8.** flesh	flash	flush
3. dead	dad	dud		**9.** mesh	mash	mush
4. hem	ham	hum		**10.** pen	pan	pun
5. kept	capped	cupped		**11.** mess	mass	muss
6. beg	bag	bug		**12.** better	batter	butter

G. PRONOUNCING /ɛ/, /æ/, AND /ʌ/ IN CONVERSATION Now use words with the sounds /ɛ/, /æ/, and /ʌ/ in conversations. Interview classmates. Ask each question until you can find a classmate who answers "Yes." Write names in the chart.

Example: **A:** Do you like to get a tan?
                  B: Yes, I do.

Find someone who . . .	Classmates
1. likes to get a tan	
2. has ever been on a trek in the mountains	
3. knows a good pun	Horry
4. has a favorite pen	Tech
5. knows how to sand wood	
6. collected bugs as a child	
7. likes mashed potatoes	Feras
8. has driven a truck	
9. has a bedroom that is a mess	Sludz

PUT IT TOGETHER

 A. TALKING ABOUT CONCERNS Work with a partner. You are going to ask your partner about his or her most important concerns in life. See the topics listed below. As you answer, use the phrases for concern, intensifiers, and stress, if appropriate. Give reasons if your partner asks for them. As you speak, try to pronounce the /ɛ/, /æ/, and /ʌ/ sounds correctly. When you are finished, find another partner. Talk to as many classmates as you can.

Example: **A:** Are you worried about getting good grades?
B: Yes, I'm very concerned about my grades.
A: Why?
B: I'm afraid that if my grades aren't good enough, I won't get my financial aid.

School/Career
• Getting good grades
• Getting a good job when you finish your education
• Making enough money

Friends and Love
• Making friends
• Finding the love of your life

Family
• Having children and raising a family
• Being able to have a family and a successful career

Health
• Your health
• The health of parents or other family members

The World/The Environment
• Conflict between national or ethnic groups
• The environment and the future of the planet

B. DISCUSSION First, on your own, **rank** (put in order) what you think are the top three concerns of your classmates. Then, in small groups, compare your rankings. Discuss the top concerns and ways to deal with them.

PART ④ BROADCAST ENGLISH A Utopian Community

BEFORE LISTENING

A. THINKING AHEAD You are going to listen to a radio program about a **utopian community** in Colombia. A **utopia** is an ideal place, especially one with ideal social conditions. Before you listen, discuss these questions in small groups.

• What is your idea of a utopia?
• Describe some utopias that you have read or heard about.

B. VOCABULARY PREPARATION
Read the sentences below. The words and phrases in orange are from the radio program. Match the definitions in the box with the words and phrases in orange. Write the correct letters on the lines.

Colombia and the surrounding areas

a. cover the ground in a random way	e. Spanish word for *ranch*
b. curve-shaped	f. a system of fixed rules for behavior
c. designed for movement through the air	g. with deep, narrow tracks
d. socially excluded	

_____ **1.** The radio crew traveled 30 miles on a deeply **rutted** road. The road was so bumpy that they ruined the tires.

_____ **2.** Hernan's dream was to retire, go back to his homeland in Colombia, and buy a big **hacienda**.

_____ **3.** Jason made a paper airplane, but because it wasn't **aerodynamic**, it wouldn't fly.

_____ **4.** Jason made a model of a plane with **contoured** sides. The curved shape allowed it to fly better.

_____ **5.** **Protocol** does not allow the senator to shake the emperor's hand; he must bow instead.

_____ **6.** The Smiths didn't follow the rules in this community, so they were **ostracized**. They finally left because no one would speak to them.

_____ **7.** Windmills **dot the landscape** like giant sunflowers.

LISTENING

Gaviotas founder Paolo Lugari walks with visitors through area of reforested pine trees.

Resin processing plant at Gaviotas turns pine tree sap into useful products.

Gaviotas is a village of about 200 people in Colombia, South America. For three decades, Gaviotans—peasants, scientists, artists, and former street kids—have struggled to build an oasis of imagination and sustainability in the remote, barren **savannas** (grasslands) of eastern Colombia. They have planted millions of trees, thus bringing back an indigenous rainforest. They farm organically and use wind and solar power. Every family enjoys free housing, community meals, and schooling. There are no weapons, no police, and no jail. There is no mayor.

Source: Friends of Gaviotas (Website)

A. LISTENING FOR MAIN IDEAS: SECTION 1

This radio program is about a model community in eastern Colombia called Gaviotas. The radio program aired in 1994, but the community still exists today. The community is a social and environmental utopia.

Listen to Section 1 of the radio program. You will hear it twice. Listen for the answer to this question:

• Why did the founders of Gaviotas choose the "hardest place" to establish their community?

Community members label water bottles. Much work is done by hand.

Using a Spider Map to Take Notes

On standardized tests, you listen to a passage and answer questions about it. The passage often seems to go by quickly, and it can be difficult to take notes on what you hear. One way to take notes is to use a graphic organizer called a spider map. In a spider map, you write the main idea in the middle circle and the supporting ideas in the outer circles. Using a spider map is one way to organize your ideas as you hear them.

Example: You read: You are going to hear a passage about computer recycling. After you listen, you will need to explain some of the negative effects of computer recycling.

You draw: A spider map such as the following and use it to jot down information as you hear it.

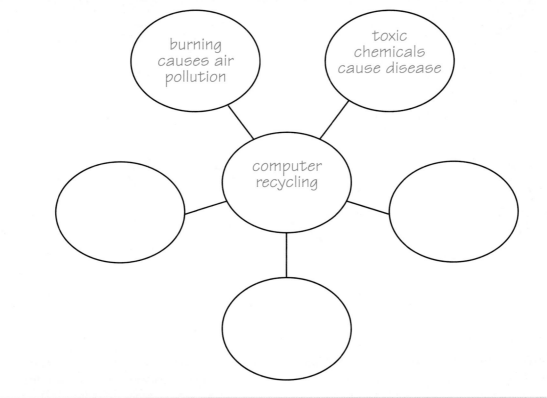

B. USING A SPIDER MAP TO TAKE NOTES: SECTION 1 Listen to Section 1 again. You'll hear it twice. Listen for details that describe eastern Colombia, the area where Gaviotas was founded. As you listen, write the descriptive words in the spider map. Listen for at least five more descriptive expressions.

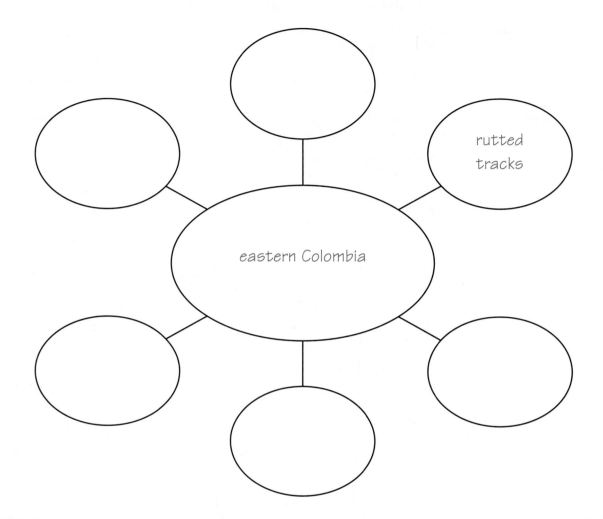

C. MAKING INFERENCES: SECTION 2 Listen to Section 2. You will hear it twice. Even though you might not understand all of the words the reporter uses, describe his first impressions of Gaviotas. Are they positive or negative? What details support your answer? (In other words, what does he see?)

First impressions: _____

_____

Supporting details: _____

_____

Now compare your answers with a partner's answers.

🎧 **D. LISTENING FOR MAIN IDEAS: SECTION 3** Listen to Section 3. You will listen twice. Listen for the answers to these questions. Write your answers on the lines.

1. Why might there be no crime in Gaviotas? _____

_____

2. Why are there no "crimes of passion" or **adultery** (sexual relationships outside of a marriage) in Gaviotas? _____

_____

👥 Now compare your answers with a partner's answers.

Listening Strategy 🔵🔵🔵

Recognizing Figurative Language

Many words can be used two ways: *literally* and *figuratively*. A literal meaning is the most common and usually the first one listed in the dictionary. A figurative meaning is different from the usual meaning; it often makes a word picture or a comparison. If you know the literal meaning of a word, you may be able to guess its meaning when it's used figuratively.

Examples: Let's get some **fresh** fruit at the market. **(Literal)**
Ramona's ideas are **fresh** and surprising. **(Figurative)**

In the first example, *fresh* is used literally; it means "food or produce that's in good condition or newly caught, picked, or prepared." In the second example, *fresh* is used figuratively; it means "new or different."

🎧 **E. RECOGNIZING FIGURATIVE LANGUAGE** Listen to parts of the radio program and guess the figurative meanings of the words in the box. Before you listen, read their literal meanings in the box below. Then use the contexts to guess the figurative meanings. Write your guesses on the lines.

> **oasis** = a place with trees and water in the desert
>
> **flourish** = to grow healthily, especially a plant
>
> **stale** = no longer fresh; not good to eat or smell

1. oasis = _____

2. flourishing = _____

3. stale = _____

AFTER LISTENING

A. DISCUSSION In small groups, discuss these questions.

1. In what ways is Gaviotas a utopia, or model community?

2. What do you think Paolo Lugari means when he says: "All our development models have been created in countries with four seasons, with totally different conditions from tropical countries. When we import solutions from northern countries, not only don't we solve our problems, but we import theirs"?

3. Does Gaviotas sound like paradise to you? Would you like to live there? Why or why not?

B. APPLYING YOUR KNOWLEDGE Look for examples of people creating or using environmentally appropriate technology, services, or products in your community. Here are some questions to ask yourself:
- Are solar panels common?
- Do you see windmills anywhere?
- Is there a recycling program?
- Do you see many electric or hybrid cars?
- Are there shops that specialize in environmentally safe products such as nontoxic cleansers?
- What other signs do you see in your community of people trying to live in harmony with nature?

Find out about the advantages and disadvantages of these technologies and products. If possible, ask people if they are satisfied with these technologies and products, and if not, why not?

In small groups, report your findings. Discuss the issues that prevent people from living a more ecologically sound lifestyle.

Solar panels

BEFORE LISTENING

A demonstrator in a Green Party parade

A. REALIZING WHAT YOU KNOW In Part 5, you are going to listen to a discussion instead of a lecture. Discussions are an important part of academic studies. In many colleges, teaching assistants (T.A.s) conduct discussion sections so students can talk about a professor's lecture and the accompanying reading material. T.A.s also give assignments and quizzes and generally help students understand difficult material.

The discussion that you will hear is about the Green Movement, a general term for Green political parties concerned with environmental and social issues. Before you listen, think about what you already know about the Green Movement (also known as Greens, or the Green Party in some countries). Read each statement below. If you think the statement is true, circle *T*; if you think it's false, circle *F*.

1. The Green Movement is concerned only with environmental issues.   T   F

2. The Green Movement is mainly active in the United States.   T   F

3. The Green Movement believes that every member of a society should participate in decision-making.   T   F

4. According to the Green Movement, it is mainly the government's responsibility to reduce waste and conserve natural resources.　　**T**　　**F**

5. Nonviolence is an important part of the Green philosophy.　　**T**　　**F**

6. Feminism and racial equality are not part of the Green Movement's key values.　　**T**　　**F**

7. The Green Party agrees with the practices of most modern industrialized societies.　　**T**　　**F**

8. The Greens believe in global responsibility, the idea that all actions must be evaluated for impact on the world environment.　　**T**　　**F**

9. The Greens believe in sustainability, which means using current resources while keeping future generations in mind.　　**T**　　**F**

10. Gaviotas is an example of a society that the Green Party would support.　　**T**　　**F**

Now discuss your answers in small groups.

B. HAVING QUESTIONS IN MIND The outline on page 256 reflects the lecture that the students heard before attending the discussion section. Looking at the outline, what questions might students have about the lecture? Write questions on the lines.

Question 1: _____

Question 2: _____

Question 3: _____

C. GUESSING THE MEANING FROM CONTEXT Read the sentences below. The words and phrases in orange are from the discussion you will hear. Guess their meanings from the context. Write your guesses on the lines.

1. Bianca said that today she is **going over** the material we read in Chapter 10. She'll begin by explaining the chart on page 125.

   Guess: _____

2. Instead of just analyzing one department in the organization, let's take **a holistic view**; that way we can see how each department interacts with the organization as a whole.

   Guess: _____

3. Instead of telling you the whole story, I'll just give it to you **in a nutshell**: I had a problem with my car, and that's why I'm late.

   Guess: _____

4. No one knows where that strange custom came from; it must **be rooted in** some ancient ritual that no one remembers anymore.

    Guess: _____

5. Jason has some **wacky** idea about going to live on a commune in Colombia, but I think he's crazy!

    Guess: _____

6. That school is a good place for kids who are **misfits**—you know, the ones who just don't fit in anywhere.

    Guess: _____

Now compare your answers with a partner's answers.

LISTENING

Listening Strategy

Listening to Accented English

Many T.A.s in the United States and Canada are non-native English speakers. Sometimes you may not understand them because, like many people, you are most familiar with standard English accents. When you can't understand a word or expression that you hear in a different accent, follow these steps:

1. Decide if knowing the word or expression is necessary for the overall meaning of what you are listening to. If it isn't, forget about it. If it is, go to Suggestion 2.

2. Supply the missing word, expression, or idea with the most logical possibility, based on the context.

    Example: **You hear:**   "The considerable recent gains in health and longevity, first in westernized countries and subsequently in others, have resulted primarily from the reduction in early-childhood [unintelligible expression]."

                      You guess: The missing part has something to do with death or disease because that's the obvious reason that people would be living longer. (The hints are *longevity* and *reduction*.)

3. If you don't understand the overall meaning and can't guess the missing word or expression, check with the person after the lecture or ask a classmate.

A. TAKING NOTES: LISTENING TO ACCENTED ENGLISH Listen to the discussion. The outline is skeletal, so it is missing many details. Listen carefully to the T.A. and to the students' questions. Notice that the T.A. is a non-native English speaker. Use the strategy in the box above to guess words and phrases that you don't understand. There are three sections. You will listen to each section twice. Fill in as much of the outline as you can. Don't worry if you can't fill in everything. (You'll listen to the whole discussion again later.) Remember to use abbreviations.

The Green Movement

Section 1

I. Ecotopia: Origins of the Concept

    A. Utopia _____

       _____

    B. Ecology _____

       _____

    C. Ecotopia _____

       _____

Section 2

II. The Green Movement

    A. Philosophy _____

       _____

    B. Ten key values of the U.S. Green Movement

       1. _____

       2. _____

       3. _____

       4. _____

       5. _____

       6. _____

       7. _____

       8. _____

       9. _____

       10. _____

Section 3

III. Conclusion _____

_____

_____

_____

Source: Adapted from a lecture by Deborah Blocker, D.Sc., M.P.H., R.D., C.D.N.

B. USING YOUR NOTES Before listening to the discussion again, look at Activity A on page 253. Use your notes to help you check your answers. For any question that you cannot answer, you will need to fill in your notes when you listen again.

C. CHECKING YOUR NOTES Listen to the whole discussion again. As you listen, review your notes and fill in any missing information. Make sure that the definitions for the 10 key values are complete.

Critical Thinking Strategy

Memorizing

In academic settings, you often have to memorize lists of concepts or definitions. Everyone has his or her favorite memory tricks, such as associating a word with something it reminds you of.

A good way to memorize a group of concepts or words and their definitions is to make flashcards using index cards. Write the word or concept on one side of the card and the definition on the back. Show yourself the word, define it, and then flip it over to see if you're right. Mix the cards up every time you study.

Example: Front of flashcard:

sustainability

Back:

not continuing a "throwaway" culture; thinking ahead to eliminate waste and pollution in the future

D. MEMORIZING Memorize the 10 key values from the outline on page 256. Use index cards to make flashcards.

With a partner, quiz each other using flashcards. Then discuss any other memory tricks that you have used to help you learn new material.

AFTER LISTENING

A. USING YOUR NOTES Use your notes to write your answers to these questions.

1. What's an ecotopia?

_____

2. What is the book *Ecotopia* about?

_____

3. What's the relationship between the book *Ecotopia* and the Green Movement, according to the lecture discussion?

_____

4. In your own words, state the basic philosophy of the Green Movement.

_____

5. When did the Green Movement begin in the United States?

_____

👥 Now compare your answers with a partner's answers.

B. REMEMBERING IMPORTANT DETAILS Without looking at your notes, write definitions of the 10 key values in the U.S. Green Movement.

1. ecological wisdom = _____

2. grassroots democracy = _____

3. personal and social responsibility = _____

4. nonviolence = _____

5. decentralization = _____

6. community-based economics = _____

7. feminism = _____

8. respect for diversity = _____

9. global responsibility = _____

10. future focus/sustainability = _____

👥 Compare your answers with your partner's answers.

C. MAKING CONNECTIONS Think about the solutions to environmental problems that your read about in Part 1, the concerns expressed in Part 2, the radio program about the utopian community in Part 4, and the discussion on the Green Party. In small groups, discuss these questions.

1. What do the Greens mean when they say that "environmental and social problems are all connected" and that "they must be solved in a holistic fashion"?

2. Are Greens realistic? Are they having any effect on the world?

3. Who has the best solutions to environmental and social problems: scientists or academics (such as the professors at Leeds University), regular citizens, utopians, political parties (such as the Greens), or someone else?

PUT IT ALL TOGETHER

GIVING A PRESENTATION In this activity, you are going to research a topic and give a presentation to your classmates.

STEP 1
Read the descriptions of the four projects. Then choose *one* project for your presentation.

Project 1
Do Internet or library research to find recent news articles on the Green Movement and learn about some of its recent activities. Find out more about the history of the Green Movement. (Who started it? Where did it start? Who or what influenced the formation of the movement? How strong is it in your country? In other countries?)

If you do Internet research, do a search with the following key words and key word combinations:

"Green Movement"
"Green Movement" + origins
"Green Movement" + [name of country]

You may also find the following websites useful:
• The Green Party of the United States
• Green Parties Worldwide
• Green Party (United Kingdom)
• Green Party of Canada
• Green (New Zealand)
• Australian Greens Online

Project 2
Do Internet or library research to find recent news articles about Gaviotas. How is the community doing now? Have there been any changes since the 1994 radio program that you listened to? If so, what are they? What does the future hold for this community?

If you do Internet research, search for *Gaviotas + Colombia*. The Friends of Gaviotas website might also be useful.

Project 3

Do Internet or library research on other utopias (or model communities) in history, such as:

- Agapemone, founded in England in 1849
- New Harmony, established in Kansas (United States) in 1825
- Oneida Community in the state of New York

Compare one of these to Gaviotas. If you do Internet research, search by using the name of one of these utopias or the key word *utopia*.

Project 4

Do Internet or library research on a mythical utopia such as Camelot or Atlantis or on a literary utopia such as those in *The Lost Horizon* by James Hilton or *Erewhon* by Samuel Butler. Compare one of these to Gaviotas.

STEP 2

Do your research and organize your notes. Think about including pictures, charts, or any other visual material that is relevant to your topic.

STEP 3

Practice presenting your information in a clear and organized way. Remember to only glance at your note cards briefly and to look up while speaking. Time your presentation to make sure it is between 3 and 5 minutes long.

Speaking Strategy

Giving Constructive Criticism

Students are often asked to give feedback or comments on the written or oral work of classmates. When you evaluate a classmate's work, it's important to use neutral language and to make positive suggestions for improvement. **Constructive criticism** is feedback with helpful suggestions that will help your classmate improve his or her presentation. When you do this, you are avoiding hurt feelings and are giving real help.

Example: Dan, I think you could look at the audience more. Why don't you try this technique: Look at your notes for one or two points and then look up at the audience as you say them.

STEP 4

Give a brief presentation (3–5 minutes) to your classmates on what you have learned. When you give your presentation, make sure you just glance at your notes—don't read them. Remember to make eye contact with your audience. Finally, listen carefully to your classmates' presentations. Try to think of a question to ask the speaker to show that you are paying attention.

STEP 5

In small groups, evaluate each other's presentations. Use the following questions to evaluate a presentation.

1. Was the presentation easy to understand? Could you understand the main ideas?

2. Were the issues interesting? Did the topic hold your attention?

3. Did the speaker use notes and make good eye contact?

4. Did the speaker support opinions with good reasons?

5. Did the speaker make clear comparisons?

6. What constructive criticism can you give to your classmate?

UNIT ④ VOCABULARY WORKSHOP

Review vocabulary that you learned in Chapters 7 and 8.

A. MATCHING Match the words to the definitions. Write the correct letters on the lines.

Words

_____ **1.** aerodynamic

_____ **2.** contoured

_____ **3.** ecosystem

_____ **4.** flourish

_____ **5.** frontline

_____ **6.** mole

_____ **7.** ostracized

_____ **8.** protocol

_____ **9.** revelation

_____ **10.** scourge

Definitions

a. surprising fact

b. cause of great suffering

c. in the most advanced position; leading a battle

d. an interrelated system of people, plants, and animals

e. a small, raised growth (usually brown in color) on the skin

f. a system of fixed rules for behavior

g. curve-shaped

h. socially excluded

i. designed for movement through the air

j. grow healthily; do well

B. TRUE OR FALSE? Read the statements below. Circle *T* if the sentence is true. Circle *F* if the sentence is false.

1. If something is **extinct**, it still exists.	T	F
2. **Indigenous** people are the original inhabitants of a place.	T	F
3. An animal that lives **in the wild** does not live in its natural environment.	T	F
4. An animal that lives **in captivity** lives in its natural environment.	T	F
5. Animals that are **camouflaged** are hidden by the use of coloring.	T	F
6. **Compost** can help plants grow.	T	F
7. If there is a **profusion** of rats, then there aren't too many of them.	T	F
8. You have good **sanitation** if you are maintaining clean, healthy conditions.	T	F
9. A child with poor nutrition is less **susceptible** to disease.	T	F
10. If there is a **unanimous** decision, leaders can move forward with plans.	T	F

C. WORDS IN PHRASES Fill in the blanks with words from the box.

chance	dot	on	over	try
concerned	loose	out	speak	up

1. Counting tigers sounds like the _____ of a lifetime. You'll probably never again have an opportunity to do something like that.

2. Hold _____! You're speaking too quickly. Can you repeat that?

3. Hey, it's Chris! _____ of the devil! We were just talking about you!

4. If Chris were turned _____ in a foreign country, he'd probably have no trouble at all because he's good at languages.

5. I know you haven't done this before, but give it a _____ anyway.

6. A lot of environmental issues are coming _____ as a result of global warming.

7. Jane has had some problems with her eyes since she returned from her trip, so she's going to have her doctor check them _____.

8. I'm _____ about all of the natural disasters we've had this year.

9. When you fly over the region, you see groups of palm trees that _____ the landscape.

10. Today we're going _____ the material from yesterday's lecture.

D. THE ACADEMIC WORD LIST In the boxes below are some of the most common academic words in English. Fill in the blanks with words from these boxes. When you finish, check your answers in the readings on pages 208–209 (for items 1–6) and page 237 (for items 7–15). For more words, see the Academic Word List on pages 315–318.

commitment	equipped	fund	goal	grant	research

Dabek uses some of her _____ money to give local schools
                                          1

much-needed pencils, paper, scissors, and other supplies. Schools are poorly

_____, she says, "and we realized that we needed to support the schools
          2

and the community if we were going to do this type of work."

Dabek even organized a scholarship for local students who want to go to college and learn to teach. "We help _____ their education," she says, "and in return they make a _____ to come back and teach for at least 10 years."

She also trains local people and students from the University of Papua New Guinea for her _____ team. "My _____ is to get some of the New Guinea students into graduate school," Dabek says. "They are going to be the world's future biologists, and we need them."

civil	economies	processing
convince	infrastructure	resources
depend	labor	unreliable

For Leeds _____ engineering professors Ed Stentiford and Duncan Mara, this is their life's work. And this year they are working on European-Union-funded projects in Vietnam, Thailand, Bangladesh, Nepal, and Colombia helping to clean up towns and cities that do not have the _____ of wealthier nations.

The key in these poorer _____ is to use locally-available technology and resources, _____ waste safely and recycling it or turning it into compost and producing irrigation water from sewage where possible.

According to Professor Mara, "Often engineers in developing countries want high-tech water treatment systems, but these are high-cost too. They _____ on _____ electricity and equipment that can break down, needing expensive spares. We try to _____ them that they should make the most of the _____ they have on hand like cheap land, plentiful _____, and sunshine."

A. Information Gap: Where in the World?, pages 212–213
Student A

Read the chart below. Ask your partner for the missing information and write the answers in your chart. Take turns asking and answering questions.

Example: **A:** What endangered species lives in the mountain forests of China?
             B: The giant panda.

Endangered Species	Habitat	Reasons for Endangerment
	Mountain forests in China	• Loss of habitat • China's warming climate • Slow rate of reproduction
Cheetah		• Loss of habitat • Inbreeding (and thus genetic anomalies) • Poaching (illegal hunting)
Eastern Lowland Gorilla	Tropical forests in Democratic Republic of Congo (central Africa)	• • • •
Queensland koala	Eucalyptus forests in Australia	•
Blue karner butterfly		• Loss of habitat due to development
Oriental white stork	Wetlands and grasslands in Russia, China, South Korea, and Japan	• •
European tree frog	Meadows and sunny forest edges in Northwest Africa, the whole of Eurasia (with the exception of Great Britain), and the Japanese archipelago	•
Short horned lizard		• Agricultural expansion • Oil and gas exploration
Florida manatee	Coastal waters of Florida and Georgia	• • •
	All oceans of the world	• Hunting

A. Information Gap: Where in the World?, pages 212–213
Student B

Read the chart below. Ask your partner for the missing information and write the answers in your chart. Take turns asking and answering questions.

Example: **B:** I have one reason for the endangerment of the giant panda: loss of habitat. What other reasons do you have?

A: The other reasons are slow rate of reproduction and China's warming climate.

Endangered Species	Habitat	Reasons for Endangerment
Giant panda		• Loss of habitat • •
Cheetah	Grasslands in a small area in the Middle East (mostly Iran) and parts of East and South Africa	• • •
	Tropical forests in the Democratic Republic of Congo (central Africa)	• Hunting • War among humans • Loss of habitat • Disease
	Eucalyptus forests in Australia	• Loss of habitat due to development
Blue karner butterfly	Open woods in North America: Wisconsin, Indiana, Minnesota, New Hampshire, New York, and Illinois	•
	Wetlands and grasslands in Russia, China, South Korea, and Japan	• Loss of habitat, especially wetlands • Human interference
European tree frog		• Disappearance of wetlands
Short horned lizard	Deserts in North America: Southern Canada to Mexico and from eastern Kansas to western Oregon and Washington	• •
	Coastal waters of Florida and Georgia	• Collisions with boats causing injury or death • Entanglement in fishing lines or other litter • Pollution of food source (grasses)
Fin whale	All oceans of the world	

Chapter 1: Cultural Anthropology
Part 2 Social Language

A. Listening for the Main Idea (page 8)

Rachel: O.K., O.K., we have to get serious.

Ashley: Yeah, you're right. I know.

Rachel: We've got that huge exam tomorrow, and—

Ashley: I know, I know. O.K., we won't get off the track again.

Rachel: Right. We'll stick to the subject.

Ashley: Now, uh, what do we still have to review?

Rachel: Well, um, you know she's gonna ask about symbolism.

Ashley: Right, like symbolism in, um, religion.

Rachel: Uh-huh, and culture in general.

Ashley: Yeah . . . but you know, I think we should sorta focus on space—um, the symbolic meaning of space—

Rachel: Gosh, you're right. She spent so much time on Edward Hall's book—

Ashley: —and personal space, his ideas on personal space—

Rachel: Yeah. I really bet that's gonna be on the exam.

Ashley: Uh-huh. I thought it was kinda interesting—you know, um, this idea that it's our culture that, um, determines how we deal with crowded places—

Rachel: —and our need for privacy.

Ashley: Yeah. You know, I never realized before that there are some languages that don't even have a word for "privacy."

Rachel: Really? Where did you hear that?

Ashley: I dunno. Maybe she talked about this the day you were absent.

Rachel: Oh.

Ashley: Yeah. But the part I don't understand, I mean, I wonder, if people don't have the word "privacy," does it mean that they don't feel a need to have time alone, you know, um, without other people around?

Rachel: I dunno. Well, what else did she say that day that I was absent?

Ashley: Um, let me find my notes. Oh, yeah. Well, she talked more about personal space—

Rachel: —the idea that we all need a certain amount of space between us and other people.

Ashley: Right. That there are invisible boundaries—

Rachel: —like borders or limits—like if I get too close to you, then I've "crossed your line," which is why we say "excuse me" when we bump into each other on the street—

Ashley: Right. Uh, but it's even more than that. According to Edward Hall, the boundaries are different in different cultures. In some countries, people stand really close when they talk to you. And in other countries, they stand farther away—

Rachel: —and it drives you nuts if you're from a culture that needs a lot of personal space, and you're talking with someone who's from a country where people stand really close—

Ashley: Exactly. And she told this great story about Edward Hall, where one time he was in the office of this guy—um, a famous psychologist from Harvard University, I mean, a long time ago when this idea was new, right?

Rachel: Uh-huh . . .

Ashley: And this famous guy is really skeptical. I mean, he doesn't believe that there's some, um, specific amount of space that we each need. So during the conversation—and they talked for about an hour—Hall moves his chair a little closer to this other guy's chair. And the other guy moves his chair a little back, a little farther away. And this is unconscious; he doesn't even realize that he's doing it, right?

Rachel: Uh-huh . . .

Ashley: So a few minutes later, Hall moves towards him again, and the other guy moves back again, to have a little more space. And this goes on for an hour. So finally, when Hall decides to leave, he points out to his friend that they started the conversation on one side of the room, and now they're on the opposite side.

Rachel: That's great. So I guess the other guy had to change his mind.

Ashley: Uh-huh. He started to understand the ideas of "personal space."

Rachel: O.K., well, what else do we hafta review?

Ashley: Well, um how 'bout some more of Hall's ideas, like how culture determines how we design our houses . . .

B. Guessing the Meaning from Context
(page 9)

1. **Ashley:** Uh-huh. I thought it was kinda interesting—you know, um, idea that it's our culture that, um, determines how we deal with crowded places—

   Rachel: —and our need for privacy.

   Ashley: Yeah. You know, I never realized before there are that some languages that don't even have a word for "privacy."

   Rachel: Really? Where did you hear that?

   Ashley: I dunno. Maybe she talked about this the day you were absent.

   Rachel: Oh.

   Ashley: Yeah. But the part I don't understand, I mean, I wonder, if people don't have the word "privacy," does it mean that they don't feel a need to have time alone, you know, um, without other people around?

2. **Rachel:** I dunno. Well, what else did she say that day that I was absent?

   Ashley: Umm, let me find my notes. Oh, yeah. Well, she talked more about personal space—

   Rachel: —the idea that we all need a certain amount of space between us and other people.

   Ashley: Right. That there are invisible boundaries—

Rachel: —like borders or limits—like if I get too close to you, I've "crossed your line," which is why we say "excuse me" when we bump into each other on the street, for example—

3. **Ashley:** Exactly. And she told this great story about Edward Hall, where one time he was in the office of this guy—um, a famous psychologist from Harvard University, I mean, a long time ago, um, when this was a new idea, right?

   Rachel: Uh-huh . . .

   Ashley: And this famous guy is really skeptical. I mean, he doesn't believe that there's some, um, specific amount of space that we each need. So during the conversation—and they talked for about an hour—Hall moves his chair just a little closer to this other guy's chair. And the other guy moves his chair a little back, a little farther away. And this is unconscious; he doesn't even realize that he's doing it, right?

C. Making Inferences (page 9)

1. **Rachel:** We've got that huge exam tomorrow, and if we don't—

   Ashley: I know, I know. O.K., we won't get off the track again.

   Rachel: Right. We'll stick to the subject.

   Ashley: Now, uh, what do we still have to review?

   Rachel: Well, um, you know she's gonna ask about symbolism.

   Ashley: Right, like symbolism in, um, religion.

2. **Ashley:** Uh-huh. I thought it was kinda interesting—you know, this idea that it's our culture that, um, determines how we deal with crowded places—

   Rachel: —and our need for privacy.

   Ashley: Yeah. You know, I never realized before that there are some languages that don't even have a word for "privacy."

   Rachel: Really? Where did you hear that?

Ashley: I dunno. Maybe she talked about this the day you were absent.

Rachel: Oh.

3. **Ashley:** And this famous guy is really skeptical. I mean, he doesn't believe that there's some, um, specific amount of space that we each need. So during the conversation—and they talked for about an hour—Hall moves his chair just a little closer to this other guy's chair. And the other guy moves his chair a little back, a little farther away. And this is unconscious; he doesn't even realize that he's doing it, right?

Rachel: Uh-huh . . .

Ashley: So a few minutes later, Hall moves toward him again, and the other guy moves back again, trying to have a little more space. And this goes on for an hour. So finally, when Hall is about to leave, he points out to his friend that they started the conversation on one side of the room, and now they're on the opposite side.

Rachel: That's great. So I guess the other guy had to change his mind.

Ashley: Uh-huh. He started to understand the idea of "personal space."

D. Noticing Grammar (page 10)

Ashley: And this famous guy is really skeptical. I mean, he doesn't believe that there's some, um, specific amount of space that we each need. So during the conversation—and they talked for about an hour—Hall moves his chair a little closer to this other guy's chair. And the other guy moves his chair a little back, a little farther away. And this is unconscious; he doesn't even realize that he's doing it, right? . . . So a few minutes later, Hall moves towards him again, and the other guy moves back again, to have a little more space. And this goes on for an hour. So finally, when Hall decides to leave, he points out to his friend that they started the conversation on one side of the room, and now they're on the opposite side.

Part 3 The Mechanics of Listening and Speaking

A. Reduced Forms of Words (page 13)

A: Dr. Roberts is gonna give a test tomorrow on the first three chapters.

B: I know, and I haven't even read 'em yet. I've gotta get busy tonight.

A: I thought you were gonna help your brother move tonight.

B: Oh no! That's right. I'll just tell 'im I can't. He'll be kinda mad, but what can I do?

A: I dunno. You can't do everything. Maybe you're tryna do too much. You have school and a job and family responsibilities.

B. Understanding Anecdotes (page 13)

One time, years ago, I was living in Greece, in Athens. I was a college student. And so one day I'm at a public library, doing some research. After a few hours, I come out, and in the street to my left is a huge crowd of men—mostly young men. They fill the entire street, from one side to the other, and they're coming toward me. They're waving their fists in the air, and they're yelling really loudly, "PAO! PAO! PAO!" Well, I dunno what's going on, I have no idea, but it doesn't look good to me. It's this enormous crowd of young men, and it seems to me that they're terribly angry. This "PAO, PAO, PAO" sounds rather, uh, violent. All I can think is, "Oh my gosh, it's a revolution or a war or something! And I'm right in the middle of it!" So, of course I turn away from the crowd. I turn to the right and walk as fast as I can. I'm tryna reach the bus stop and take a bus back to my apartment. But the problem is that each time I turn a corner, there's another huge crowd of young men shouting "PAO! PAO! PAO!" I keep turning corners and changing direction, tryna get away from this crowd. It just seems as if they're coming after me, but I dunno why. My heart is pounding fast, and now I'm really running. I've never been so scared before! It's like a nightmare—a horrible dream.

Finally, after what seems like hours, I get back safely to my apartment. I lock the door and turn on the radio to hear the news. It turns out that there was a big soccer game that day between

Greece and Yugoslavia. Greece won. And all those "angry" crowds of men in the streets? Well, they weren't angry. They were *happy*. They were celebrating the fact that their team had won the game. As it turned out, "PAO" was *not* a violent expression. It meant "Panhellenic Athletic Organization,"—P-A-O— which was the name of their soccer team. And I felt *really stupid*.

Part 4 Broadcast English

B. Listening for Supporting Ideas: Section 1 (page 19)

Section 1

Penkava: Robert Sommer is one of our guests. He's a professor of psychology at the University of California at Davis, and he's the author of many books, including *Tight Spaces, Hard Architecture and How to Humanize It* and *Personal Space: The Behavioral Basis of Design*. Robert Sommer joins us from Davis, California. Welcome to "Talk of the Nation."

Sommer: Very pleased to be here.

Penkava: And Deborah Pellow is a professor of anthropology at Syracuse University and editor of *Setting Boundaries: The Anthropology of Spatial and Social Organization*. She joins us from WAER in Syracuse, New York. Thanks for being with us, Deborah Pellow.

Pellow: Hi, Melinda. Thanks for having me.

Penkava: And if you'd like to join our conversation, our number is 1-800-989-8255; 1-800-989-TALK. Well, are we seeing more personal space invaders than before, Robert Sommer?

Sommer: I think there's simply more people around and more settings where people come into direct contact with one another, so more opportunities for invasions.

Penkava: Mm-hm. And, and these rules of uh, "you've stepped into my space," they're, they're, they're things that we don't speak about, are they?

Sommer: Right, and there are more heterogeneous meetings there where you meet people from different backgrounds and the spatial rules change, which—um, make collisions in space.

Penkava: Mm-hmm. Mm-hmm. Are people more sensitive about that, Deborah Pellow?

Pellow: Well, what I was just thinking was, as Bob was saying, you know, it's more heterogeneous. In a sense the world has become so much smaller because we travel more, we go more places, we come across people from so many different cultural traditions, um, each of which may have a different rule book, shall we say, on how people interact, how closely, you know, they stand next to each other and that, and that sort of thing.

Penkava: Mm-hm. And this does go down culture by culture. You've studied this, have you not?

Pellow: Yes. Yes. Um, I, I guess that, um, what I would say is that generally when we talk about culture, we're talking about—culture in its entirety is about communication. And so we can talk about talking, and writing, and so on and so forth, but there's also non-verbal communication: um, the gestures that we use, tones and accents, and that sort of thing. And the cultural organization of space: the way in which we understand space; the way in which we distance ourselves from one another; how we organize our houses; how we design our cities. Um, all of that, also, comes out of a cultural backdrop, shall we say. Um, and as you said, it's often not conscious. It's sort of a hidden system, although people always know it's there when it's been trespassed.

Penkava: Mm-hm. Mm-hm. You know when somebody has crossed your line, right?

Pellow: Uh, you certainly do.

C. Listening for Supporting Ideas: Section 2 (page 19)

Section 2

Penkava: We'll go to Frankfurt, Germany. Rita's on the line. Welcome to "Talk of the Nation," Rita.

Rita: Yeah, hi. How are you?

Penkava: O.K. How are you doing?

Rita: I'm fine. Yeah, I wanted to talk about, uh, the cultural thing, or was it an age factor? I wondered about it, because I used to live in India for 25 years, and then I lived in the U.S. for 16 years, and now I'm in Germany. And every time I visit, uh, India, I feel, gosh, you know, I'm giving up my personal space. And yet, when I lived there, I didn't feel it. And so the thing is, is this something I acquired while in the U.S.? Or is it that I'm just getting older and I'm noticing it more just because I'm older and I need more space?

Pellow: Is it so much age, or is it, um, more the cust—

Rita: Culture.

Pellow: Well, yeah, and the customs, you know, that one becomes used to. Um, I mean, spatiality—when we talk about space and how you use space, it's not exactly a language, but it certainly does, uh, function, to some extent, the way languages do; it does communicate. Um, and you can—and so you—just as you can learn language, you can learn, you can internalize, uh, different ways of, you know, operating in space. And I think that India's a very crowded place.

Rita: Mm-hm.

Pellow: And if you're—you know, when you're there, it's sort of, uh, "do as the Indians do," shall we say.

Rita: Mm-hm.

Pellow: I mean, you know, you were there for a long time. You were living in that system, shall we say, and I would say it's a cultural system. When you leave that—you know, if you're away for any length of time, it's, it's, I think it's like many other traditions. You know, they become more diluted. You lose a bit of it.

Sommer: And probably your privacy needs did change after spending time in the U.S.

Rita: Mm-hm.

Sommer: You just became accustomed to being able to close doors, or to be able to walk in and not bump into people.

D. Listening for Examples: Section 3
(page 19)

Section 3
Rita: Mm-hm. Yeah.

Penkava: But I wonder if it's an age thing, too, because I find myself more, um, more sensitive to that. If I'm sitting down on the Metro or on a train and somebody sits right in front of me—

which happened a few weeks ago and they had headphones on that were bleeding. And I could hear that music and I didn't like it. And I, actually, just got up and moved about five seats ahead of that person, because I just didn't want to deal with it.

Pellow: Mm-hm. But of course, we—

Sommer: Well, particularly if you live alone, that's—

Pellow: Mm-hm.

Sommer: If you live with other people, then then, the privacy needs change, too.

Rita: Yes, that's true, and if you have children.

Pellow: And we also have more—pardon?

Penkava: I'm sorry. Rita?

Rita: With children, too. If you have children, your privacy needs—you, you're just more tolerant, I think.

Pellow: Exactly, but we also have more different kinds of apparatus now that bleed all over us. I mean, it drives me nuts when people sitting in restaurants have their cell phones go off.

Penkava: Mm-hm.

Pellow: I really see that as an incursion on my space. A restaurant's a public place. It's not my, you know, it's not our home. It's sort of, it's like our agreement to share, you know, this public space, this commons, which I really see people trespassing, when they have—whether it's their pager or their cell phone. And the same thing would be true with kids with their Walkman, you know, that are booming at you.

Penkava: Well, thank you for your call.

Rita: Sure. Thank you. Bye-bye.

E. Listening for Details (page 19)

(See Sections 1–3 of the audio script, pages 269–271.)

F. Making an Inference (page 20)

Penkava: Well, are we seeing more personal space invaders than before, Robert Sommer?

Sommer: I think there's simply more people around and more settings where people come into direct contact with one another, so more opportunities for invasions.

Part 5 Academic English

A. Taking Notes: Sections 1 and 2 (page 25)

Section 1

Hi everyone. We have a lot to cover.

Today we're going to take a look at the way that culture influences or determines people's use of space. The anthropologist whose name is most associated with research in this area is Edward T. Hall. He was the one who coined the term *proxemics.* So what is proxemics? The term proxemics refers to theories about how each culture affects people's beliefs about space and about how the use of space affects personal relations. Let me repeat that. Proxemics refers to theories about how each culture affects people's beliefs about space and about how the use of space affects personal relations.

Before we turn to various human cultures, let's consider the animal kingdom. Biologists point out that we can put most animals into one of two groups. Some animal species are "contact species." Contact species need to be very close to each other. They need physical contact, touching. Examples of contact species are walruses and parakeets. Other species are non-contact species. They avoid touching. Examples of non-contact species are horses, hawks, and swans.

A famous animal psychologist from Switzerland, Hediger, coined the term "personal distance" to refer to the spacing between animals that non-contact animals seem to feel is normal. He noticed that dominant animals—bigger, stronger animals that have a high position in the group—these dominant animals have a larger personal distance than animals in lower positions.

Section 2

O.K., what about humans? Well, just like animals, humans have a need for a certain amount of space [holds hands far apart] between them and other people. The difference—and this is Edward Hall's main point—the difference is that an animal's need for space is determined by biology while a human's belief about space is also determined by culture.

If you travel from country to country, pay attention to people in conversation in different cultures. Notice the distance between the two people as they talk. What you'll see is that in some cultures people stand very close to each other [holds hands close together]. For example, in the Arab world, people stand extremely close to someone they're talking with. In other cultures, such as Japan, people feel the need for more space between them and a person they're talking with.

However, within each culture, there are variations, differences, depending on the relationship between the two people and the type of conversation. Edward Hall points out four different distance zones that are common in cultures such as Europe and the United States. First is intimate distance, when people are touching or almost touching [holds hands close together]. This is the distance of love and protection . . . but also of physical fighting. In many cultures, intimate distance is not considered appropriate in public. For this reason, people become tense when on a crowded elevator or subway, where it's difficult to avoid physical contact with strangers. O.K.

The second distance zone is personal distance—close enough, for example, to shake hands or talk with a husband, wife, or friend. Social distance—the distance for impersonal business, common for people who work together or people at a casual social meeting. And fourth is public distance—for more formal situations, such as a public speech or performance. At this distance, the voice must be quite loud.

Edward Hall notes, however, that this pattern—intimate, personal, social, and public—may not be universal. In other words, it might not be found in all cultures. In some cultures, the pattern may, instead, have just two distances—one for family members and one for people to whom one is not related.

B. Taking Notes: Section 3 (page 27)

Section 3

Let's move on to another area of proxemics—the use of space in the design of the home. I'm going to give you examples from several different cultures, and you'll notice, I think, how the home itself reflects people's need for privacy.

In American culture, privacy is highly valued: It's very important to most people, even to those who like to spend time with others. In a typical home, parents share a bedroom, of course, but it's very common for each child to have his or her own bedroom. The idea here, although this is a little off track, is for each child to learn responsibility for one area, for a certain amount of space which is "his" or "hers." It's a step towards that child's future independence. It's also common, in a medium-sized or larger home, for each parent to have one room—perhaps an office or studio—which is considered just his or hers. The important point here is that when an American wants some privacy, wants to be alone, he or she will simply go into a room and close the door. Everyone understands what the closed door means; they know there is no reason to worry, but they also know that they have to knock before entering.

Now. A different culture. In the Arab world, at least for people who can afford it, the home has lots of space [holds arms apart], but this is quite different from the space of American homes in that the Arab home doesn't have many partitions or walls breaking the house up into a number of rooms. The reason? According to Edward Hall [points to board], Arabs do not like to be alone. For much of the time, they like to have the family together in one large room. Even if they aren't engaged in conversation, they can at least see each other on the other side of the room [points across room]. Clearly, then, there is no true physical privacy in an Arab home—and, indeed, the Arabic language itself doesn't even have a word for "privacy." But does this mean that an Arab feels no need for privacy? No. It doesn't. When an Arab needs to be "alone," he simply stops talking. Everyone around him understands what this means and is not worried. However, cross-culturally, you can imagine that this could lead to misunderstandings. When an American "stops talking," for example, it may be interpreted as an expression of quiet anger.

Now. One more culture. Japanese is another language in which the word "privacy" does not exist. In a traditional Japanese home, there are many interior walls, but they are thin. They screen out visually, but they don't screen out sound, in contrast to homes in the Netherlands or Germany, say, where people want very thick walls to screen out sound, too. In addition, walls in a traditional Japanese home are moveable.

They slide back and forth [mimes sliding a door] to create a changing environment, depending on the season or the purpose for the room. The same room can serve as a dining room, bedroom, or living room for socializing. In Japanese-style sleeping arrangements, the family members sleep close together. Perhaps the essence of Japanese character may be found in a typical home on a cold winter day, when everyone sits close together around a sort of fireplace in the center of the room. They all sit under the same quilt or blanket, and this holds in the warmth. So you see that the design of the Japanese home emphasizes the need for closeness. In such a small, crowded country, there is little privacy. What little there is may be found in quiet corners of traditional gardens.

Well, I see our time is up. Before our next session, I want you to read the section in Hall's book about the design of cities. I'll give you a hint: I'm including this on your exam, so make sure you understand the two types of designs that he focuses on. O.K. See you on Friday.

C. Checking Your Notes (page 27)

B. Listening for Specific Information (page 28)

(See Sections 1–3 of the audio script, pages 271–273.)

Chapter 2: Physical Anthropology Part 2 Social Language

A. Listening for the Main Idea (page 36)

B. Listening for Details (page 37)

Victor: So, are you guys gonna stick with this? Next quarter it's physical anthro.

Jennifer: I have to because I'm majoring in anthro, but I'm looking forward to it.

Brandon: I dunno. What *is* physical anthropology, anyway?

Jennifer: You study primates, primate evolution, early humans, stuff like that.

Victor: You mean like chimpanzees and gorillas, and all?

Jennifer: Yeah, exactly. And like *you,* too.

Victor: Whaddaya mean?

Jennifer: I mean you're a primate, too.

Victor: Oh, yeah? I know that . . .

Jennifer: In fact, there are a lotta similarities between us and nonhuman primates. Didja know *that?*

Victor: I knew that . . . like what?

Jennifer: Well, both humans and chimps use tools.

Brandon: Wait a minute, Jennifer, I'm not so sure about that.

Jennifer: Sure they do. Chimps use twigs to dig out insects from tree trunks so they can eat them.

Brandon: Yeah, but it's not the same thing . . .

Jennifer: Why not?

Brandon: Because we plan ahead. We know we need to accomplish a task, like get food, and we design an implement specifically for that purpose. Chimps just grab anything that's handy . . .

Jennifer: Well, that may be, but I—

Victor: Hey, hey, that reminds me of a show I saw on TV once about a chimp that could communicate using sign language—

Jennifer: Victor, don't interrupt me—

Victor: But that's cool, isn't it? I mean, it's an example of what you were talking about, doncha think?

Jennifer: Yeah, that's Koko. She's a gorilla, not a chimpanzee. And yes, that is a good example. That's another thing we have in common with primates—language.

Brandon: Well, I don't know . . . can this gorilla use sign language to make up *original* sentences? If so, then I would say that's "language." If not, then it's just imitative behavior or something . . .

Victor: Hey, Brandon, my man, sounds like you take exception to being compared to a chimpanzee . . . hey, I was at the zoo last Sunday, and I saw your twin brother at the monkey house! On the inside of the cage . . .

Brandon: Oh, yeah? [Victor begins chasing Brandon.]

Jennifer: Hey you guys . . . hey . . . hey, you guys! Hey, hey aren't we supposed to study some more?

C. Listening for Emotions (page 38)

1. **Victor:** So, are you guys gonna stick with this? Next quarter it's physical anthro.

   Jennifer: I have to because I'm majoring in anthro, but I'm looking forward to it.

2. **Jennifer:** I mean you're a primate, too.

   Victor: Oh, yeah? I know that . . .

3. **Jennifer:** In fact, there are a lot of similarities between us and nonhuman primates. Didja know that?

   Victor: I knew that . . . like what?

4. **Brandon:** Wait a minute, Jennifer, I'm not so sure about that.

   Jennifer: Sure they do. Chimps use twigs to dig out insects from tree trunks so they can eat them.

5. **Jennifer:** Well, that may be, but I—

   Victor: Hey, hey, that reminds me of a show I saw on TV once about a chimp that could communicate using sign language—

Part 3 The Mechanics of Listening and Speaking

B. Listening for Intonation to Express Disagreement (page 42)

1. **A:** It seems to me that humans aren't much smarter than chimpanzees.

   B: I disagree. [soft]

2. **A:** I think zoos are horrible places.

   B: Well, I'm not so sure I agree with that. [soft]

3. **A:** Physical anthro is really hard.

   B: I completely disagree. [strong]

4. **A:** Dr. Taylor is a really good teacher.

   B: I agree, but I think he should be better organized. [soft]

5. **A:** I think they should close all the zoos and put the primates back in their natural environment.

   B: You're wrong. [strong]

6. **A:** This is the hardest class I've ever taken.

B: I understand what you're saying, but we're learning an awful lot, aren't we? [soft]

C. Guessing the Meaning from Intonation
(page 42)

Part 1

1. **A:** This class is really hard.
   B: I agree.

2. **A:** Chimps are so similar to humans!
   B: I completely agree . . . [will probably disagree]

3. **A:** It's amazing how much language Koko has learned.
   B: I agree . . . [will probably disagree]

4. **A:** Humans are the most destructive animals on Earth.
   B: I agree with that . . . [will probably disagree]

5. **A:** The new primate section at the zoo is great!
   B: I agree with that.

Part 2

1. **A:** This class is really hard.
   B: I agree. It's one of the most difficult ones I've taken.

2. **A:** Chimps are so similar to humans!
   B: I completely agree, but they are only really similar to an infant or baby.

3. **A:** It's amazing how much language Koko has learned.
   B: I agree, but she is just being trained to respond to commands.

4. **A:** Humans are the most destructive animals on Earth.
   B: I agree with that, but humans are not naturally destructive.

5. **A:** The new primate section at the zoo is great!
   B: I agree with that. It's wonderful.

D. Hearing the Difference Between /θ/, /s/, and /t/ (page 43)

E. Pronouncing /θ/, /s/, and /t/ (page 43)

1. tank
2. thin
3. pass
4. thick
5. force
6. sigh
7. mat
8. tent
9. ace
10. Bess

Part 4 Broadcast English

A. Listening for the Topic in an Introduction (page 47)

Brand: While they were not our ancestors, Neanderthals were our nearest relatives as a species. But our cousins didn't survive. Something happened. They vanished about 30,000 years ago. Here to explain is the host of NPR's "Science Friday," Ira Flatow. And he joins us every Thursday.

B. Listening for the Main Idea (page 47)

C. Listening for Details (page 47)

Brand: I'm Madeleine Brand, and this is "Day to Day."

While they were not our ancestors, Neanderthals were our nearest relatives as a species. But our cousins didn't survive. Something happened. They vanished about 30,000 years ago. Here to explain is the host of NPR's "Science Friday," Ira Flatow. And he joins us every Thursday.

Hi, Ira.

Flatow: Hi, Madeleine.

Brand: Now this has been a big mystery, has it not?

Flatow: Yeah, this has been one of those great, uh, mysteries of all time. Here, you had pretty successful cousins of we humans, the Neanderthals. They were roaming around Europe for thousands of years. And then suddenly, in the fossil record, we find out that they died, they died out about 30,000 years ago and we've always been wondering what happened to them. There have been, you know, all kinds of different theories. But a new study out says that they think they have figured this out. And they think it's because the Ice Age, which was developing in Europe, actually did them in. I mean, they were not able to adapt climatically. It turns out that the cold weather moved down southward and the Neanderthals just could not, you know, hack it.

Brand: What do you mean? They couldn't gather enough fur skins? They couldn't dress warmly enough?

Flatow: That's right, they—well, we could say they really were not dressed for success in the most meaningful part of the way. Success—no, as a culture, a species or whatever they were, not only did they not adapt their clothing, but they didn't change their eating habits. For example, as the weather was changing gradually around them over a period of 10,000 years—they had some time to do this, but they didn't.

Brand: And so despite the opinions of some women, that's why we're not descendents of them?

Flatow: Well, not quite. I mean, our European ancestors were living at that time, too, in the neighborhood, the origination, but they retreated to the south, actually to the southwest of France—I guess you would call it the Riviera of the day 'cause it was warmer down there—and they survived.

And what happens, according to this study by a team of scientists at the University of Cambridge, is that about 30,000 years ago, there appears on the scene the Gravicians, complete with their own high-tech tools and warm clothing. I guess these are the kinds of things we'd see in the, in the movies if they made movies of cave people those days. They're carrying those javelin-like spears to catch the animals. They've got fishing nets to catch fish. There's a new high-tech concept for you.

Brand: Mm-hmm.

Flatow: And they have the latest in high-tech clothing, which are furs that are sewn together. And they even have woven cloth. So they're much better equipped to survive this colder weather.

Brand: And hence, all those Raquel Welch movies.

Flatow: That's right. And they come back and they flourish and they rejuvenate, the populations of our ancestors, while the Neanderthals never quite make it.

Brand: So does this prove once and for all that the Neanderthals were not our ancestors?

Flatow: Well, you know, there's always been a debate about where do we, where do we really fit them in. Were they a subspecies of humans that contributed to the evolution of humans in Europe, or were they a distinct species? And a new study by Katerina Harvati at NYU appears to add heavy weight to the idea that the Neanderthals were a separate species within the, uh, genus of homo. So we're homo sapiens, they were—'homo' being the genus; they were the 'homo,' but they were not the species. So if you're a Neanderthal fan, it's a bad week for you because they just sort of wimped out and never survived.

Brand: Ira Flatow hosts NPR's "Science Friday," and he joins us every Thursday.

Thanks, Ira.

Flatow: Thank you, Madeleine.

D. Understanding Humor (page 48)

Flatow: For example, as the weather was changing gradually around them over a period of 10,000 years—they had some time to do this, but they didn't.

Brand: And so despite the opinions of some women, that's why we're not descendents of them?

Flatow: Well, not quite.

Part 5 Academic English

A. Listening for the Meanings of New Words and Phrases (page 53)

1. It wasn't until approximately 1.4 million years ago that a new type of tool, stone hand axes, also known as Acheulean stone tools, were developed.

2. This raises the question, why did humans become bipedal if not to free their hands? Well, many hypotheses have been proposed

and one idea is that bipedalism allowed individuals to carry food back to some central place for sharing with other members of the group.

3. Human paternal care involves, first, extensive provisioning; in addition, human fathers provide protection from predators; they also provide defense of the territory, and, last, the transport of infants. As a result, the level of mortality in young humans is much lower than in nonhuman primates.

4. Since Jane Goodall made these observations of what is now referred to as "termite fishing" among the Gombe chimpanzees, other primatologists have also observed tool-using behavior in other nonhuman primate populations.

5. Well, many hypotheses have been proposed and one idea is that bipedalism allowed individuals to carry food back to some central place for sharing with other members of the group.

C. Listening for the Lecture Subtopics in an Overview (page 54)

D. Taking Notes: Introduction (page 54)

Lecturer: Good morning. Today, I'm going to be discussing human and nonhuman primate behavior. Um, humans, apes, monkeys, and prosimians have many traits in common and they're all classified as primates. According to fossil and behavioral and genetic data, humans and all other primates shared a common ancestor millions of years ago.

In today's lecture, I'm going to compare the behavioral patterns of human and nonhuman primates. Specifically, I'm going to identify several of the behavioral similarities between these two groups, and then I'm going to discuss a few of the differences.

Naturally, there are, uh, lots of them, so I will focus on only a few of the more important behavioral similarities and differences. Specifically, I am going to discuss locomotor patterns, tool use, parental care, and, uh, meat eating. Throughout this lecture, you will see that these behaviors are related to each other in complex ways.

E. Taking Notes: Sections 1, 2, 3, and 4 (page 54)

Section 1

Lecturer: Good morning. Today, I'm going to be discussing human and nonhuman primate behavior. Um, humans, apes, monkeys, and prosimians have many traits in common and they're all classified as primates. According to fossil and behavioral and genetic data, humans and all other primates shared a common ancestor millions of years ago.

In today's lecture, I'm going to compare the behavioral patterns of human and nonhuman primates. Specifically, I'm going to identify several of the behavioral similarities between these two groups, and then I'm going to discuss a few of the differences.

Naturally, there are, uh, lots of them, so I will focus on only a few of the more important behavioral similarities and differences. Specifically, I am going to discuss locomotor patterns, tool use, parental care, and, uh, meat eating. Throughout this lecture, you will see that these behaviors are related to each other in complex ways.

One important difference between humans and all other primates is the way they each move around in their environments. That is, they differ in their locomotor patterns. Some nonhuman primates move in a vertical manner: they cling, they leap. These small primates grasp the sides of small trees while remaining upright, and they also leap around on the ground. An example of a vertical clinger is the *sifaka*. By the way, there's a picture of a *sifaka* on page 55 of your textbook.

Other nonhuman primates move around on all four limbs—the arms and legs—on the ground. These animals are called "terrestrial quadrupeds." That's a mouthful. "Terrestrial quadrupeds." An example is the baboon.

Species that use all four limbs to move around in trees are referred to as "arboreal quadrupeds." Nonhuman primate species that are classified as arboreal quadrupeds include macaques and capuchin monkeys. An example of a terrestrial quadruped is the baboon, *Papio*. Our nearest relatives, the African great apes—you know them as chimpanzees and gorillas—exhibit an unusual type of locomotor style called "knuckle-walking." You've seen this at the zoo. Knuckle walking is a form of terrestrial quadrupedalism in which the primate does not use its hands flat on the ground when walking, but instead bears its weight on its knuckles.

The locomotor style of gibbons, also known as "the lesser apes," is referred to as "brachiation." This is a very acrobatic form of locomotion in which they swing through the forest using their very long arms. Brachiation differs from quadrupedalism in that it relies heavily on the arms and not the legs to propel the primate's body forward.

Um, the locomotor style of humans is distinct from that of all other primates. It is referred to as "*bi*pedalism." Bipedalism is defined as walking on the two hind limbs. The human body's entire weight is distributed to the two legs via the pelvis—that is, the hips. The earliest evidence for bipedalism is found in a hominid fossil ancestor who lived approximately six million years ago in the Tugen Hills in East Africa. The fossil evidence suggests that our ancestors walked bipedally *long* before they first made tools. The earliest stone tools were made around 2.5 million years ago, but the first bipedal human ancestor began to walk approximately *six* million years ago.

This raises the question, why did humans become bipedal if not to free their hands? Well, many hypotheses have been proposed and one idea is that bipedalism allowed individuals to carry food back to some central place for sharing with other members of the group. This differs dramatically from *non*human primates who don't carry their food from one location to another, but consume it where they find it.

Section 2

Another behavioral difference between human and nonhuman primates concerns the use of tools. As I mentioned before, the first stone tools date to around 2.5 million years ago. These tools are no more than crude choppers and are part of what is called the Oldowan tool tradition. Oldowan is the name of the east African area

where the tools were first identified. The Oldowan tradition began about $2\frac{1}{2}$ million years ago, and it ended about $1\frac{1}{2}$ million years ago.

During this period, the Oldowan tradition remained fairly unchanged. These Oldowan tools are believed to have been created by our human ancestor, known as *Australopithecus garhi*. It wasn't until, approximately 1.4 million years ago that a new type of tool, stone hand axes, also known as Acheulean stone tools, were developed. That's "Acheulean"—A-C-H-E-U-L-E-A-N. These tools were used until about 300,000 years ago. There is quite a lot of variation in the form and function of the Acheulean tools. These tools are believed to have been used for cutting meat, scraping animal hides, digging up tubers. Another human ancestor, *Homo ergaster*, chose these hand axes as their primary tool.

Up until a few years ago, tool use was believed to be the defining characteristic of what it meant to be human, because non-human primates were not known to modify or use tools in any way. Um, but it was Jane Goodall, the famous primatologist, who found that some populations of chimpanzees *do* in fact use tools in their natural environments. Goodall observed chimpanzees using sticks to dig for termites. Termites are a high quality food, but they're very difficult to remove from their termite mounds. To obtain these nutritious insects, the chimpanzees find and then modify slender tree branches or twigs. They then use these modified twigs to dip into the entrance holes of the termite mounds. When the termites attack the twig, the chimpanzees slowly withdraw the twig and eat the termites that are clinging to it.

Since Jane Goodall made these observations of what is now referred to as "termite fishing" among the Gombe chimpanzees, other primatologists have also observed tool-using behavior in other non-human primate populations. For example, there was another researcher who found chimpanzees in Ivory Coast, West Africa using rocks to crack open nuts. In fact, these chimpanzees hide their mortar and pestles (tools for cracking open nuts) in tree holes. When they want to crack a nut, they go to the tree hole, remove their mortar and pestle, crack open the nuts, and then return the mortar and pestle to its hiding place. These, uh, observations of chimpanzees suggest that tool-using behavior is not exclusive to humans, nor is it the defining feature of humankind.

Nonetheless, it is important to recognize that tool use by nonhuman primates is much simpler than that observed in modern humans, or even that observed in our human ancestors—*Australopithecus garhi* and *Homo ergaster*. Even early human tool use involved modifying stones for specific purposes. In addition, early humans sometimes used several different items together as tools. This is known as "composite tool use." Neither modifying stone tools, nor the use of composite tools, have yet been observed in the tool-using behavior of the nonhuman primates. Another major difference in tool use between chimpanzees and hominid ancestors relates to the observation that hominids use many different types of materials in the development of tools—for example, bone, antler, stone, teeth, and wood. Chimpanzees have not been observed using any materials besides stone and wood.

Section 3

All right. Another behavioral distinction between human and nonhuman primates concerns parental care. Primates, in general, provide much more parental care to their offspring than do most mammals. Both nonhuman primates and humans are born helpless and are dependent on their parents' care.

However, this period of dependency is much longer in humans. You see, nonhuman primates must find their own food after being weaned from their mother's milk. However, humans have an extended period of dependency, and they require enormous amounts of direct parental investment past weaning and throughout young adulthood. For example, in the United States, children live with and are financially supported by their parents until they reach the age of 18 because most are incapable of earning enough money to take care of themselves.

In addition to the fact that humans provide more parental care to their offspring, scientists have observed that human fathers provide much of this care. Human paternal care involves, first, extensive provisioning; in addition, human fathers provide protection from predators; they also provide defense of the territory, and, last, the

transport of infants. As a result, the level of mortality in young humans is much lower than in nonhuman primates.

Although some nonhuman primate fathers do provide care for their offspring, it's very rare. Most scientists believe that the lack of paternal care in nonhuman primates relates to the species' social system. Humans have a monogamous social system; that is, in which a male-female pair mate together. Consequently, the male—the father—is confident that the offspring is his. In most nonhuman primates, the social system is more promiscuous; that is, uh, females mate with many males—resulting in low paternity certainty. In this case, the male is not certain that the offspring is his so he does not provide paternal care.

Section 4

Lastly, another related behavioral distinction between humans and nonhuman primates concerns meat eating. Much of the food that is provided by human fathers to their families comes in the form of meat. The only nonhuman primate known to hunt for meat on a regular basis is the chimpanzee. Um, however, meat from hunting does not make up a substantial part of the chimpanzee's diet, but it has an important social function. Chimpanzee hunting is often cooperative and occurs most often when females are in estrus—that means, the females are sexually receptive. So, after the hunt, the male hunters often exchange the meat for sex with the females.

Chapter 3: Developing Nations Part 2 Social Language

A. Listening for the Main Idea (page 73)

B. Listening for Details (page 73)

Mike: This way. Hi. I'm doing interviews for Campus TV. May I ask you one question?

Speaker 1: Um . . . uh, I guess so. Sure.

Mike: What do you think should be done to end poverty?

Speaker 1: You mean here in the States, or anywhere?

Mike: Anywhere.

Speaker 1: Well, I think the government has to get involved. Um, the government needs to create more jobs.

Speaker 2: No, no, no. Not more government intervention! People need to start taking responsibility for themselves, you know, take care of their own families. You know the expression, "There's no free lunch"? Well, that's what I think.

Mike: Well, thank you very much for your time. Hey, I'm gonna try and get this guy on the bike. Hey, uh, I'm doing an interview for Campus TV. Can I ask you a few questions?

Speaker 3: Uh, sure.

Mike: O.K.

Speaker 3: I guess so.

Mike: What do you think should be done to end poverty?

Speaker 3: Well, um, I think more job-training programs.

Mike: So, you mean education.

Speaker 3: Well, I, I don't mean, an education like people going to the university to get degrees in anthropology or philosophy or something like that. I mean really practical classes in how to do stuff that's gonna get people jobs.

Mike: O.K. What do think can be done to end poverty?

Speaker 4: Well, uh, just handouts from the government don't seem to work very well.

Mike: So, you mean welfare isn't a good idea?

Speaker 4: Right. Nothing ever seems to change. This may sound harsh, but, maybe we should think about ending these programs.

Mike: That's great, thank you. What do you think can be done to end poverty?

Speaker 5: Uh, that's a pretty big question. I think that the government needs to have more social welfare programs like, um, Europe. Uh, basic health care for everyone. Free education. Stuff like that. Um, a safety net.

Speaker 6: It's easy. People need to work harder. There's lots of work out there. Look at all the signs in the window. People just don't want to work hard.

Mike: Well thank you very much, for your time.

Speaker 6: You're welcome. Take it easy.

Mike: What do you think can be done to end poverty?

Speaker 7: Um, well, you know there, there's this great proverb about fishing, you know? Um, if you give a man a fish, he'll . . .

Mike: . . . eat for a day?

Speaker 7: Yeah, right. But if you teach 'im how to fish, he eats for a lifetime. Yeah.

Mike: So, so you mean—

Speaker 7: Well, we need more job training. Education.

Mike: O.K. Thank you very much for your time. I appreciate it.

C. Guessing the Meaning from Context
(page 73)

1. **Speaker 2:** Not more government intervention! People need to start taking responsibility for themselves, you know, take care of their own families. You know the expression, "There's no free lunch"? Well, that's what I think.

2. **Speaker 5:** Pretty big question. Uh, I think that the government needs to have more social welfare programs like, um, Europe. Uh, basic health care for everyone. Free education. Stuff like that. Um, a safety net.

D. Managing a Conversation (page 75)

Mike: Hi. I'm doing interviews for Campus TV. May I ask you one question?

Speaker 1: Umm, I guess so. Sure.

Mike: What do you think should be done to end poverty?

Speaker 1: You mean here in the States, or anywhere?

Mike: Anywhere.

Speaker 1: Well, I think the government has to get involved. The government needs to create more jobs.

E. Guessing the Meaning from Context: Proverbs (page 75)

Speaker 7: Um, well, you know there, there's this great proverb about fishing, you know? Um, if you give a man a fish, he'll . . .

Mike: . . . eat for a day?

Speaker 7: Yeah, right. But if you teach 'im how to fish, he eats for a lifetime. Yeah.

Mike: So, so you mean—

Speaker 7: Well, we need more job training. Education.

Part 3 The Mechanics of Listening and Speaking

A. Listening for Tone of Voice (page 78)

1. **A:** Do you understand the term "microcredit"?

   B: Uh-uh. [No.]

2. **A:** Thank you for participating in the interview.

   B: Uh-huh. [You're welcome.]

3. **A:** Some of the people we interviewed had excellent suggestions.

   B: Uh-huh! [I really agree!]

4. **A:** Most people on welfare are just lazy.

   B: Yeah. [Yes.]

5. **A:** Most people on welfare are just lazy.

   B: Yeah . . . [I don't think so.]

6. **A:** Most people on welfare are just lazy.

   B: Yeah, right. [You're wrong.]

B. Giving Advice and Suggestions (page 79)

1. **A:** I don't understand these economic terms.
2. **A:** Oh, no! I've lost my economics book!
3. **A:** Wow, this economics paper is due tomorrow!
4. **A:** My report is only five pages long.
5. **A:** You know, I'm really not prepared for the exam.

6. **A:** Gee, I really need more information on that economist for my paper.

C. Commenting on Past Actions (page 79)

1. **A:** We only have a few hours to prepare this presentation.
2. **A:** Oh, no. I can't find my economics text!
3. **A:** I got a "C" on my presentation.
4. **A:** I didn't understand the last assignment.
5. **A:** I'm not prepared for the exam.
6. **A:** I can't afford to go to the movies with you.

D. Reduced Forms of Words (page 80)

1. Microsoft outta build the factory here.
2. Microsoft shuddena built the factory there.
3. Why doncha take that class?
4. The government shudda started a microcredit program.
5. The government otto uv started a microcredit program.
6. They shuddena raised taxes.

Part 4 Broadcast English

A. Listening for Background Information: Section 1 (page 82)

Section 1

Host: Bangladesh is the country that used to be East Pakistan. When the British left the Indian subcontinent in the 1940s, it was partitioned, and the newly created Moslem country, Pakistan, straddled majority Hindu India, separated by a thousand miles. Bangladesh broke away, became independent in 1971. Here to talk with us a bit about Bangladesh is Ambassador Teresita Schaffer, who is director for South Asia at the Center for Strategic and International Studies in Washington. She lived in Bangladesh in the 1980s.

B. Listening for Main Ideas: Section 2
(page 83)

C. Listening for Supporting Statistics
(page 83)

D. Listening for a Reason (page 84)

Section 2

Host: In the case of Bangladesh, I suppose, Ambassador Schaffer, it's fair to say that geography is destiny.

Schaffer: Well, geography has certainly marked the place. Uh, Bangladesh is about the size of Minnesota, and, uh, is flat as a pancake. In a normal dry season, about one-third of its land area is rivers. It's the delta of the Ganges and the Brahma Putra, which come together. And in a normal monsoon season, that percentage goes up to over half. The floods that you read about in the newspapers are in the abnormal monsoon seasons, when two-thirds of the country may be under water.

Host: But even a normal monsoon season, you're saying, uh, leaves the country awfully wet.

Schaffer: That's right. Uh, it's also very crowded. Uh, the distance at which people stand and stare at you is markedly closer than it is in either India or Pakistan.

Host: The social distance. Between people.

Schaffer: That's right. That's right. But I think that's in part at least a function of how crowded the place is.

E. Listening for Details: Section 3 (page 85)

Section 3

Host: As we've heard, Bangladesh is a major recipient of U.S. aid. Uh, what has the U.S. been trying to do for Bangladesh with that money?

Schaffer: Well, this has shifted a bit over the years. In the early years when U.S. aid was very capital intensive, uh, we focused on building major infrastructure projects, including a dam which to this day appears on the basic postage stamp in Bangladesh. But more recently, the focus has been on community development and on grassroots development—and also on family planning. And there have really been some amazing success stories in this area.

Host: But in the overall picture, has the country developed any significant export industries?

Schaffer: It's developed one significant export industry, and that is ready-made garments. Bangladesh is the third or fourth largest supplier of ready-made garments to the U.S. economy. Uh, but it's got another potential one, which at the moment is not an export industry by Bangladesh policy. Uh, and that is natural gas. Uh, they have had natural gas—they've known about natural gas—there for a long time but in recent years have discovered that the quantities probably are very exciting on a world scale, and this has sparked a big inflow in investment, and it holds the possibility for really transforming the economy.

Host: We heard in Vicky O'Hara's report reference made to people who were beneficiaries of this mi—microcredit program, which is the kind of orientation of U.S. aid that you mentioned that is different from underwriting big public works and dams and the like. Has this really affected lots and lots of people in such a populous country as Bangladesh, or is it just the odd happy village story that celebrates—

Schaffer: No, it has really affected a lot of people. Uh, in a country of, uh, it's now 120 million people, you don't go all the way nationwide very easily, uh, but, uh, the Grameen Bank and the Bangladesh Rural Advancement Committee known as BREC have gone almost nationwide. They have an extraordinary number of beneficiaries, and they have touched the lives of the people who've participated with very small loans that have permitted people to go from below subsistence level to a level at which they were actually earning some cash income.

Part 5 Academic English

A. Taking Notes: Sections 1, 2, and 3
(page 89)

Section 1

Lecturer: The 1998 recipient of the Nobel Prize for Economics, Amartya Sen, was a child growing up in urban Bengal, India at the time of the terrible famine of 1943. Now, his family was well-to-do, and he didn't personally know anyone who went hungry during this time, but the streets of Calcutta were full of dead and dying people. Three million people starved to death in that famine.

Now, let's stop here for a second. I want you to consider just some of the famines in recent history. You've no doubt seen famine victims on the evening news on TV: think of the famines in Niger, Ethiopia, Somalia, Sudan, and North Korea. Or, if you reach back a little further, there was the 1974 famine in Bangladesh and the famine in China from 1958 to 1961. Between 23 and 30 million people died in that one. O.K. Let's do a little brainstorming. What causes a famine? Crop failures? O.K., so what causes crop failures? Poor agricultural methods? Lack of water? Drought? Yeah, maybe. Too much water? Floods? O.K. Maybe an invasion of locusts; billions and billions of insects come along and eat everything in sight? Well, all these appear to many people to be the causes of famine. But not to Amartya Sen. Amartya Sen's specialization is an area of economics called development economics or welfare economics—in other words, the study of how societies make choices about allocating resources. So, he examines poverty and what is perhaps the most extreme form of poverty—famine. In focusing on this area, Sen is giving a voice to the world's poor.

Section 2

According to Amartya Sen, famines are not caused by any natural disaster per se. Famines are not caused by the simple absence of food. Instead, he says, the causes of famine are sociological and political. Specifically—and here is the essence of his argument—he points out that there has never been a famine in a democratic country with a free press. Why is this the case? Well, think about it. What happens in a democracy if crops fail and people begin to die of hunger? There are reports of this in the country's newspapers and magazines. People get upset with the government and demand action. And—because politicians need votes if they're going to keep their jobs—the government has to find a way to distribute food to the areas of the country that are affected.

Now, all of the countries that I just mentioned—Niger, Somalia, Sudan, North Korea, and China during the period of the Great Leap Forward—all of these nations were nations with dictatorships or authoritarian regimes. And what about India? Although it's a democracy today, in 1943, remember, it was still a colony of England. The British rulers didn't have much interest in listening to the poor.

Section 3

Who is it who dies in a famine? Poor people in a dictatorial society. Sen quite rightly points out that, quote, "the kings and the presidents, the bureaucrats and the bosses, the military leaders and the commanders never starve." Unquote. Amartya Sen says that a famine never affects more than ten percent of a population. The people affected are the poor, usually the rural poor, and this often happens even when the food supply is just fine, when there is no food shortage. For example, in the Bangladesh famine of 1974, the amount per capita of food available was quite high. But floods interrupted the transplanting of rice. This caused unemployment among rural workers. They weren't making any money, so they couldn't buy food. Then the situation was made worse when people started hoarding food. This caused prices to rise, and the poor simply couldn't afford to buy it.

B. Listening for Quoted Material (page 90)

Who is it who dies in a famine? Poor people in a dictatorial society. Sen quite rightly points out that, quote "the kings and the presidents, the bureaucrats and the bosses, the military leaders and the commanders never starve." Unquote.

C. Taking Notes: Sections 4 and 5 (page 90)

Section 4

So what can be done to avert famines in the future? Growing more food would help because it would lower the cost and also provide work—and therefore money—to people in rural areas. But according to Sen, this is too simple. He says—and here I'm referring to an article that he wrote in 1993—you can find this in the journal, uh, *Scientific American*, if you're interested; it's called "The Economics of Life and Death"—anyway, he says that the purchasing power—that is, the ability to buy things—the purchasing power of the poorest people, the people with the least ability to obtain food—must be increased.

How? With public employment programs. These can rapidly provide an income that allows the poorest people to compete with the rest of the population for a share of the food supply. Now, although this creation of jobs does cause prices to rise, it actually turns out to be beneficial because this price increase causes, in turn, other groups in the population to reduce their consumption. The result is that if a food shortage comes along, this shortage will be distributed more equitably throughout the population, and mass starvation will not result.

Section 5

So we see that underlying all famines are two factors: poverty and lack of democracy. Amartya Sen has said that it's a mistake for economists to look at just the gross national product to determine the wealth of a nation because, as he says, GDP, quote, ". . . overlooks the fact that many people are terribly poor." Unquote. His quote unquote "poverty index" counts not just how many people are living below the poverty line, but also the degree of poverty among the poorest of the poor.

Sen says that taking care of the poorest members of society is both the ethical thing to do and good for business. See, he likes to point to societies that have high standards in education and health. The economic growth of modern China, for example, surpasses that of India because China is providing an education for its masses. Costa Rica is another good example. We might think of Costa Rica as a poor country. After all, it does rank low in gross domestic product per person. In other words, the average income is low. However, Costa Rica focuses its spending on health and education. So, as a result, the quality of life is very good. For example, life expectancy there is 78.2 years. That's very high—almost what it is in the country with the highest life expectancy, Japan. And the adult literacy rate—the percentage of people who can read and write—is also quite high: 96%. From the example of Costa Rica, we see that a country's gross domestic product per se does not necessarily determine the quality of life of the people.

So as we see, when a society takes care of its most vulnerable—the very poor—not only can disastrous famines be prevented, but the quality of life improves for the entire society.

D. Noting a Point of Greater Importance
(page 91)

So what can be done to avert famines in the future? Growing more food would help because it would lower the cost and also provide work—and therefore money—to people in rural areas. But according to Sen, this is too simple. He says—and here I'm referring to an article that he wrote in 1993—you can find this in the journal, uh, *Scientific American*, if you're interested; it's called "The Economics of Life and Death"—anyway, he says that the purchasing power—that is, the ability to buy things—the purchasing power of the poorest people, the people with the least ability to obtain food—must be increased. How? With public employment programs. These can rapidly provide an income that allows the poorest people to compete with the rest of the population for a share of the food supply.

Chapter 4: The Global Economy
Part 2 Social Language

A. Listening for the Main Idea (page 104)

B. Listening for Details (page 104)

Tanya: What're you guys gonna do this summer?

Jennifer: I don't know. I wanna do some writing, but I need money . . .

Tanya: Me, too. I'll probably have to get some dumb job because it's been impossible to get a good internship this summer!

Jennifer: Brandon's the lucky one. He always seems to get jobs that are career-related, donchu, Brandon?

Brandon: Well, I was lucky last summer.

Tanya: Whadju do?

Brandon: I had this great job writing code all summer for this computer game developer.

Tanya: Cool. Did you get games to keep and all?

Brandon: I got a copy of the game I worked on, *Escape from Volcano Island*.

Tanya: Wow! I love that game! And you're gonna do that again this summer?

Brandon: Well, I wanted to, but I dunno.

Jennifer: Whaddya mean?

Brandon: I keep in touch with a couple people I worked with there. They told me the boss let go of three people last spring, so . . .

Jennifer: Oh, so that doesn't look too good for you, huh?

Tanya: How come they're layin' people off? *Escape from Volcano Island* is one of the biggest selling games right now.

Brandon: That doesn't have anything to do with it. Apparently they're contracting with programmers in Eastern Europe.

Jennifer: Why's that?

Tanya: It's cheaper, right?

Brandon: Exactly. They work for a lot less. And they do great work, too.

Jennifer: That's such a drag! What does that mean for you? I mean, you were planning on getting a great job at a company like that as soon as you graduated, right?

Brandon: Well, it's not like I'm gonna write code for the rest of my life. I've been doin' it since I was 13.

Tanya: That's a long time!

Brandon: Yeah, so my goal is to *develop* games, and hire *other* people to do the programming. Actually, my goal is to have my own company.

Jennifer: If you have your own company, would you hire cheap labor overseas?

Brandon: Definitely. I'd wanna keep overhead low. I'd hire the best work force I could, for the least amount of money.

Jennifer: Even if it meant taking jobs away from U.S. citizens?

Brandon: Sure. That's how you make a profit. Besides, it creates jobs for people who really need them.

Tanya: . . . and it helps you keep the product affordable so that poor students like myself can have some fun once in a while.

Jennifer: Yeah, I see your point.

Brandon: Speaking of fun, I'm outta here. See you guys later. Don't study too hard.

C. Making Inferences About Attitudes or Feelings (page 105)

1. **Tanya:** What're you guys gonna do this summer?

   Jennifer: I don't know. I wanna do some writing, but I need money . . .

   Tanya: Me, too. I'll probably have to get some dumb job because it's been impossible to get a good internship this summer!

2. **Jennifer:** That's such a drag! What does that mean for you? I mean, you were planning on getting a great job at a company like that as soon as you graduated, right?

   Brandon: Well, it's not like I'm gonna write code for the rest of my life. I've been doin' it since I was 13.

3. **Brandon:** Well, it's not like I'm gonna write code for the rest of my life. I've been doin' it since I was 13.

   Tanya: That's a long time.

   Brandon: Yeah, so my goal is to *develop* games, and hire *other* people to do the programming. Actually, my goal is to have my own company.

4. **Jennifer:** If you had your own company, would you hire cheap labor overseas?

   Brandon: Definitely. I'd wanna keep overhead low. I'd hire the best work force I could, for the least amount of money.

   Jennifer: Even if it meant taking jobs away from U.S. citizens?

5. **Jennifer:** Even if it meant taking jobs away from U.S. citizens?

   Brandon: Sure. That's how you make a profit. Besides, it creates jobs for people who really need them.

   Tanya: . . . and it helps you keep the product affordable so that poor students like myself can have some fun once in a while.

Part 3 The Mechanics of Listening and Speaking

A. Asking for Confirmation and Offering an Explanation (page 108)

1. **A:** Kathleen's going to Harvard in the fall. She must be smart, huh?

   B: True, but she's exactly the kind of person they're looking for.

2. **A:** Your brother is a straight-A student, isn't he?

   B: Right. He gets excellent grades.

3. **A:** You always get summer jobs, don't you?

   B: That's not true. Last summer I didn't work at all.

4. **A:** Brandon got a high score on the test. He must be smart, huh?

   B: Nah, he was just lucky.

5. **A:** Brandon got a high score on the test. He's lucky, isn't he?

   B: I wouldn't call it luck . . . he really studied hard.

B. Hearing Tag Question Intonation (page 109)

1. Chrissy's smart, isn't she? [Rising intonation]

2. Evan has a great job this summer, doesn't he? [Rising intonation]

3. You always land on your feet, don't you? [Falling intonation]

4. Brandon's lucky, isn't he? [Falling intonation]

5. That video game is doing well, isn't it? [Falling intonation]

6. Using programmers in Eastern Europe isn't fair to American workers, is it? [Falling intonation]

7. You're not leaving now, are you? [Rising intonation]

8. You worked in a video store last summer, didn't you? [Falling intonation]

D. Reduced Forms of Words (page 110)

1. You got a great summer job, didncha?

2. You didn't study last night, didja?

3. You're pretty lucky, arncha?

4. You think you're pretty smart, doncha?

5. You're working for a computer company, arncha?

6. You didn't get an internship this summer, didja?

Part 4 Broadcast English

A. Listening for the Main Idea in an Introduction (page 114)

Host: T. R. Reid is back in Tokyo, just in time to celebrate the opening of the one thousandth Mister Donut shop.

Reid: *Mista Donatsu* has just taken Japan by storm, and there's a very good reason for this: You know what? Mister Donut in Japan is vastly better than any Mister Donut in America.

B. Listening for Comparisons: Section 1 (page 114)

Host: T. R. Reid is back in Tokyo, just in time to celebrate the opening of the one thousandth Mister Donut shop.

Reid: *Mista Donatsu* has just taken Japan by storm, and there's a very good reason for this: You know what? Mister Donut in Japan is vastly better than any Mister Donut in America.

Host: And why is that?

Reid: Well, I don't, you know, you go to, you go to the Mister Donut near my house in America, and you wait around a while, and some guy with a greasy apron comes out and gives you a donut on a piece of wax paper and sloshes some coffee in a cup, you know, a paper cup.

Here, you go in, these stores are absolutely clean: they're bright, they're beautiful, they have gleaming hardwood floors, and there's six people in these perfect uniforms with a little white cap and a bow tie. And they say, "Oh, thank you, honorable customer for entering our respected store in the middle of your busy day." And then, you know, they serve you on china, the coffee is in a beautiful china cup. They're falling all over themselves. You see, they really do it right.

And then they have this thing called "the lucky *kaado,*" the lucky card? Uh, you scratch off the numbers and see if you won. And they've got it rigged so that, like, every other time that you go in, you win. And you win some stupid little prize, but it feels pretty good. But, then, they have this guy in the background who purports to be a disk jockey at a radio station in Boston. He's always t—his name is Josh—he's always talking English, 'cause English is cool, right? And he plays only American goldie oldies—Chuck Berry, Elvis, Supremes—that's all he does.

C. Listening for Details: Section 2 (page 114)

Reid: There's just a couple of things they've done wrong.

Host: Oh, O.K., what?

Reid: They can't make a donut.

Host: [Laughs]

Reid: I mean, it's beautiful, it's clean, the people are bowing to you in their perfect uniforms, but the donuts just don't taste like donuts. This morning in *Mista Donatsu,* I had a, a caramel and sweet potato donut, and, uh, it was a concoction, but it wasn't a donut. The coffee's O.K., though.

Host: Well, now, what's the draw? Because a lot of Japanese businesses are, are clean and give you very gracious service, right?

Reid: Well, it's American, that's cool, you get the free *kawari* on coffee. *Missu Do*—that's *Mista Donatsu*—has appealed very brilliantly to a core audience. These high school girls in their uniforms come pouring out of the high schools and they immediately go to *Missu Do* to talk over the latest gossip and everything.

Host: Now, are they there for the donuts, the refill, or Josh?

Reid: [Laughs] Maybe Josh, I don't know. They're there because it's *kakkoi*—it's cool.

Host: Mmm-hmm. So, we do sushi bars here, and they do Mr. Donatsu . . .

Reid: Exactly.

Host: Who do you think got the better end of the bargain?

Reid: Sushi is better than a donut in either country, but, uh, I'm telling you, *Mista Donatsu* is so bright, and fun. Maybe it's a draw.

Host: T. R. Reid, in Tokyo, Japan is on leave from *The Washington Post.*

D. Japanese Words and Phrases (page 114)

1. **Reid:** *Missu Do*—that's *Mista Donatsu*—has appealed very brilliantly to a core audience. These high school girls in their uniforms come pouring out of the high schools and they immediately go to *Missu Do* to talk over the latest gossip and everything.

2. **Reid:** And then they have this thing called "the lucky *kaado,*" the lucky card? Uh, you scratch off the numbers and see if you won.

3. **Reid:** This is the only place in Japan that gives you a free refill on coffee. They even had to make up a Japanese word for this— *kawari. Kawari* kind of means "exchange" or "turn over."

4. **Host:** Now, are they there for the donuts, the refill, or Josh?

   Reid: [Laughs] Maybe Josh, I don't know. They're there because it's *kakkoi*—it's cool.

Part 5 Academic English

A. Listening for the Meanings of New Words and Phrases (page 119)

1. To produce some of these things, nations are constrained by their scarce resources to produce less of other things. This is called a "trade-off," and this is at the very heart of economic reality.

2. One way—this is referred to as socialism—it tried to centralize the decision-making by putting it under government control.

3. For example, economists often use an expression that gets at the essence of costs: "There's no such thing as a free lunch." You've all heard that, right? No such thing as a free lunch. By this, they mean that every choice and every decision made by

individuals or collectively by nations, necessarily involves a give and take.

4. By contrast, the other way—generally referred to as market capitalism—tired to resolve the dilemma of economic trade-offs by, by allowing the decisions of millions of buyers and sellers in decentralized and competitive markets to determine resource allocation and distribution.

5. Under socialism, government planners—often called "technocrats" —developed elaborate and intricate plans for how the nation's scarce resources would be used. They would decide what would be produced, and for whom the output would be used or distributed.

6. Since most, if not all, of the productive resources of these nations were owned or controlled by the state and not the private sector, the plan was plausible, huh, at least theoretically.

7. Regardless of their political philosophies or ideologies or the magnitude of their wealth, all nations are constrained by the scarcity of the resources they have to produce a seemingly unlimited amount of things—the necessities and luxuries—that people want and need.

8. The technocrats generally used the nation's res—scarce resources to produce what consumers wanted and needed. They gave priority to so-called "strategic output": industries such as steel, tools, machinery, ships, and national defense systems.

9. Governments slowly replaced the practice of freely printing money to pay bills with more fiscally sound measures of raising funds through taxation and borrowing.

10. The transition from one economic system to another occurred as former socialist governments disassembled state bureaucracies and privatized state enterprises.

B. Listening for the Main Points in an Introduction (page 119)

Lecturer: Good morning! Let's get started. All right, as I mentioned last week, today we're going to take a look at economic issues that affect all nations of the world and two main ways that nations have chosen to deal with those issues. We'll also examine the disadvantages of one system that have led to a major trend in global economics in the last decade: the transition from *central* economic planning to *market* economies.

C. Taking Notes: Using a Variety of Graphic Organizers (page 120)

Section 1

Lecturer: Good morning! Let's get started. All right, as I mentioned last week, today we're going to take a look at economic issues that affect all nations of the world and two main ways that nations have chosen to deal with those issues. We'll also examine the disadvantages of one system that have led to a major trend in global economics in the last decade: the transition from central economic planning to market economies. [Writes on board] Central economic planning, market capital.

There are nearly 200 nations in the world today, each, as you know, quite different and unique. Some are centuries old; others have only recently been created from the collapse of the Soviet Union in 1991 and the emergence of some 12 independent republics.

Some nations are large geographically but are rather sparsely populated. Australia and Canada are two examples, while other nations are tightly packed with people, such as Canada, excuse me, such as *China* and India. And some nations are extremely wealthy. But, of course, riches are not measured in terms of money. Rather, the wealth of a nation is measured by human resources—its people. Now, what do we mean by this? Its collective knowledge, talents, and skills.

And what else? Its accumulation of productive machinery and equipment; and its stockpile of natural resources such as oil, natural gas, timber, navigable rivers, and proximity to deep water seaports and airports.

Some nations are endowed, in varying degrees, with these resources; and others are *not* so fortunate. While nations may be rich in human productive and creative talents, some are natural-resource poor. Can you think of any examples? Did I hear Japan, I did yes, Japan. And also Singapore.

Section 2

Lecturer: O.K. Think about a mosaic for a minute. The nations of the world—whether old or new, small or large, populous or not, rich or impoverished—are as *dissimilar* as the separate tiles or pieces of a mosaic. However, taken as a whole, these seemingly different nations somehow fit together to form a beautifully textured, yet complicated mosaic called the global economy. [Writes on board] Global, global economy.

While dissimilar in one sense, all the nations of the world share one thing in common: each must confront the same limitations inherent in economic reality. Uh, yes?

Student: What do you mean by, "same limitations"?

Lecturer: Good question, um, what I mean by that is, regardless of their political philosophies or ideologies or the magnitude of their wealth, all nations are constrained by the scarcity of the resources they have to produce a seemingly unlimited amount of things—the necessities and luxuries that people want and need.

Now, only a fool would suggest that the world's economies are not constrained by scarcity. What I mean is, even for the most wealthy nations, the richest of nations, it's impossible to produce nutritious food, housing, clothing, education, and medical care simply by *boop, boop, boop* [makes button pushing motions], pressing a few buttons. The reality is that we do not *live* in a world where perpetual abundance rules, where people and nations lack nothing, where everything is free just for the taking and just for the asking. All of the resources nations need to produce the things that people desire are *never* free; there's always a cost involved.

But, like the expression "the wealth or the riches of a nation," the term "cost" [writes on board]—the term "cost" means more than *monetary* value. For example, economists often

use an expression that gets at the essence of costs: "There's no such thing as a free lunch." You've all heard that, right? No such thing as a free lunch. By this, they mean that every choice and every decision made by individuals or collectively by nations, necessarily involves a give and take.

Here's an example: a farmer's decision to use an acre of land to produce, uh, corn means that the same acre cannot be used at the same time to graze and raise sheep. So, economists say that the cost of producing more corn to make breakfast cereal means that fewer wool sweaters and dresses can be produced. Well, more generally, if a nation decides—however these decisions are reached—to devote more of its scarce resources to manufacture steel, to build ocean-going ships, to construct super highways and defense systems, the fewer resources will be available to produce *other* things such as health care, food, housing, stereos, DVDs, and education.

So, to produce some of these things, nations are constrained by their scarce resources to produce less of *other* things. This is called a "trade-off," [writes on board] trade-off, so, a "trade-off," and this is at the very *heart* of economic reality. How have the nations around the world addressed this universally shared problem of economic [taps board] *trade-off*?

O.K. Let's take a look at the ways that nations have dealt with economic trade-offs. During the 20th century, for example, nations tried, with varying degrees of success, to—two alternate ways to cope with economic trade-offs. One way—this is generally referred to as *central economic planning*—Um, yes?

Student: I'm sorry, what was that?

Lecturer: Um, central economic planning, [points to board] central economic planning. Um, it tried to centralize the decision-making by putting it under government control. By contrast, the other way—generally referred to as [points to board] *market capitalism*—tried to resolve the dilemma of economic trade-offs by, by allowing the decisions of millions of buyers and sellers in decentralized and competitive markets to determine resource allocation and distribution. O.K.?

Section 3

Lecturer: Under [points to board] central economic planning—now that I've explained that a bit, what's another name for it? C'mon . . . socialism, right? Government planners—often called "technocrats"—developed elaborate and intricate plans of how the nation's scarce resources would be used; they would decide *what* would be produced, and for *whom* the output would be used or distributed.

Now, since most, if not all, of the productive resources of these nations were owned or controlled by the state and not the private sector, the plan was plausible, huh, at least theoretically. Now, as you can imagine, this was not simple, however. The central plan had to cover every single aspect of a large, complex economy, and was carried out by superimposing the dictatorial authority of the few—the central planners and the state bosses, the bureaucrats—over the many, the many—the mass of consumers. And the technocrats generally used the nation's res— scarce resources to produce what consumers wanted and needed. However, they gave greater priority to so-called "strategic output."

[Recognizes student's hand] Yes?

Student: What do you mean by "strategic output"?

Lecturer: Yes, good question, I was just getting to that. "Strategic output" means that industries such as steel, tools, machinery, ships, and national defense systems. Consumers, of course, with no voice in this central plan, had to do without the things they needed.

O.K. Now, under [points to board] central economic planning the power of the state over the control and ownership of resources was used to produce whatever the *planners* believed was necessary to maintain and expand the nation's position in the world community. For example, in the 1960s, a leader of the former Soviet Union claimed that socialism would "bury" the nations of the West, which represented competitive markets and democracy. By "bury," that Soviet leader meant economic domination of the free, democratic world. Of course, with their economic power, the Soviets also hoped to use their *military* strength to eliminate democracy. To achieve these objectives, the Soviet brand of socialism meant placing an *inordinate* amount or emphasis on strategic industries by taking resources away from the production of consumers' necessities such as food, clothing, housing, and automobiles.

D. Taking Notes: Sections 4 and 5
(page 122)

Section 4

Lecturer: So, while undemocratic and often harsh, this strategy produced some rather impressive economic results. For example, there was virtually no unemployment in the Soviet Union; all workers had their place in the labor force. Whether the position workers held was what they *wanted*, huh, or for which they were *qualified* was, of course, another issue. Freedom to choose employment opportunities was not part of the technocrat's plan. Workers went where and when they were needed.

Now, the emphasis on strategic production left fewer resources for housing, home appliances, food, clothing, and mass education. The technocrats determined, without the need of consulting or considering those who would be affected, that producing more strategic output was well worth the cost as measured by less production of the things consumers needed. With more consumer-oriented goods sacrificed to produce strategic output, there were persistent shortages. Why? Because consumers' demand always exceeded the supply of things consumers wanted.

Here's an example: Building materials and workers were directed by central planners to construct factories, and those productive resources could just as easily have been used to construct much needed apartment buildings. A serious shortage of housing quickly followed. Those who received apartments were generally among the bureaucratic elite; others who were not so fortunate had to put their names on long lists and wait maybe several years before a flat became available. Also, butcher shops had little to sell hungry consumers, so lines of eager buyers would form *hours* before the shops would open. Only the few who were fortunate to be first in line went home with meat to put on the dinner table. So shortages not only posed a great hardship on consumers but also encouraged corruption and perpetuated inequalities in a political system that *claimed* to believe in fairness.

So, with government enterprises virtually the only employer, workers' wages were rather predictable. But with widespread shortages, there was very little to buy. Consumers had little choice but to save in government-owned banks. The banks recycled these savings into low-interest or even interest-free loans or credits to state-controlled enterprises. And more often than not, these loans were not intended to be repaid; they were, in fact, grants the government technocrats made to strategic industries, industries enabling them to command more of the nation's scarce resources.

Also, the government's bank—called the *central bank*—supplemented bank loans and credits with more spending power by freely printing money. What do you think this led to?

Well, this generally resulted in periods of chronic inflation, which only added to the burdens on consumers because they had to pay even *higher* prices for increasingly harder-to-find things that they needed.

And on top of the persistent shortages and inflated prices, central planning also resulted in the depletion of resources, environmental pollution, and the infliction of damage on the health and safety of workers and non-workers alike. These conditions sparked discontent. People seemed to be saying, "Enough! We want change!" So, socialism—as a way in which the problems of economic [points to board] trade-offs could be effectively and fairly addressed—was an utter catastrophe. Rather than "burying" the Western democracies, central planning managed to bury itself! Hm.

Section 5

O.K. Now let's turn to the somewhat difficult transition to [points to board] market capitalism that many nations face today. The path that many centrally planned economies have chosen has generally led to an alternate political economic system: market capitalism. [points to board] Now, of course, market capitalism—which we generally identify with Western Europe and the United States—has its own problems and challenges. Market capitalism substitutes the decentralized power of the "invisible hand" of competitive markets for the "visible hand" of [points to board] centralized planning. And it substitutes supportive and transparent demo-democratic institutions and accountable governments for self-serving state bureaucracies. But the transition was slow and difficult.

The transition from one economic system to another occurred as former socialist governments disassembled state bureaucracies and privatized former state enterprises. The result was costly: unemployment rose sharply because workers had to compete for positions on the basis of talent and merit and not political party affiliation or connections. Other results included financial problems as governments slowly replaced the practice of freely printing money to pay bills with more fiscally sound measures of raising funds through taxation and borrowing.

Now, even after several economies made this transition, a mindset—if you will—of central economic planning has remained to some degree in some of these economies. But, in conclusion, the alternate economic system of that market capitalism that addresses economic trade-offs and economic and social fairness offers greater promise to citizens, who are eager to exercise their right to choose how a nation will use its scarce resources to meet their own unlimited needs and wants.

All right. We have time for a few questions?

Chapter 5: Poetry
Part 2 Social Language

A. Listening for the Main Idea (page 141)

Pam: . . . Yes, that's right. Could I make an appointment for next week? Uh, I have classes in the afternoon. Is there any opening in the morning? That would be great. O.K. All right. I'll see you then. Thanks a lot. O.K. Bye-bye . . . Hi.

Victor: Do you have a few minutes?

Pam: Sure. I'm Pam.

Victor: I'm Victor.

Pam: Hi Victor. Have a seat. How can I help?

Victor: Well I'm in Dr. Sears' American lit class . . . and I'm having a lotta trouble with that poetry unit. I'm thinking of dropping the class.

Pam: Oh. I hate to tell you, but Friday was the last day to drop.

Victor: Oh no. I *knew* I should have dropped last week.

Pam: Well, it's all right. Let's see what we can do to get you through the class. Guess literature isn't your thing, huh?

Victor: It's just this unit on poetry. I did O.K. with short stories.

Pam: What's giving you problems?

Victor: I just don't get a lot of this modern stuff. It just doesn't seem like *poetry* to me.

Pam: What exactly bothers you?

Victor: I understood the poems by Robert Frost and Maya Angelou. But the poems in last night's homework don't rhyme or have rhythm or anything.

Pam: Yeah, I see. That is true. See, most contemporary poetry has dropped those older conventions. A lot of it's even conversational.

Victor: And like prose.

Pam: Um, in some ways. But it might seem more difficult because it's more *concise;* there are fewer words, so fewer clues to meaning. The reader needs to become sort of a detective.

Victor: O.K.

Pam: I think the homework for Monday should help. The reading compares the conventions of poetry from the past with poetry today.

Victor: All right . . .

Pam: It's very clear.

Victor: Yeah . . .

Pam: You still seem hesitant. Is there something else?

Victor: Yeah. That assignment for next week—to write a poem ourselves? I just can't do it.

Pam: Mm-hm. I'm hearing that from a lot of students.

Victor: I'm not a writer. I'm not creative.

Pam: You're probably more creative than you think. You want some ideas for how to get started?

Victor: Yeah! Please!

Pam: Well, you can describe a dream that affected you deeply—but in the poem don't say that it's a dream that you're talking about, O.K.?

Victor: Yeah.

Pam: Or you can describe an old family photo and then—somewhere in the poem—you *become* one of the people in that photo.

Victor: Yeah?

Pam: Or you could start by writing a short *prose* paragraph about something that happened to you in the past.

Victor: O.K.

Pam: And one more suggestion. This might sound weird . . . are you right-handed?

Victor: Yeah.

Pam: Try writing your first draft with your left hand.

Victor: Really?

Pam: I know. It'll look terrible, probably, but sometimes this helps to get your brain working in a different way.

Victor: Cool. Well, I'll try it. Thanks.

Pam: O.K. Good luck.

B. Listening for Inferences (page 141)

Victor: Do you have a few minutes?

Pam: Sure. I'm Pam.

Victor: I'm Victor.

Pam: Hi Victor. Have a seat. How can I help?

Victor: Well I'm in Dr. Sears' American Lit class . . . and I'm having a lotta trouble with that poetry unit. I'm thinking of dropping the class.

Pam: Oh. I hate to tell you, but Friday was the last day to drop.

Victor: Oh no. I knew I should have dropped last week.

Pam: Well, it's all right. Let's see what we can do to get you through the class. Guess literature isn't your thing, huh?

Victor: It's just this unit on poetry. I did O.K. with short stories.

Pam: What's giving you problems?

Victor: I just don't get a lot of this modern stuff. It just doesn't seem like *poetry* to me.

Pam: What exactly bothers you?

Victor: I understood the poems by Robert Frost and Maya Angelou. But the poems in last night's homework don't rhyme or have rhythm or anything.

C. Guessing the Meaning from Context
(page 142)

D. Listening for Important Details
(page 142)

Victor: I understood the poems by Robert Frost and Maya Angelou. But the poems in last night's homework don't rhyme or have rhythm or anything.

Pam: Yeah, I see. That is true. See, most contemporary poetry has dropped these older conventions. A lot of it's even conversational.

Victor: And like prose.

Pam: Um, in some ways. But it might seem more difficult because it's more *concise;* there are fewer words, so fewer clues to meaning. The reader needs to become sort of a detective.

Part 3 The Mechanics of Listening and Speaking

A. Questions and Statements (page 146)

1. Yes?
2. No.
3. Oh.
4. Really?
5. You couldn't get an appointment?
6. The office is closed on Tuesdays?
7. The appointment was for 9:00.
8. You can't make it earlier?

B. Hearing Questions with *Or* (page 146)

1. **A:** Do you prefer short stories [up] or novels [down]?

   B: Short stories.
2. **A:** Did we have to read Chapter 5 [up] or Chapter 6 [up]?

   B: No.

3. **A:** Do you like Frost [up] or Whitman [down]?

   B: Frost.
4. **A:** Could you use some help on the research [up] or the organization [up] of the term paper?

   B: Yes, please.
5. **A:** Are you going to the library tomorrow [up] or Saturday [down]?

   B: Saturday.
6. **A:** Next semester, are you taking American literature [up] or world literature [down]?

   B: World literature.
7. **A:** Do you want to get together to study Wednesday [up] or Thursday [up]?

   B: Sure.
8. **A:** Did you talk to the professor [up] or the T.A. [up]?

   B: No, not yet.

G. The Medial *T* (page 150)

1. certain	6. forgotten
2. batter	7. letter
3. gotten	8. fatter
4. flatter	9. bitten
5. fountain	10. potter

Part 4 Broadcast English

B. Listening for Main Ideas (page 155)

Stephen Banker: You stood out from the crowd beginning at a very early age, and it was for a variety of reasons.

Angelou: Well, um, I kind of stood out because, one of the reasons was the crowd didn't accept me. That was one reason. Um, so I was, sort of stood out as a pariah, almost. Uh, my survival, uh, of the conditions of, of discrimination and bias—on many levels, not just race—but, I mean, even within the—my community. Uh, my survival can be credited to art, to literature, almost directly—well, my family and literature.

Banker: Well, when you say your family, you're talking about, uh, well, not your parents for the first few years.

Angelou: No. I was thinking of my grandmother, my brother, and my uncle, for the first few years, and another, and a woman in the town in which I grew up—a Mrs. Flowers, who encouraged me to read.

Banker: Rose T. Flowers.

Angelou: Well, that's according to the rewrite and a television, um, movie made on, on my book. The woman's name was Mrs. Beulah Flowers, and she was a . . . great woman, and she somehow had, uh, had connections in the white school in my little town. And she used to bring me books. I read all the books in the black library, uh, the library of the black school.

Banker: But she, she thought you should have a sense of self, a sense of pride, a sense of being very glad of being who you were and what you were.

Angelou: Yes, and she thought I would be able to, to, uh, achieve self—a, a sense of self if I could, if I would read. And, um, she encouraged me to speak. I, I was a volunteer mute for a number of years, and, um, I simply could not—

Banker: Let's, let's pause there and talk about it. A volunteer mute. That means to say you made a decision not to say anything. And you kept your mouth shut for years. Well, I, I think people who are listening to us will want to hear more about that and why you did it and how it ended.

Angelou: Well, um, I—at seven and a half I was raped, and, uh, I said so. I mean, I, after pressure from my brother, who I loved a lot, um, I named the man. Um, the man was subsequently killed, I mean, almost immediately. And, uh, I believed that because I had spoken, um, the man was dead. And it was suggested that he was kicked to death. Um, I thought that my saying his name caused—directly caused his being killed, and I guess it is so. But I, I just decided I would never speak—I couldn't—my words had such—I was almost eight by that time—and I thought that my words had such power that they could get people killed. People could stop living. At, at eight years old you really don't know, and I—

Banker: Well, no, but it's true. Words *do* have enormous power, and even though what

happened to you is an extraordinary incident and doesn't happen to many people, still we know that, uh, that words are responsible for wars. So in a way it was, uh, maybe an unfortunate but a very apt preparation for the life of a writer.

Angelou: Well, it's a terrible crucible—no more terrible than other people's, but of course one's own distinct one is, is, because one is so close to it . . . I found I could talk to my brother, but somehow that was because I figured out I loved him so much that, um, my words couldn't hurt him. But they might hurt almost anyone else . . . Um, after a while . . . I no longer knew why I didn't speak. I just didn't speak.

Banker: Well, if you went to the dentist, for instance, would you say "ouch"?

Angelou: Probably not.

Banker: That much commitment to the silence. And how did you come out of it?

Angelou: Well, that same Mrs. Flowers, um, used to read to me, and she read poetry, and I had memorized by then large sections of Shakespeare, Paul Lawrence Dunbar, Countee Cullen, Langston Hughes. Uh, I had memorized portions of Charles Dickens because I had nothing else to do, and I loved to memorize things. Uh, and Mrs. Flowers told me that poetry was music written for the human voice and that I would, I must speak it. To really understand it, I must put it on my tongue and use my lips to form the words.

Banker: So they weren't your words.

Angelou: No, they weren't mine, but I loved them, and I began, um, under the bed—we had the high country beds, you know—and I used to crawl under the bed and sit way back against the wall and read Poe—and I loved Edgar Allen Poe. My brother and I called him "Eap." And, uh, so I, I, started reading Poe aloud and Paul Lawrence Dunbar aloud. And then I would try with my brother, and finally, it was poetry alone that, um, that lured my voice out of its hidden place.

C. Understanding the Passive Voice
(page 156)

Angelou: Well, um, I—at seven and a half I was raped, and, uh, I said so. I mean, I, after pressure from my brother, who I loved a lot, um, I named the man. Um, the man was subsequently killed, I mean, almost immediately. And, uh, I believed that because I had spoken, um, the man was dead. And it was suggested that he was kicked to death. Um, I thought that my saying his name caused—directly caused his being killed, and I guess it is so.

D. Listening for Inferences (page 157)

Angelou: Well, that same Mrs. Flowers, um, used to read to me, and she read poetry, and I had memorized by then large sections of Shakespeare, Paul Lawrence Dunbar, Countee Cullen, Langston Hughes. Uh, I had memorized portions of Charles Dickens because I had nothing else to do, and I loved to memorize things. Uh, and Mrs. Flowers told me that poetry was music written for the human voice and that I would, I must speak it. To really understand it, I must put it on my tongue and use my lips to form the words.

Banker: So they weren't your words.

Angelou: No, they weren't mine, but I loved them, and I began, um, under the bed—we had the high country beds, you know—and I used to crawl under the bed and sit way back against the wall and read Poe—and I loved Edgar Allen Poe. My brother and I called him "Eap." And, uh, so I, I, started reading Poe aloud and Paul Lawrence Dunbar aloud. And then I would try with my brother, and finally, it was poetry alone that, um, that lured my voice out of its hidden place.

Part 5 Academic English

B. Vocabulary Preparation (page 160)

Lecturer: The first creative impulse that I'm going to cover today is the pleasure of wordplay. The term *wordplay* refers to the simple joy—the, uh, *fun*—that poets find in using new words— and also colorful and unusual rhyme, rhythm, and punctuation. You can immediately recognize some of the best-loved American poets from their unique use of humor and punctuation.

C. Taking Notes: Using an Outline (page 161)

Section 1

Lecturer: Good morning everyone. Well, I imagine some of you are glad that we finished with *British* poetry last week, and—[a student interrupts]—yes, I do hope to get your exams back to you on Wednesday. Anyway, today it's on to *American* poetry. O.K., well, as you can probably guess, American poets, like Americans in general, are diverse, and they're highly individualistic. Their reasons for writing and their creative processes are as varied as their backgrounds. Although generalizing about such a diverse group is difficult, it's possible to identify three separate impulses that create "voice" in American poetry.

The first creative impulse that I'm going to cover today is the pleasure of wordplay. The term *wordplay* refers to the simple joy—the, uh, *fun*— that poets find in using new words—and also colorful and unusual rhyme, rhythm, and punctuation. You can immediately recognize some of the best loved American poets from their unique use of humor and punctuation.

The second creative impulse is the desire to represent the common dramas of a multi-racial, multi-ethnic society. In other words, poets with this impulse are either celebrating cultural diversity or expressing social and political convictions.

Now, the third creative impulse is an attempt to express intensely personal and private emotions and experiences. By giving voice to their individual feelings, many American poets have transformed emotions, from deeply felt love to crippling feelings of alienation and loneliness, into powerful and moving poetry. These three creative impulses: the joy of wordplay, the celebration of diversity, and the expression of the individual emotion will be discussed in terms of several specific American poets.

Section 2

Lecturer: O.K. Our first creative impulse— wordplay. Two poets—Emily Dickinson and E.E. Cummings—are both famous for playing with words and ideas. Both writers were born in Massachusetts, and their lives were otherwise very dissimilar. Emily Dickinson, a woman poet of the 19th century, became a rather famous recluse. She remained unmarried and refused visitors. Cummings, a man of the 20th century, was well educated, well traveled, and married several times. Dickinson had few published poems in her lifetime, while Cummings was quite popular. And yet their poetry has obvious similarities, most striking of which is their development of unique and unusual styles of punctuation. Dickinson's poems can be identified at a glance by her frequent dashes and her liberal use of capitalization. Dickinson was deeply philosophical, and she thought deeply about faith and death. You can easily recognize her poems from their idiosyncratic use of punctuation and capitalization—as well as the absence of titles. She had a wonderful sense of humor, irony, and wonder. Cummings' poems can also be identified at a glance. Writing after the advent of the typewriter, Cummings played with commas, parentheses, and spaces almost in the manner of a musical score, sometimes squeezing, sometimes stretching and separating words, phrases, and lines. His subjects were more various than Dickinson's, but his innovative arrangements of punctuation marks and spacing express a similar sense of struggle, surprise, and ironic wit. Both writers established their voices through wordplay.

Section 3

Lecturer: Now, as I've already mentioned, other American poets are moved to write about the diversity of the country; they write poetry out of political or social conviction. Walt Whitman, a contemporary of Dickinson, was raised in Brooklyn, and spent his youth reading. He traveled through the eastern United States as a journalist and as an army nurse during the Civil War. In doing so, he searched for a poetic voice that would express the grandeur and expansiveness—the, um, *hugeness*—of the North American continent. He wanted his poems to voice the energy and abundance of this land's diverse people. In his poetry, in particular his masterpiece "Song of Myself," you'll find lists, or sort of catalogues, of the details of both 19th-century urban life and of nature. His lines are long, and they often spill over the narrow limits of the printed page. His poetry can be seen as a love song to the ideals of American democracy and to the joy of simply being alive.

Another American poet whose voice grew from his social awareness and who was moved to write because of his egalitarian convictions was

Langston Hughes. Hughes was an important member of the literary movement called the Harlem Renaissance. This movement sought to celebrate the music and lives of black Americans and incorporated jazz and gospel rhythms, as well as black dialect, into poetry. Hughes, like Whitman, had read widely in his youth. Also, like Whitman, he traveled extensively. When he returned from a year in Paris, he took a job as a busboy in a hotel in New York City and one night he showed several poems to Vachel Lindsay, a well-established poet of the day, who admired and read them during one of his own performances, and that established Hughes' reputation. Hughes used the voices of the people he knew directly in his poetry, and he created characters—in other words, *speakers*—to narrate many of his poems. In his poems, there is a realistic portrayal of the daily lives of these characters. And you can actually *hear* the jazz rhythms and blues atmosphere. These two American poets, Walt Whitman and Langston Hughes, are examples of American poets whose creative impulses led them to portray the culture, the society.

Section 4

Lecturer: Now, in contrast to these highly social writers, John Berryman and Anne Sexton are example of poets who explored deep and often dark emotions. They discovered their voices through intense self-consciousness and isolation. Berryman's loneliness was rooted in the suicide of his father during Berryman's childhood, and he himself suffered from alcoholism and mental instability. He wrote of himself as "Henry." In other words, Henry was the main character and the speaker in many of his poems. By using Henry as his speaker, he was able to both disguise and describe his *own* feelings and encounters. He used a strict poetic form that he called "dream song." In the center of Berryman's book, *Dream Song,* Henry kills himself. Berryman admitted he hoped writing Henry's suicide would help in his own struggles with despair. Another poet who turned to poetry out of intense personal crisis was Anne Sexton. Sexton's psychotherapist suggested that she begin to write poetry as therapy, as a way to grapple with her unstable feelings and perceptions. Anne Sexton began writing poems to give voice to her personal psychological demons. Her poetry, like psychoanalysis, is rich with references to folk tales. Like Berryman, Sexton felt that discovering her poetic voice kept her alive.

Section 5

Lecturer: No matter which of the three impulses—creative wordplay, social concerns, or emotional need—inspires a poet, the voice he or she creates results from choices the poet makes about poetic technique. Although the poets discussed here—Dickinson, Cummings, Whitman, Hughes, Berryman, and Sexton—can easily be assigned a *primary* creative impulse, readers of American poetry will find that most practicing poets today try to cultivate all three impulses in their work to create their voice.

Chapter 6: Heroes in Literature Part 2 Social Language

A. Listening for the Main Idea (page 174)

B. Listening for Details (page 174)

Rachel: O.K. let's get started . . . the assignment says, uh: "Describe the heroic characteristics of your favorite movie character."

Ashley: Gee, I haven't been to a movie in ages . . .

Rachel: Why not?

Ashley: Too much work. I'm at the library most weekends . . .

Rachel: Yeah, I know what you mean . . . hey, we can rent a couple of movies and take notes. It'll be fun.

Ashley: I guess so . . . but what movies? I don't want to waste time with, you know, uh, stuff we can't use.

Rachel: Yeah, um, well I've got a great idea—how about those old Clint Eastwood movies?

Ashley: Sounds boring . . .

Rachel: Yeah, but I've read a lot about these movies, ah, especially, *A Fistful of Dollars*—

Ashley: Isn't that one of those "spaghetti westerns?"

Rachel: Yeah, that's right. Eastwood's character is a perfect hero to write about.

Ashley: Whaddaya mean?

Rachel: Well, in this movie, he doesn't talk much. He's a man of few words. And he represents a kind of Old Testament, eye-for-an-eye-type justice.

Ashley: What's the character's name?

Rachel: I dunno. Ah, you never know his name. He's anonymous. You don't know where he comes from . . . he's a loner. Uh, he has no friends, no, ah, allies—

Ashley: Sounds like something from a samurai movie.

Rachel: That's right! In fact, I think I heard that *A Fistful of Dollars* is based on a Japanese movie called *Ju*—uh, *Yojimbo*. Supposedly, the main character in *Yojimbo* is just like the Eastwood character. He's a samurai who's hired to protect a village—

Ashley: I think I saw that—

Rachel: Yeah, well, Eastwood plays the same kind of character—uh, you're not really sure what it is that he represents. He's morally ambiguous. Um, he hates weakness. He's actually kind of an *anti*-hero.

Ashley: Sounds familiar.

Rachel: Yeah, in fact, I think this character paved the way for a whole new generation of American movie heroes.

Ashley: Whaddaya mean?

Rachel: You know, uh, all those Bruce Willis and Arnold Schwarzenegger characters of the 80s and 90s . . . ?

Ashley: Oh yeah.

Rachel: O.K., well, let's get back to work. Uh, you make the popcorn and I'll go get the movies . . .

C. Making Inferences (page 174)

Rachel: Hey, we can rent a couple of movies and take notes. It'll be fun.

Ashley: I guess so . . . but what movies? I don't want to waste time with, you know, stuff we can't use.

Rachel: Yeah, um, well, I've got a great idea—how about those old Clint Eastwood movies?

Ashley: Sounds boring.

Part 3 The Mechanics of Listening and Speaking

A. Hearing Question Intonation (page 177)

1. What did you do this weekend?
2. How was your weekend?
3. Did you see a movie last night?
4. You saw a Clint Eastwood movie?
5. What have you been doing lately?
6. You're going to the library tonight?

C. Reduced Forms of Words (page 178)

A: Hi, Sarah. Whadja do this weekend?

B: Hi, David. I went to the beach.

A: Whendja go?

B: On Sunday.

A: Wheredja go?

B: To Mariner Point. It was great.

A: Wow. Whodja go with?

B: Jeff.

A: Didja go surfing?

B: No, it was too cold to go in the water, so we just sat on the sand and talked.

D. Hearing /ð/ (page 179)

1. Zen	6. worthy
2. breeding	7. closing
3. bathe	8. dough
4. Dan	9. they've
5. they	10. load

Part 4 Broadcast English

A. Listening for the Main Idea: Section 1
(page 183)

Dowell: By now, everyone knows that *Star Wars* tells a story that's been told in one form or another for a very long time. Foundling princes, kidnapped princesses, and brave warriors who must defeat dragons and monsters appear in many cultures, says Mary Henderson. She curated the popular exhibition about *Star Wars* that ran for more than a year at the National Air and Space Museum in Washington, D.C. She also wrote a book about it, *Star Wars: The Magic of Myth.*

Henderson: George Lucas studied mythology in college. He was an anthropology and sociology student, and he was particularly interested in folk tales. He was particularly interested in the work of Joseph Campbell and Joseph Campbell's book, *The Hero with a Thousand Faces*, and I think actually may have done a book report on this.

When he decided to switch over to film school, he carried many of those ideas with him. And one of the things that he really wanted to do was to create some kind of mythic story using the basic hero's journey pattern but set with metaphors and imagery that would be appropriate for today.

B. Listening for Details: Section 2
(page 183)

Dowell: The hero's journey, as told by George Lucas, is a pattern of quest and initiation that has variations in many different cultures, says C. Scott Littleton, who teaches comparative mythology at Occidental College in Los Angeles.

Littleton: Wherever we find hero stories, whether it be in Japan or in Native American traditions or, uh, in traditional European, Indo-European, Semitic, etc., there's an attention played to the birth. The hero, as a young child, usually loses his patrimony, he is fostered, and then finally rediscovers it. In fact, some have even looked at the story of Jesus that way. You have a difficult birth, a birth in a stable and flight, then a period of quiescence, sort of an exile, and then he returns.

C. Listening for Influences: Section 3
(page 184)

[Audio from *Star Wars*]

Obi-Wan Kenobi: Now the Force is what gives a Jedi his power. It's an energy field created by all living things. It surrounds us and penetrates us. It binds the galaxy together.

Dowell: The idea of the Force incorporates elements of Buddhism and other faiths of the Pacific Rim. Some of *Star Wars'* visual details also echo Buddhist culture as well as more secular influences. The robes of the Jedi Knights resemble those of Japanese Samurai, and George Lucas has long acknowledged a 1958 Japanese Samurai movie as an influence.

Akira Kurosawa's *The Hidden Fortress* has a plot similar to *Star Wars*. It's an adventure tale about a plucky young princess fleeing the overthrow of her father's kingdom, protected by a master swordsman and helped reluctantly by two bumbling peasant soldiers.

[Audio from *The Hidden Fortress*]

Unidentified Actor: [Japanese spoken]

Dowell: There are other elements of the *Star Wars* movies that echo westerns, says historian Richard Slotkin. He examined western movies in *Gunfighter Nation*, the last of a trilogy of books tracing the influence of the frontier on the American imagination.

Slotkin: Captivity and rescue is the basic western plot, and also the characters, certain of the characters. The Han Solo character is the good mercenary, the good gunfighter who would be a character out of something like *The Magnificent Seven*, cynical on the surface, but in the end, he's going to lay down his life for the woman, the village. And Chewbacca would be the Indian sidekick, who speaks in a funny language and is seemingly a more primitive type than the *Lone Ranger*, who would be Han Solo.

D. Listening for Influences: Section 4
(page 184)

Dowell: In borrowing the mythology of the western, Slotkin says *Star Wars* carries some of the western's ideological baggage, too.

Slotkin: The myth is always made, you know, in a sense by the winners in the society so that in the way that the classic western movies developed, there were certain exclusions from the history that belonged to the period when the genre was originating. The society that produced westerns was essentially a white supremacist society, which, uh, treated Indians as generic enemies and which never represented women or peoples of color as historically significant actors.

Dowell: Neither does *Star Wars*, Slotkin says. Nevertheless, it does what myths are supposed to do. It simplifies complex moral dilemmas in a way that makes answers seem clear and solutions possible. And that, says Slotkin, is exactly what *Star Wars* is offering right now.

Part 5 Academic English

A. Guessing the Meaning from Context
(page 192)

1. As you recall, Carl Jung developed the idea of the *collective unconscious*. It describes the thoughts and dreams that humans from *all* cultures share.

2. The saga of Pecos Bill is entertaining, but it is more than that. It also and this is the second purpose for those of you who are careful note-takers—it also symbolically depicts Americans remaking the wilderness.

3. Pecos Bill is a bigger-than-life cowboy. He represents individualism and personal prowess, which has long been admired in American culture.

4. The hero experiences an event, which is sometimes traumatic, that leads to an adventure or a quest.

5. Now, the heroes and heroines of folktales often play much more humble roles than do the heroes of mythology.

6. Some folk heroes gain riches or wisdom. And, there's also the folk hero who is a simpleton but who brings riches back to his family.

7. Finally there's Trickster Hero, the hero who uses his wits to get out of a bad situation. This hero is often smaller or weaker than his opponent, but succeeds by using his brains.

8. The dog is a benevolent symbol of protection and faithfulness.

9. When Momotaro and his companions defeat the ogres, they are overcoming death.

B. Taking Notes: Listening for Topic Signals (page 192)

Section 1

Lecturer: Hi everybody, good morning. Today, we're going to be talking about the characteristics of the hero in folklore.

But, before we start, what is a hero? What—or who—comes to mind when you hear the word "hero"? Can somebody give me some examples?

Student: Wonder Woman.

Lecturer: Good.

Student: Robin Hood.

Lecturer: Good, that's a good one.

Student: Superman.

Lecturer: Right. Those are good examples.

O.K. Heroes—or heroines—appear in the mythologies, religions, and stories of all cultures. Basically, the hero is an idealized super-human with abilities beyond those of a normal person. According to Joseph Campbell, the hero is a manifestation of a culture's collective unconscious quest to discover our identity and the true meaning of life.

As you may recall, Carl Jung developed the idea of "collective unconscious." It describes the thoughts and dreams that humans of *all* cultures share.

Anyway, this is what Campbell calls the "archetypal hero." An archetypal hero is a model for *all* heroes.

Campbell's ideas explain the common characteristics found in heroes that appear in myths and religions around the world. Like the archetypal hero, the *folk* hero also has similarities across cultures.

Every nation and region in the world has its own set of folk heroes. Interestingly enough, the heroes from different geographical regions are sometimes strikingly similar. When this is true, the stories connected with these figures can reveal similarities between two seemingly different cultures. Often, however, heroes from one culture or region are quite distinctive. When this is the case, the heroic figure demonstrates the unique aspects of, of specific people, not merely universal responses to similar circumstances.

Section 2

Lecturer: Before we turn to the folk hero, let's take a closer look at Campbell's archetypal hero.

As we said, an archetype is a model on which other things are based. To Campbell, it's a repeating pattern in mythology and religion.

After spending several years studying and comparing myths from around the world, Campbell determined that all archetypal heroes share certain characteristics. These characteristics are:

- The hero has unusual birth circumstances; [points to board] sometimes he's born in dangerous circumstances or is born into a royal family.
- The hero leaves his family or land and lives with others. [points to board]
- Now, I'm using "hero" and "he" here, but of course, the hero can be female.
- The hero experiences an event, which is sometimes traumatic, that leads to an adventure or a quest.
- The hero has a special weapon [points to board] that only he knows how to use.
- The hero has supernatural help. [points to board]
- The hero must prove himself many times while on adventure.
- The hero must either [points to board] seek revenge for his father, or [points to board] make up for some wrongdoing that his father committed.
- And finally, when the hero dies, he's rewarded spiritually.

Now, the heroes and heroines of folktales often play much more humble roles than do the heroes of mythology. In fact, Jane Bolen refers to folktales as "the small bits and fragments of the great hero myths."

We relate to folk heroes because through their experiences, we feel a sense of control over the unexplained, the unknown, and the frightening aspects of life. Let me say that again. Folk heroes and their adventures give us a sense of control over the unexplained, the unknown, and the frightening aspects of life. This is why these stories have been with us for thousands of years.

Section 3

Lecturer: O.K. So what are folk heroes? Folk heroes are figures from stories that change over time. They appear in legends that cannot be identified with one particular author. In fact, folk heroes evolve through time and reflect the efforts and creativity of several storytellers, most of whom are unknown. And the stories are primarily oral, not written.

Folk heroes and their stories are created informally by people who perform in face-to-face contact with their audience. One example is the poet Homer, who recited his heroic tales to small but attentive audiences in ancient Greece. This was a favorite form of entertainment in an era long before the advent of the movies and television.

What are the characteristics of a folk hero? To what extent are these characteristics universal or culture-specific?

Some folk hero characteristics can be found in many stories from around the world. Here are a few examples: As you listen, try to think of folk heroes that you know who fit these characteristics:[indicates these points on the board as he goes through them.]

- A folk hero may have unusual birth circumstances.
- He often has animal companions or helpers.
- A folk hero is sometimes an animal with human characteristics.
- He often leaves his family and goes on a journey.
- He may accomplish a heroic deed such as killing a monster.
- Some folk heroes gain riches or wisdom. And there's also the folk hero who is a simpleton but who brings riches back to his family.
- Folk heroes are sometimes responsible for creating things in nature such as geological formations or for the existence or characteristics of certain animal species.
- Finally there's the Trickster Hero, the hero who uses his wits [points to head] to get out of a bad situation. This hero is often smaller or weaker than his opponent, but succeeds by using his brains.

Now, in addition to these characteristics, folk heroes—and their deeds—often reflect a culture's belief and values; that is, the *deep structure* of the culture, the core concepts that distinguish it from other cultures. In addition, folktales can reflect a culture's issues and challenges at any given point in history.

Section 4

Lecturer: Let's take a look at how two folk heroes, one American—Pecos Bill—and one Japanese—Momotaro, or "Peach Boy"—reflect the cultures in which they appear.

Pecos Bill represents American culture at a time when the country was still young, when people came—mostly from Europe—and then started moving west. There were enormous opportunities in this New World. In addition, the social and economic position of people was not as clearly defined as in Europe, Africa, and Asia. As a result, people were able to do things that they couldn't do in the Old World. Storytellers created heroes who actively confronted the unique opportunities and challenges that America provided.

Pecos Bill is a classic example of how many Americans viewed themselves and their world. Pecos Bill is a bigger-than-life cowboy. He represents individualism and personal prowess, which has long been admired in American culture. The character of Pecos Bill serves two purposes. First, the exploits of Pecos Bill are used to explain various natural phenomena such as dust storms and the shape of geological formations. In other words, Pecos Bill *transforms the world*.

The saga of Pecos Bill is entertaining, but it's more than that. It also—and this is the second purpose for those of you who are careful note-takers—it also *symbolically depicts Americans remaking the wilderness*. An implicit moral of these stories is that Americans could literally change the world. The story of Pecos Bill reflects the spirit of those who tamed the frontier and suggests the opportunities possible in the unsettled West.

Now, let's turn to the story of Momotaro, or "Peach Boy." Unlike the stories about Pecos Bill, Momotaro is not fixed in any particular era in Japanese history. It's a timeless tale that reflects the values that are at once Japanese and universal. It's rich with symbolic creatures that reflect humanity's desire to survive.

For example the peach from which the hero, Momotaro, is born, represents fertility and reproduction. It's basically a symbol for the womb. Momotaro appears to an older, childless couple—they represent humanity at risk of dying out—to save them. As such, Momotaro symbolizes life and hope.

Animals traditionally held a special place in Japanese culture due to the influence of Buddhism. Their appearance in folktales therefore is often symbolic. Momotaro's three animal helpers include a pheasant, a dog, and a monkey. According to Casal, the pheasant represents the soul in Japanese folk literature. The dog is a benevolent symbol of protection and faithfulness. And the monkey traditionally embodies the spirit of fun and curiosity. Combined, the three represent the essential qualities of life, not only to survive and reproduce, but to think and feel, as well.

When Momotaro and his companions defeat the ogres, they are overcoming death. Their reward is enough riches for them all with plenty to bring back to Momotaro's family. In the end, Momotaro has given the dying family prosperity and hope for future generations.

Section 5

So, in conclusion, by looking at a variety of folk heroes, we can understand not only some of the problems and issues that members of a particular society or culture have confronted, but also tap into the bigger concerns and desires of humanity in general—the collective unconscious, if you will.

While each of the folk hero types we've discussed differ from each other, they all deal with the cultural, social, and technological problems facing humanity. Because they do, these folk heroes combine compelling stories with important commentaries on life and how to best live it.

Do I have any questions?

C. Understanding a Summary in the Conclusion to a Lecture (page 195)

Lecturer: So, in conclusion, by looking at a variety of folk heroes, we can understand not only some of the problems and issues that members of a particular society or culture have confronted, but also tap into the bigger concerns and desires of humanity in general—the collective unconscious, if you will.

While each of the folk hero types we've discussed differ from each other, they all deal with the cultural, social, and technological problems facing humanity. Because they do, these folk heroes combine compelling stories with important commentaries on life and how to best live it.

Do I have any questions?

D. Checking Your Notes (page 195)

(See Sections 1–5 of the audio script.)

Chapter 7 Endangered Species
Part 2 Social Language

A. Listening for the Main Idea (page 211)

Evan: Hello. He's not here right now. Would you like me to give him a message? O.K. Hold on, yep, tomorrow, 10:00 AM Grayson Hall. O.K. I'll tell him. Yep. Speak of the devil—Annie just called.

Victor: Oh, thanks. You guys, I've got a great idea for the summer!

Chrissy: Oh yeah?

Victor: Yeah. In one word—adventure! Exotic locations, research, adventure!

Evan: That's four words.

Chrissy: Exotic locations? Hawaii?

Victor: Yeah, we could do Hawaii! We could, we could volunteer at the marine mammal laboratory there to observe humpback whales, or we can be part of a study on dolphin intelligence.

Evan: "Volunteer"? That sounds like work.

Chrissy: Sounds like biology.

Evan: What is that?

Victor: It's this cool organization that sponsors scientific research all over the world.

Chrissy: All biology?

Victor: Yeah, well, they've got some studies in archaeology and stuff, but, a lotta their programs are in ecology.

Evan: Like what else?

Victor: You can count jaguars in the Mexican forest or, or help save sea turtles in Costa Rica.

Chrissy: And you don't have to be an expert in this stuff?

Victor: No. Wow, Kenya! You can do something—it doesn't say what—about animals in Kenya.

Chrissy: I don't get it. You don't have to know anything about this at all?

Victor: No. They just need volunteers to spend a couple of weeks. The team leader tells you what to do. C'mon! It'll be great.

Chrissy: So what's the catch?

Victor: No catch.

Evan: Here's the catch. You gotta pay for the opportunity to count jaguars. $1600 for ten days. $1300 for a week with the dolphins.

Chrissy: Well, I'm out. I can't pay that kinda money. I gotta work this summer.

Evan: I gotta take summer school. I can't go anywhere.

Victor: This is the chance of a lifetime.

Evan: Yeah, well, it'll have to be another lifetime for some of us.

Chrissy: Send us a postcard, O.K.?

[Phone rings.]

Evan: Hello? Yeah hi, speaking. He's here now, but he's on his way to count jaguars.

B. Listening for Details (page 211)

Victor: Yeah, well, they've got some studies in archaeology and stuff, but, a lotta their programs are in ecology.

Evan: Like what else?

Victor: You can count jaguars in the Mexican forest or, or help save sea turtles in Costa Rica.

Chrissy: And you don't have to be an expert in this stuff?

Victor: No. Wow, Kenya. You can do something—it doesn't say what—about animals in Kenya.

Chrissy: I don't get it. You don't have to know anything about this at all?

Victor: No. They just need volunteers to spend a couple of weeks. The team leader tells you what to do. C'mon! It'll be great.

Chrissy: So what's the catch?

Victor: No catch.

Evan: Here's the catch. You gotta pay for the opportunity to count jaguars. $1600 for ten days. $1300 for a week with the dolphins.

C. Listening for Inferences (page 212)

1. **Evan:** . . . O.K. I'll tell him. Yep. Speak of the devil. Annie just called.

   Victor: Oh, thanks. You guys, I've got a great idea for the summer!

   Chrissy: Oh yeah?

   Victor: Yeah. In one word—adventure. Exotic locations, research, adventure!

2. **Victor:** Yeah. In one word—adventure. Exotic locations, research, adventure!

   Evan: That's four words.

   Chrissy: Exotic locations? Hawaii?

3. **Victor:** Yeah, we could do Hawaii. We could, we could volunteer at the marine mammal laboratory there to observe humpback whales, or we can be part of a study on dolphin intelligence.

   Evan: "Volunteer"? That sounds like work.

4. **Victor:** You can count jaguars in the Mexican forest or, or help save sea turtles in Costa Rica.

   Chrissy: And you don't have to be an expert in this stuff?

   Victor: No. Wow, Kenya. You can do something—it doesn't say what—about animals in Kenya.

   Chrissy: I don't get it. You don't have to know anything about this at all?

5. **Evan:** Hello? Yeah hi, speaking. He's here now, but he's on his way to count jaguars.

Part 3 The Mechanics of Listening and Speaking

A. Taking a Message (page 214)

1. **A:** Hello.

   B: Hi. This is Tim. Is Evan there?

   A: No. He's not here right now. Can I give him a message?

B: Oh . . . just tell him Tim called.

A: O.K.

B: Thanks. Bye.

A: Bye-bye.

2. **A:** Hello.

B: Hello. May I please speak with Victor?

A: He just stepped out. May I take a message?

B: Yes. Please tell him to call Dr. Taylor.

A: All right.

B: Thank you. Good-bye.

3. **A:** Hello.

B: Hi! Is Tanya there?

A: Oh, no. She isn't. Can I take a message?

B: Sure. Tell her to call Bob. My number is 555-6321.

A: O.K.

B: Thanks. Bye.

A: Bye-bye.

4. **A:** Hello.

B: Hello. May I please speak to Brandon?

A: He isn't available right now. Can I give him a message?

B: Yes. Uh, tell him Mike called. And would you ask him to bring his English book to class tomorrow?

A: Sure.

B: Thanks.

A: You're welcome.

B: Bye.

A: Bye.

C. Listening for Clarification (page 216)

1. **A:** Would you tell him Professor Walters called?

B: Could you please repeat that?

A: Professor Walters.

2. **A:** Can I take a message?

B: Yeah. Tell her Desmond called.

A: Des—uh, how do you spell that?

B: Desmond: D as in dog, E-S as in Sam, M-O-N-D.

A: Thanks.

3. **A:** Would you tell her to call Tim? I'm at 323-555-5489.

B: Can you say that again, please?

A: Sure. It's 323-555-5489.

B: Thanks

4. **A:** Would you tell Tanya to call Dr. Vandross?

B: How do you spell that?

A: That's V as in Victor, A-N-D as in dog, R-O-S-S.

B: Thanks.

E. Hearing the Difference Between *Can* and *Can't* (page 217)

1. I can afford that.

2. I can help you.

3. I can't take a message.

4. You can't leave yet.

5. She can't hear you.

6. We can't see the board.

7. He can drive us.

8. We can go with you.

9. I can take a message.

10. She can't help us.

11. He can't graduate this year.

12. She can take it at summer school.

F. Understanding Outgoing Messages
(page 218)

1. Hello. This is Robert Walker. At the tone, please leave a message, and I will call you back as soon as possible.

2. Hi. This is Jason. I'm not here, so leave a message, and I'll get back to you.

3. Hello. You have reached 302-555-6791. If you'd like to leave a message, please do so at the tone.

4. Hey! This is Janine. Leave me a message, and I'll call ya back!

5. Hi. This is the Brier residence at 555-2309. Please leave a message, and we'll get back to you as soon as we can.

Part 4: Broadcast English

A. Listening for Main Ideas: Section 1
(page 221)

Section 1

Plotkin: Well, what makes life in the rain forest possible is plants. I mean, when you go into these villages, what you see is people and plants. The houses are made from palm thatch; they may be shaped like igloos; they may be shaped like beehives; they may be shaped—nothing more than lean-tos. The poles in the houses are forest saplings. The women are sitting there grating cassava, which is a forest plant which has been domesticated by these people, grating, grating, grating—you always hear that *ch ch ch ch ch ch* sound in every indigenous village. The little girls may be making, uh, bread from the cassava. The men are sharpening their arrows, which are made from forest plants, to get ready to go out hunting. Their bows are made from forest trees of the fig family—to go out hunting. Everything is made from forest plants.

Moss-Coane: How would you describe their relationship with the forest around them?

Plotkin: Well, I'd say pretty much, they're very much a part of the ecosystem, and I mean that as the highest compliment. They're in and of the ecosystem itself. They know the ecosystem better than any university-trained botanist does. And remember that none of these plants were learned of by Harvard or Yale or Cambridge or Oxford-trained botanists. They were all discovered like Columbus discovered America: the Indians got there first. And when they're living their traditional lifestyle, they're part of the ecosystem, but when we go in there with our religion or our technology and begin to disrupt their traditional relationship, uh, with even the best of intentions in many cases, they start to lose their dependence on the rain forest and that cycle is broken.

B. Listening for Details: Section 2
(page 222)

Section 2

Moss-Coane: Describe for us if you can your, your introduction, and there was a guide you had named Fritz, and, and it, it seemed the way you wrote about it, this was really your first introduction into, into the rain forest, where, where the job was to, to try to understand the plants that were all around you.

Plotkin: Well, Fritz van Troen is the greatest botanist I've ever met. This is a barely literate man of a Maroon tribe, which is a tribe of Afro-Americans. These were Africans brought to the Amazon in the 17th and 18th century to be slaves on the sugar plantations. These guys took one look around and said, hey, this is equatorial rain forest, we'll see you white boys later, and took off for the interior, where they main—maintained what are essentially West African tribal lifestyles to the current day. And Fritz van Troen—it sounds like a good Dutch name.

Moss-Coane: Yeah, it sure does.

Plotkin: —I expected this little Dutch boy with a pageboy haircut and wooden shoes—and here was this huge, muscular, uh, Afro-American man who turned out to know more about botany than I could ever hope to learn.

Moss-Coane: Well, describe for us how he, how he took you into the forest and, and how he related to the plants around him.

Plotkin: Well, he took me into the forest and began to show me the many uses they have for plants, not just medicines, but drinks, but vines to make ropes or hammocks, uh, plants used by his ancestors to survive when they'd escaped into the jungle to escape the overseers. And it was really an eye-opener because I began to see this wasn't something just beautiful, but really something that could provide the, the, all the sources to make life possible.

C. Listening for Main Ideas and Details: Section 3 (page 222)

Section 3

Moss-Coane: Well, I got the feeling, the way you wrote, that every step of the way was, at least for you, this, this, this whole new, um, drugstore, if we can use that again, of, uh, of plants. And, and around the next corner was a whole other one.

Plotkin: Every step into the rain forest the first time was a revelation because every few feet, every few feet there'd be a medicine or a fiber or an essential oil or some sort of useful plants, and it just showed me how with my western education, being turned loose in the rain forest, I was just in a sea of green. But with an indigenous or a semi-indigenous guide, all of a sudden you understand how to use the forest, how these things can benefit us. And it makes you appreciate not only the potential of these species, which are being lost, but the importance of the knowledge of these species, which really exists in the heads of the men and women who know the forest best.

Moss-Coane: What kinds of sicknesses do people get who, uh, the indigenous tribes who live in the rain forest?

Plotkin: Well, of course the great tragedy is these introduced diseases for which they often have no cure. Now, you give these guys another 20,000 years, and maybe they can find a cure for the common cold, but they haven't had 20,000 years to find plants against it, only 500 years since it's been introduced. But nonetheless, I think a very important point worth underlining is that the greatest scourge in human history is malaria. Malaria has killed more people than any other two diseases combined, and the frontline drug for malaria is quinine, which comes from western South America. Now quinine was first discovered and taught to us by the South American Indians. So they did in those 500 years find the cure to the greatest disease from which people have ever suffered.

D. Listening to Fast English (page 224)

Plotkin: Well, what makes life in the rain forest possible is plants. I mean, when you go into these villages, what you see is people and plants. The houses are made from palm thatch; they may be shaped like igloos; they may be shaped like beehives; they may be shaped—nothing more than lean-tos. The poles in the houses are forest saplings. The women are sitting there grating cassava, which is a forest plant which has been domesticated by these people, grating,

grating, grating—you always hear that *ch ch ch ch ch ch* sound in every indigenous village. The little girls may be making, uh, bread from the cassava. The men are sharpening their arrows, which are made from forest plants, to get ready to go out hunting. Their bows are made from forest trees of the fig family—to go out hunting. Everything is made from forest plants.

Moss-Coane: Well, describe for us how he, how he took you into the forest and, and how he related to the plants around him.

Plotkin: Well, he took me into the forest and began to show me the many uses they have for plants, not just medicines, but drinks, but vines to make ropes or hammocks, uh, plants used by his ancestors to survive when they'd escaped into the jungle to escape the overseers.

Part 5 Academic English

A. Taking Notes: Using an Outline
(page 227)

B. Listening for Signals (page 230)

Lecturer: O.K. Good afternoon everybody. As I mentioned last time, today we're going to take a little departure and look at the role of one individual in the effort to save endangered species: Gerald Durrell. That's [writes on board] D-U-R-R-E-L-L.

Gerald Durrell saved many of the world's rarest animals by turning zoos into safe places for endangered species. *Before* Gerald Durrell, zoos were primarily amusement parks. *After* Durrell, they became important as centers for conservation and education.

Now, let's take a look at Gerald Durrell's early life. He was born in India in 1925 and lived in both England and Greece as a young child. And it was in Greece that Durrell first learned to love animals. As a child, he collected many wild creatures and he would keep them for a long period of time to observe their behavior. He also had a wide variety of traditional pets such as cats and dogs. Now, Durrell's family fled to England at the beginning of World War II, and by the end of the war, Durrell had found a job as a zookeeper at the London Zoo. Within a few years, he was taking part in experiments to collect animals for zoos, and he quickly began supervising his own collecting trips.

It was on his expeditions that we can first see how Gerald Durrell was different from other zoo professionals. At that time, zoos collected all their animals from the wild, and death within a short time after capture was common. Why? Well, for two reasons. Animal collectors had no idea how to capture animals without harming them. Also, to be honest, most did not know much about caring for animals after capture, either. Collectors would catch as many animals as they could, knowing that most would die right away. Animals that survived the trip back to England usually perished within a few months of their arrival. Many zoos didn't seem to care about animal welfare at all, and would simply order more animals from collectors to replace those that had died.

So how was Durrell's approach different? Well, he captured animals humanely, and he gave his hunters extra money to ensure that specimens were uninjured. So, each animal received the best care that could be provided for it. In fact, while on expedition, Durrell rarely had an opportunity to go into the forest because he spent so much time caring for the animals he had captured. He even went so far as to train his specimens to eat the artificial diets they would be getting in the zoo. This helped their adjustment to captivity, and also undoubtedly saved the lives of many animals.

Durrell had many special qualities that ensured his success. First and foremost, he was a keen observer of wildlife, a good scientist, and an excellent collector. He knew how to locate and capture animals, and he was especially good at catching rare species. However, to keep a species alive in captivity, you have to know its biology, and many animals he captured had never been observed alive. No one knew anything about their diet, habitat preference, or behaviors. However, Durrell was such a good scientist that he was able to overcome these problems.

Now, Durrell's dream was to have his own zoo, but he was penniless, and he needed money. Durrell's older brother, Lawrence, was a successful writer and novelist. He believed that Gerald had a gift for writing, and he encouraged his brother to write about his experiences as an animal collector. So Gerald Durrell wrote a novel entitled *The Overloaded Ark*, which described his experiences collecting animals in Cameroon, West Africa. The book became a huge commercial success. In fact it was wildly entertaining and very funny. So Durrell used the profits from his first novel to get out of debt, and used advances from future novels to secure a loan from—for his *own* zoo. However, he wanted *his* zoo to be different from existing zoos.

Durrell thought that most zoos were little more than amusement parks for people. The object of most large zoos was to have one or two individuals of as many different kinds of animals as they could. Status and success were based on collection size. Smaller zoos often attracted visitors with amusement rides and entertaining shows in which trained animals performed tricks while dressed in costumes. In nearly all zoos, animals were fed and caged poorly. Breeding was more by accident than by design, and there was almost no attempt to provide public education.

Durrell was also concerned with the problem of extinction. Many animals and plants no longer existed due to human activity, and an increasing number of species were becoming rare. Durrell saw this phenomenon firsthand. On successive trips to Africa, he saw how animals that were once common were now impossible to find because their forest habitat had been destroyed for planting crops, or because hunters had killed them.

Now, Durrell knew that many species were rapidly approaching extinction, but that zoos could prevent extinction by providing safe havens for animals. Animals could be maintained in safety, and populations increased by captive bree—breeding. Now the factors causing extinction, such as over-hunting, could be controlled, and when conditions were better, animals could be released back into the wild. Zoos needed to become an ark of refuge for endangered species.

So, how would Durrell make his zoo different? Well, he developed a plan for a zoo guided by four principles:

Let's write those on the board, [writes on board]. First, zoos should set up breeding groups [writes on board], breeding groups of animals that had become so rare that they could no longer survive in the wild. Offspring from these breeding groups could be released back into the wild when conditions were better for survival.

Second—and this was really quite innovative—zoos should set up breeding groups of animals in their countries of origin. [writes on board] Durrell believed that conservation was a worldwide effort, and should *not* take place only at zoos in developed countries.

Thirdly, zoos should promote studies to learn more about animals. [writes on board] Promote studies . . . promote studies to learn more about animals, both in captivity and in the wild. And the knowledge from these studies could be used to help prevent extinction.

And finally, zoos should promote conservation education for visitors. [writes on board] Education for visitors. Visitors should learn something about the animals they see, and should better understand the problem of extinction.

O.K. So what was Durrell's vision of this new kind of zoo? First, according to Durrell, the modern zoo would have *fewer* species, but they would be displayed better. Animals would be housed in natural family groups, in habitats that allowed them to engage in natural behaviors. In other words, and this is an important point, the environment would be as similar to the animals' natural habitats as possible.

Next, diets would be nutritionally balanced, and as close as possible to foods eaten in the wild. Third, animal care would focus on long-term survival, and every effort would be made to facilitate breeding. Also important as I've mentioned already, educational specialists would look for ways to teach visitors about animals.

And most importantly, conservationists and zookeepers from the countries where endangered species were found would be brought to the zoo for training. This way each country with endangered species could have trained personnel who could act locally, and conservation would occur outside of developed countries.

O.K. So what happened with his ideas? Well, Durrell discussed his ideas with other zoo directors and conservationists, who told him unanimously that his ideas would never work, that visitors would never attend his style of zoo, and the entire project would fail and leave him bankrupt. Well, Durrell refused to listen, and he purchased an estate on an island off the southern coast of England that he converted into a zoo. The Jersey Zoological Park opened in 1959, and was renamed the Jersey Wildlife Preservation Trust in 1963. Now, the first years were difficult. Durrell sometimes didn't have enough money to pay his staff, and he was often taking out new loans to pay back existing loans. He was forced to beg for contributions from wealthy individuals, and to make unprofitable collecting expeditions to gather new material for books. However, his books *did* grow in popularity, and his writing kept the trust alive for many years until it could become more secure financially. Durrell also enlisted the assistance of many famous actors and even the British royal family. Eventually, the trust did become self-sustaining. Durrell then joined the Jersey facility with other organizations to form an international conservation group.

To the surprise of everyone *except* Durrell, the facility attracted visitors, and the zoo became one of the most popular visitor attractions on the island. However, it was only after years of work that Durrell was able to turn his attention to his *primary* goal of the re-establishment of endangered animals in their natural habitats.

Durrell died in 1995 after a year-long battle with complications of a liver transplant. He left behind an extremely successful zoo, but was that his greatest legacy? Not in the least. His ideas about the role of zoos spread throughout the world, and today nearly every one of the world's zoos follows his principles. Zoos have become centers for conservation and education, and visitors expect and demand this approach. Rather than make zoos *less* appealing, the new focus has actually had a positive effect on attendance. Nearly every zoo participates in captive breeding and conservation programs, and nearly every zoo has a conservation department. In fact, zoos have become focal points for conservation, and have brought many species back from the brink of extinction. So Gerald Durrell's vision was achieved not only for his own zoo, but for nearly every zoo in the world.

All right. I see our time's up. Next week, we'll take a look at environmental organizations such as the Green Movement. O.K. See you then.

Chapter 8: Environmental Health
Part 2 Social Language

A. Listening for the Main Idea (page 240)

B. Listening for Details (page 240)

C. Listening for Emotions (page 240)

Chrissy: Hi, my name is Chrissy. And your name is?

Speaker 1: I'm David.

Chrissy: Uh, I'm doing an interview for Campus TV. Can I ask you a few questions?

Speaker 1: Give it a try.

Chrissy: Great. Are you worried about the effects of environmental hazards on your health?

Speaker 1: Somewhat. I mean they are there and I probably, in one sense, I, I don't want to say I should worry more. I'm concerned about it, but I don't think worrying about it is the way to deal with it.

Chrissy: What, what are you concerned about?

Speaker 1: Concerned about the quality of the air, concerned about the quality of, of food and whatever poisons are in it.

Speaker 2: Well, a couple years ago I worked on a science project where we looked at soil for radioactivity and it was for the government, um, and we found that there were some high levels of radioactivity, so it is a concern to me and I have, uh, done scientific research on it. But, uh, I think that you just have to realize that there are different, uh, environmental hazards out there and, and know that even, even though that there are so many hazards out there, you know, everybody—it affects everybody and it's something you just have to deal with. It's part of living.

Speaker 3: I'm concerned about the ozone depleting. I'm concerned about the effect it has on my skin. I'm very fair. I have a lot of moles. So I go to the dermatologist, have them checked out, they're very healthy. And try and wear a lot of sunscreen, stay out of the sun. That sorta thing.

Speaker 4: Um, I guess more like environmental illnesses, like now, how that's coming up—so many people are getting sick because of just being in their normal environment because, bec—but it's becoming so much more polluted.

Chrissy: Do you worry about the effects of environmental hazards on your health?

Speaker 5: Yes, I do. I really worry about the toxins in the water. That really scares me sometimes to think about that.

Chrissy: Does that prevent you from going into the ocean or anything?

Speaker 5: No, but I think twice.

Speaker 6: Yes, I worry about it. I think most people should especially in the city. You have a lot of young children who suffer from asthma because of all of the smoke and the exhaust and the dirt and the heat.

Chrissy: Do you worry about the effects of environmental hazards on your health?

Speaker 7: Not really, no. Um, I guess that's why I'm living here in New York. It doesn't really bother me too much.

Part 3 The Mechanics of Listening and Speaking

A. Listening for Intensity (page 242)

1. I'm worried about air pollution. [Not intense]

2. I'm very concerned about overpopulation. [Intense]

3. I'm quite concerned about ozone depletion. [Intense]

4. My main concern is that we'll run out of resources soon. [Not intense]

5. I really worry about toxins in the water. [Intense]

6. I'm concerned about air quality. [Not intense]

7. I'm worried about my grades. [Not intense]

8. I'm extremely worried about air pollution. [Intense]

B. Listening for Emotional Intensity with Stress (page 243)

1. I'm concerned about the quality of our drinking water. [Neutral]

2. I'm *really* worried about my grades this quarter. [Emotional]

3. I am *very* concerned about your health. [Emotional]

4. I'm afraid that I didn't study enough this quarter. [Neutral]

5. I'm *really* afraid that I didn't study enough this quarter. [Emotional]

6. We should all be concerned about toxins in the environment. [Neutral]

7. Jim is worried about the exam tomorrow. [Neutral]

8. Jim is *really* worried about the exam tomorrow. [Emotional]

D. Hearing /ɛ/, /æ/, and /ʌ/ (page 244)

1.	sunned	7.	hem
2.	lag	8.	pen
3.	trek	9.	cupped
4.	flush	10.	mass
5.	dud	11.	beg
6.	mash	12.	batter

E. Hearing /ɛ/, /æ/, and /ʌ/ in Sentences (page 244)

1. That's a funny pen.

2. Is that butter?

3. Do you have a tan?

4. It's just a short trek.

5. I capped it.

Part 4 Broadcast English

A. Listening for Main Ideas: Section 1 (page 248)

B. Using a Spider Map to Take Notes: Section 1 (page 250)

Weisman: Driving to Gaviotas takes 16 hours over a rutted track through the Llanos of Colombia, a barren plain that stretches over half the country, clear to the Venezuelan border. The road bumps for miles, past huge cattle haciendas belonging to drug barons, and through check points where travelers are searched and questioned, sometimes by the army, sometimes by leftist guerrillas.

Except for a few sparse grasses, little grows in these thin, sun-baked soils. The sluggish rivers swarm with pirhanas and malarial mosquitoes. But I recall what Paolo Lugari, a Colombian founder of Gaviotas, told me back in Bogota.

Lugari: [Speaks in Spanish.]

Translator: They always put social experiments in the easiest, most fertile places. We wanted the hardest place. If we could do it there, we could do it anywhere. The only deserts are deserts of the imagination. Gaviotas is an oasis of imagination.

Weisman: Twenty-three years ago Paolo Lugari, the brilliant son of a tropical geographer, flew across the Andes behind Bogota, over the Llanos, and had a vision. One day, Lugari thought, savannas like these would be the only place to put growing populations. This was a perfect setting, he decided, to design the ideal civilization for the tropics.

Lugari: [Speaks in Spanish.]

Translator: All our development models have been created in countries with four seasons, with totally different conditions from tropical countries. When we import solutions from northern countries, not only don't we solve our problems, but we import theirs.

C. Making Inferences: Section 2 (page 250)

Weisman: A few miles from Gaviotas, I see the first signs of the new civilization Lugari has in mind. What appear to be bright, aluminum sunflowers begin to dot the landscape. They are windmills, unlike any I've ever seen. Light, compact units, whose blade tips are contoured like airplane wings, to trap soft, equatorial breezes. They were designed by engineers that Lugari lured here from Bogota's finest universities to create the right technology for the tropics.

The first thing I see as I enter Gaviotas, are the town's steeply vaulted, nearly aerodynamic roofs, studded with solar panels. The buildings are shaded by mango trees and bougainvillea, filled with yellow warblers and dazzling crimson tanangers. The air smells like gardenias.

For the next few days, my guide is Gonzalo Bernal, administrator of Gaviotas. Paolo Lugari is meeting in Bogota with the president of Guyana and the prime minister of Jamaica, who want Caribbean versions of Gaviotas. Gonzalo, formerly a journalist, tells me he arrived here in 1978.

Bernal: [Speaks in Spanish.]

Translator: I grew up in the 60s. My friends and I had romantic dreams of a better world. Back then, there were just two alternative paths—become an artist, or become a guerrilla. Then I saw a TV program on Gaviotas and learned that what I dreamed already existed.

D. Listening for Main Ideas: Section 3
(page 251)

Weisman: We're joined by Gonzalo's wife, Cecilia, who's a therapist, and their son Federico. Besides schooling for their children, I learn that housing, health care, and food are free here. And everyone earns the same, above-minimum wage salary. With no poverty, Gonzalo and Cecilia suggest, perhaps that's why families remain a manageable size and why there's no crime in Gaviotas.

Gonzalo Bernal: [Speaks in Spanish.]

Translator: We have no police or jail because nothing gets stolen. There is no need for laws or written rules. In Gaviotas, we just have codes of common sense.

Weisman: Anyone who violates these unwritten social protocols, Cecilia adds, is simply ostracized by the community. What about crimes of passion, I ask, or adultery?

Cecilia Bernal: [Speaks in Spanish.]

Translator: It's not a problem because no one gets married here. Couples live in free union.

Gonzalo Bernal: [Speaks in Spanish.]

Translator: There is no church and no politicians, either. Politics and religion don't matter here. We respect what others believe but we don't need them in Gaviotas.

Weisman: Cecilia points to a family of monkeys swinging over the children's heads.

Cecilia Bernal: [Speaks in Spanish.]

Translator: For me, God is in the birds, in the monkey, in the trees—that's how I explain it to the kids. People ask how I left a world where I was a successful professional. But here, I feel I am in paradise.

Weisman: It's been years since I've heard anyone talk like this. Yet these aren't free love hippies—they're serious people committed to flourishing in a world of shrinking resources. After nearly a quarter century, Gaviotas makes already stale phrases like "sustainable development" and "appropriate technology" seem not just believable, but fresh and surprising.

E. Recognizing Figurative Language
(page 251)

1. **Lugari:** They always put social experiments in the easiest, most fertile places. We wanted the hardest place. If we could do it there, we could do it anywhere. The only deserts are deserts of the imagination. Gaviotas is an oasis of imagination.

2. **Weisman:** It's been years since I've heard anyone talk like this. Yet these aren't free love hippies—they're serious people committed to flourishing in a world of shrinking resources.

3. **Weisman:** After nearly a quarter century, Gaviotas makes already stale phrases like "sustainable development" and "appropriate technology" seem not just believable, but fresh and surprising.

Part 5 Academic English

A. Taking Notes: Listening to Accented English (page 255)

C. Checking Your Notes (page 257)

Section 1

Student 1: Bianca, would you mind going over Professor Samuels' lecture from Thursday? Particularly the Green Movement.

Bianca: No, not at all. He also covered the concept of "ecotopia"—do you want to review that? That's really the foundation of the Green Movement, so let's review that. As you recall, in 1516, in England, Sir Thomas More wrote a book titled *Utopia,* where he described an ideal place. Since then the word "utopia" has been used to describe an ideally perfect place, especially in its social, political, and moral aspects. Now, as you know, ecology is the science that studies the relationships between humans and their environment. This includes their physical as well as their social environment.

O.K., in 1975, the writer Ernest Callenbach combined the concepts of utopia and ecology in a novel titled *Ecotopia.* In it, Callenbach describes the fictional state of Ecotopia, which was created when the states of Northern California, Oregon, and Washington seceded from the United States. In Ecotopia, there is a perfect balance between human beings and their environment. It's a place where poverty, overcrowding, and environmental pollution have been eliminated. A place where there is devotion to nature that is so extreme it can be considered worship. Women dominate the government—ah, that sounds like a good idea to me—and workers own all the businesses and farms in Ecotopia.

So an "ecotopia" is a place where there's optimal human health: physical, mental, emotional, social, and spiritual. Even though *Ecotopia* is a work of fiction, it was influential in the development of the international environmental movement also known as the Green Movement. So O.K., you guys, any questions about that?

Student 1: So an ecotopia is an environmental utopia?

Bianca: Well, not exactly. It also includes what?

Student 2: Well, it's also a political and economic utopia—no poverty, women rule . . .

Section 2

Bianca: Right. O.K. Now, what did Professor Samuels say about the Green Movement? Uh, well, starting with the philosophical foundations. When we think of the environment, we usually think about the air, land, and water that surround us and keeping it clean and safe. This however, is a very, very narrow view of our environment. The Green Movement takes a more wide-ranging or holistic view because it includes not only traditional concerns about the environment but also concerns for peace, social justice, racial equality, feminism, and human rights as well. Also, the Green Movement is truly, truly international, with followers in virtually every nation. The Green Movement offers an alternative to the political and social structures that dominate human societies. Any questions?

Student 1: So, in a nutshell, their philosophy is, quote, "the Greens believe that our current system is based on exploitation and domination of both the environment and people and that the pursuit of economic growth has led to an ecological and social crisis." Unquote. Right?

Bianca: Right. The Green Movement recognizes that environmental and social problems are all connected and that they must be solved in a holistic fashion.

Student 1: So would you mind going over the "10 Key Values" again?

Bianca: Sure, the 10 Key Values of the U.S. Green Movement; here we go. In 1984, people from throughout the United States with concerns about the environment, political and social justice, and similar issues, met to discuss the creation of a Green Movement in America. They developed the 10 Key Values of the U.S. Green Movement.

O.K. The first one is Ecological Wisdom. What was that?

Student 2: "A respect for the environment and the wise use of our natural resources is essential for the health of our planet."

Bianca: Right. The second, Grassroots Democracy. Anyone? Try to summarize . . .

Student 2: Uh, when a few people in power control most of the resources, um, there's greater potential for selfish gain and abuse. So, every member of the society should participate in decision-making.

Bianca: Good. O.K. The third one, Personal and Social Responsibility.

Student 1: That one refers to the fact that every member of the society must act responsibly with respect to the environment, reducing waste and conserving natural resources.

Bianca: Right! The fourth is Nonviolence.

Student 2: Oh! Uh, violence is destructive to humans and the environment. Peace and mutual respect will enable all members of the society to reach their potential.

Bianca: Next is Decentralization.

Student 1: I forget that one.

Student 2: Decentralization means local empowerment and control. Communities should be free to set policies for the promotion of health locally. A self-governing society.

Bianca: Right! Number six was Community-Based Economics. Economics for the good of the community is less likely to be destructive to the environment and is less likely to be rooted in selfish, narrow interests. And, seven, Feminism: In order for a society to flourish, women must be given equal opportunities to participate in every aspect of that society. The eighth was Respect for Diversity, that is, racism and ethnic or religious intolerance will ultimately destroy any society and its environment. Every member of the society should be valued and treated with respect.

The ninth, Global Responsibility was that all actions must be evaluated for impact on the world environment because we have only one planet, and all of us must live on it in harmony with nature and with each other. And finally, the tenth?

Student 1: Uh, Future Focus/Sustainability.

Bianca: And that was . . .?

Student 1: Uh, to eliminate shortsighted decisions based on immediate need or want, and consider the impact of those decisions on future generations. I think there was something else . . .

Bianca: Yeah. What do they mean by "sustainability"?

Student 2: They maintain that we can't continue to live in a "throwaway" culture. We can't continue to waste and pollute our natural resources so that we can live comfortably today.

Section 3

Bianca: Right. O.K. Any questions about those?

Student 1: So the Green Movement is really a bunch of wacky misfits who can't get along in society.

Bianca: Anyone?

Student 2: Not exactly. They just oppose the practices of the modern, industrial, high-technology world. They oppose the domination and exploitation of nature and people. That's not so wacky. They just oppose the accumulation of wealth and power today at the expense of the environment and humanity.

Bianca: Yeah. Basically, The Green Movement advocates changes that would result in the creation of societies that promote the health of individuals and their environment. What was an example of one of these that you read about in the text?

Student 2: Gaviotas.

Bianca: Right. However, how likely is it that, considering human history and the current state of affairs in the world, the sweeping changes advocated by the "Greens" will take place?

Student 2: But, more and more societies are becoming aware that a wasteful and environmentally-hostile way of life has to change. There's some effort to clean up polluted air, land, and water, recycle waste products, conserve energy. So, social and economic change is occurring, but very slowly.

Bianca: Right. Well, on that optimistic note, let's move on. Were there any questions about Chapter 10?

APPENDIX 3 ACADEMIC WORD LIST

The list on pages 315–318 is Sublist One of the most common words on the Academic Word List, a list compiled by Averil Coxhead. To view the entire list, go to Averil Coxhead's AWL website (http://language.massey.ac.nz/staff/awl/index.shtml).

Each word in italics is the most frequently occurring member of the word family in the academic corpus. For example, *analysis* is the most common form of the word family *analyse*.

The Academic Word List includes both British and American spelling.

analyse
    analysed
    analyser
    analysers
    analyses
    analysing
    analysis
    analyst
    analysts
    analytic
    analytical
    analytically
    analyze
    analyzed
    analyzes
    analyzing
approach
    approachable
    approached
    approaches
    approaching
    unapproachable
area
    areas
assess
    assessable
    assessed
    assesses
    assessing

assessment
    assessments
    reassess
    reassessed
    reassessing
    reassessment
    unassessed
assume
    assumed
    assumes
    assuming
    assumption
    assumptions
authority
    authoritative
    authorities
available
    availability
    unavailable
benefit
    beneficial
    beneficiary
    beneficiaries
    benefited
    benefiting
    benefits
concept
    conception
    concepts

conceptual
conceptualisation
conceptualise
conceptualised
conceptualises
conceptualising
conceptually
consist
    consisted
    consistency
    consistent
    consistently
    consisting
    consists
    inconsistencies
    inconsistency
    inconsistent
constitute
    constituencies
    constituency
    constituent
    constituents
    constituted
    constitutes
    constituting
    constitution
    constitutions
    constitutional
    constitutionally

constitutive
unconstitutional
context
   contexts
   contextual
   contextualise
   contextualised
   contextualising
   uncontextualised
   contextualize
   contextualized
   contextualizing
   uncontextualized
contract
   contracted
   contracting
   contractor
   contractors
   contracts
create
   created
   creates
   creating
   creation
   creations
   creative
   creatively
   creativity
   creator
   creators
   recreate
   recreated
   recreates
   recreating
data
define
   definable
   defined
   defines
   defining
   definition

definitions
redefine
redefined
redefines
redefining
undefined
derive
   derivation
   derivations
   derivative
   derivatives
   derived
   derives
   deriving
distribute
   distributed
   distributing
   distribution
   distributional
   distributions
   distributive
   distributor
   distributors
   redistribute
   redistributed
   redistributes
   redistributing
   redistribution
economy
   economic
   economical
   economically
   economics
   economies
   economist
   economists
   uneconomical
environment
   environmental
   environmentalist
   environmentalists

environmentally
environments
establish
   disestablish
   disestablished
   disestablishes
   disestablishing
   disestablishment
   established
   establishes
   establishing
   establishment
   establishments
estimate
   estimated
   estimates
   estimating
   estimation
   estimations
   over-estimate
   overestimate
   overestimated
   overestimates
   overestimating
   underestimate
   underestimated
   underestimates
   underestimating
evident
   evidenced
   evidence
   evidential
   evidently
export
   exported
   exporter
   exporters
   exporting
   exports
factor
   factored

factoring
factors
finance
  financed
  finances
  financial
  financially
  financier
  financiers
  financing
formula
  formulae
  formulas
  formulate
  formulated
  formulating
  formulation
  formulations
  reformulate
  reformulated
  reformulating
  reformulation
  reformulations
function
  functional
  functionally
  functioned
  functioning
  functions
identify
  identifiable
  identification
  identified
  identifies
  identifying
  identities
  identity
  unidentifiable
income
  incomes

indicate
  indicated
  indicates
  indicating
  indication
  indications
  indicative
  indicator
  indicators
individual
  individualised
  individuality
  individualism
  individualist
  individualists
  individualistic
  individually
  individuals
interpret
  interpretation
  interpretations
  interpretative
  interpreted
  interpreting
  interpretive
  interprets
  misinterpret
  misinterpretation
  misinterpretations
  misinterpreted
  misinterpreting
  misinterprets
  reinterpret
  reinterpreted
  reinterprets
  reinterpreting
  reinterpretation
  reinterpretations
involve
  involved
  involvement

involves
involving
uninvolved
issue
  issued
  issues
  issuing
labour
  labor
  labored
  labors
  laboured
  labouring
  labours
legal
  illegal
  illegality
  illegally
  legality
  legally
legislate
  legislated
  legislates
  legislating
  legislation
  legislative
  legislator
  legislators
  legislature
major
  majorities
  majority
method
  methodical
  methodological
  methodologies
  methodology
  methods
occur
  occurred
  occurrence

occurrences
occurring
occurs
reoccur
reoccurred
reoccurring
reoccurs

percent
percentage
percentages

period
periodic
periodical
periodically
periodicals
periods

policy
policies

principle
principled
principles
unprincipled

proceed
procedural
procedure
procedures
proceeded
proceeding
proceedings
proceeds

process
processed
processes
processing

require
required
requirement
requirements
requires
requiring

research
researched
researcher
researchers
researches
researching

respond
responded
respondent
respondents
responding
responds
response
responses
responsive
responsiveness
unresponsive

role
roles

section
sectioned
sectioning
sections

sector
sectors

significant
insignificant
insignificantly
significance
significantly
signified
signifies
signify
signifying

similar
dissimilar
similarities
similarity
similarly

source
sourced

sources
sourcing

specific
specifically
specification
specifications
specificity
specifics

structure
restructure
restructured
restructures
restructuring
structural
structurally
structured
structures
structuring
unstructured

theory
theoretical
theoretically
theories
theorist
theorists

vary
invariable
invariably
variability
variable
variables
variably
variance
variant
variants
variation
variations
varied
varies
varying

VOCABULARY INDEX

Vocabulary Workshop:
Unit 3
Academic Word List

analysis
analyze
context
criteria
cultures
elements
framework
literary
logic
mentioned
myths
psychology
theory

UNIT 4
Chapter 7

ambles
bankrupt
breeding
camouflaged
catch
chance of a lifetime
concerned about
disrupt
ecosystem
endangered
ensure
extinct
founded
frontline
habitat loss
hammocks
hold on
humanely
I'm out
in captivity
in one word
in the wild
indigenous
interior
keen
legacy
local
nibble
offspring
perished

plight
revelation
safe havens
saplings
scourge
speak of the devil
susceptible
thatched
tree kangaroo
turned loose
unanimous
vice versa
yep

Chapter 8

adultery
aerating
aerodynamic
affect
algae
break down
capitalize
check it out
coming up
compost
conduct
constructive criticism
contoured
deal with
dot the landscape
effect
flourish
give it a try
going over
hazards
holistic
make the most of
misfits
mole
neutral
nutshell
oasis
ostracized
other half of the equation
out of the question
profusion
protocol
rank
rooted in
rutted

sanitation
savannas
stale
the other half of the equation
utopia
utopian community
wacky

Vocabulary Workshop:
Unit 4
Academic Word List

civil
commitment
convince
depend
economies
equipped
fund
goal
grant
infrastructure
labor
processing
research
resources
unreliable

SKILLS INDEX

Text

p. 33: "Apes and Sign Language" adapted from Conrad Kottak, *Anthropology: The Exploration of Human Diversity, Fifth Edition*, copyright © 1989 by McGraw-Hill, Inc. Reprinted with the permission of the McGraw-Hill Companies. p. 44: From "Homo Dmanisi" by Stephen Oppenheimer which appeared on Bradshaw Foundation website, www.bradshawfoundation.com. Reprinted by permission of the Bradshaw Foundation. p. 69: From "International Year of Microcredit 2005" from United Nations Department of Economic and Social Affairs website, www.un.org. p. 99: Adapted from "Solar Oven Society Hopes to Make a Difference" by Mary Losure, Minnesota Public Radio, May 27, 2003, as appeared on, www.news.minnesota.publicradio.org. © ℗ 2003, Minnesota Public Radio. All rights reserved. Used by permission of Minnesota Public Radio and MPR News. p. 100: Adapted from "Reaching the Far Reaches of the World—without wires, less affluent, more remote areas benefit from wireless" by Greg Botelho, CNN website, www.cnn.com. Courtesy of CNN. p. 101: "Ghana Gets a Fab Lab" by Michelle Delio as appeared on Wired News website, www.wired.com, September 21, 2005. © Copyright 2006, Lycos, Inc. Lycos is a registered trademark of Lycos, Inc. All Rights Reserved. Reprinted with permission. p. 135: "Gypsies" by Alden Nowlan from *Playing the Jesus Game: Selected Poems* by Alden Nowlan, 1970. Copyright by Claudine Nowlan. Used by permission. p. 135: "Totally like whatever, you know?" by Taylor Mali. Reprinted by permission of the author, www.taylormali.com. p. 136: "Thinking Twice in the Laundromat" by Harley Elliott, first appeared in *Hanging Loose* magazine. Reprinted with permission of the author. p. 142: "A Sunday Morning After a Saturday Night" by LoVerne Brown from *View from the End of the Pier*, 1983. p. 142: "Without Stopping" from *Before Our Very Eyes* by Cherry Jean Vasconcellos, 1996. Reprinted by permission of the author. p. 154: "Caged Bird," copyright © 1983 by Maya Angelou, from *Shaker, Why Don't You Sing?* by Maya Angelou. Used by permission of Random House, Inc. p. 169: "Why the Parrot Repeats Man's Words" from *Ride with the Sun* by Harold Courlander, 1955. p. 188: "Momotaro," from *Japanese Fairy Tales* by Lafcadio Hearn. Copyright 1953 and renewed © 1981 by Liveright Publishing Corporation. Used by permission of Liveright Publishing Corporation. p. 207: From "Zoos Unite to Keep Animals in the Wild" by Laurie Toupin, originally appeared on *Christian Science Monitor*, (www.csmonitor.com) March 2, 2004, p. 18. Reprinted by permission of Laurie Toupin. p. 237: "Success Story:

Where there's muck there's hope," *The Reporter*, No. 449, #7, June 2004. Used with permission of the University of Leeds. p. 315: "Academic Word List Sublist One" by Averil Coxhead, as appeared on website www.language.massey.ac.nz/staff/awl/index.shtml. Reprinted by permission of Averil Coxhead.

Photo

Cover (top right): The McGraw-Hill Companies, Inc.; (middle left): © Comstock/SuperStock; (bottom right): © Ron Cohn, The Gorilla Foundation/koko.org.

Unit 1. p. 1: © Peter Adams/Getty Images; p. 3: © Stuart McClymont/Getty Images; p. 4 (top left) : © Nancy R. Cohen/Getty Images; p. 4 (bottom right): © Michael Freeman/CORBIS; p. 8: © The McGraw-Hill Companies, Inc.; p. 11: © BananaStock/ JupiterImages; p. 12: © Comstock/PictureQuest; p. 15 (top left): © Brand X Pictures /PunchStock; p. 15 (top right): © Steve Mason/Getty Images; p. 15 (bottom left): Jennifer Bixby; p. 15 (bottom right): © oote boe/Alamy; p. 16 (all): Jennifer Bixby; p. 21 (top left): © PhotoLink/Getty Images; p. 21 (top right): © Kristian Cabanis/Age Fotostock; p. 21 (bottom left): © Mark Duffy/Alamy; p. 21 (bottom right): © Royalty-Free/CORBIS; p. 25: © The McGraw-Hill Companies, Inc.; p. 31: © Ron Cohn, The Gorilla Foundation/koko.org; p. 32: © 20th Century Fox/Everett Collection; p. 33 (top): Nina Leen/Time & Life Pictures/Getty Images; p. 33 (bottom): © Ron Cohn, The Gorilla Foundation/koko.org; p. 35: Courtesy of the National Library of Medicine; p. 36, 40: © The McGraw-Hill Companies, Inc.; p. 45: Painter: Gianni Coniglio. Association: Alfamodel Club, Roma. Photo by: Riccardo Lazzarini; p. 48: © Digital Vision; p. 49: © Kennan Ward/CORBIS; p. 50: © PhotoLink/Getty Images; p. 54: © Brand X Pictures/PunchStock; p. 55 (left): © Alan and Sandy Carey/Getty Images; p. 55 (right): © PhotoLink/Getty Images.

Unit 2. p. 65: © Zubin Shroff/Getty Images; p. 67: PhotoDisc/Getty Images; p. 68: AP/Wide World Photos; p. 69: Courtesy of Grameen Foundation; p. 70: Rohanna Mertens for ACCION International; p. 72: © The McGraw-Hill Companies, Inc.; p. 76: © Jeff Greenberg/The Image Works; p. 83: © Howard Davies/CORBIS; p. 86: AP/Wide World Photos; p. 88: © BananaStock/JupiterImages; p. 97: © Peter Adams/Getty Images; p. 98 (left): © Ted Wood/Stockphoto.com; p. 98 (right): © PhotoLink/Getty Images; p. 99: Courtesy of www.solarovens.org, phone: 612.623.4700, e-mail:

sos@solarovens.org, mail: 3225 East Hennepin Avenue, #200, Minneapolis, MN 55413; p. 100: © Andrew October; p. 101: courtesy of Jason Taylor, Massachusetts Institute of Technology, 2002; p. 104: © The McGraw-Hill Companies, Inc.; p. 107: © Ken Chernus/Getty Images; p. 112: © Michael S. Yamashita/CORBIS; p. 118: © The McGraw-Hill Companies, Inc.; p. 123 (top): Andre Durand/AFP/Getty Images; p. 123 (bottom): © Antoine Gyori/CORBIS.

Unit 3. p. 131: © Denis Felix/Getty Images; p. 133: © Syracuse Newspapers/Frank Ordonez/The Image Works; p. 134 (top): © Bettmann/CORBIS; p. 134 (bottom): Linda S. O'Roke; p. 141: © The McGraw-Hill Companies, Inc.; p. 142: Salvador Dali, *The Persistence of Memory*, 1931. © The Museum of Modern Art/Licensed by SCALA/Art Resource, NY. © 2007 Salvador Dali, Gala-Salvador Dali Foundation/Artists Rights Society (ARS), New York; p. 145: © The McGraw-Hill Companies, Inc.; p. 148: © Jacobs Stock Photography/Getty Images; p. 149: © image100; p. 152: © Syracuse Newspapers/Frank Ordonez/The Image Works; p. 154: PhotoLink/Getty Images; p. 161: © Bettmann/CORBIS; p. 162 (top): Library of Congress; p. 162 (bottom): The Granger Collection/New York; p. 164: © The McGraw-Hill Companies, Inc.; p. 167: © Columbia/Everett Collection; 172 (left): Everett Collection; p. 172 (right): The Kobal Collection; p. 173: © The McGraw-Hill Companies, Inc.; p. 174: © BananaStock/JupiterImages; p. 178: © Comstock Images/JupiterImages; p. 181: Lucasfilm/20th Century Fox/The Kobal Collection; p. 184: Lucasfilm/20th Century Fox/The Kobal Collection/Merrick Morton; p. 191, 196: © The McGraw-Hill Companies, Inc.

Unit 4. p. 203: © Michel Touraine/Getty Images; p. 205: © Alan and Sandy Carey/Getty Images; p. 206: © Comstock/PunchStock; p. 207: © Melanie Stetson Freeman/The Christian Science Monitor via Getty Images; p. 208: © Toby Ross/Woodland Park Zoo; p. 211: © The McGraw-Hill Companies, Inc.; p. 213: © Digital Vision/Getty Images; p. 218: © TRBfoto/Getty Images; p. 219: © Mark Edward/Peter Arnold; p. 225: © Channel Island Pictures/Alamy; p. 227: © The McGraw-Hill Companies, Inc.; p. 228: Durrell Wildlife Conservation Trust, Photo by Peter Trenchard; p. 235: © Will & Deni McIntyre/Getty Images; p. 236 (both): © Digital Vision/PunchStock; p. 238: © Peter Turnley/CORBIS; p. 240: © The McGraw-Hill Companies, Inc.; p. 248 (all): Photos by Hollister Knowlton; p. 252: © C. Sherburne/PhotoLink/Getty Images; p. 253: © Linda Robshaw/Alamy.

Audio

Chap. 1: From "Talk of the Nation," November 10, 1999 interview with Melinda Penkava, Robert Sommer and Deborah Pellow. © 2005, National Public Radio, Inc. Reprinted with permission. Chap. 2: "What Happened to the Neanderthals?" hosted by Madeleine Brand and Ira Flatow, "Day to Day," 2004. © 2005, National Public Radio, Inc. Reprinted with permission. Chap. 3: "Bangladesh Primer" with Ambassador Teresita Schaffer with host Bob Edwards, "All Things Considered," March 20, 2000. © 2005, National Public Radio, Inc. Reprinted with permission. Chap. 4: "T.R. Reid on Mr. Donut in Japan," "Morning Edition," March 26, 1997. © 2005, National Public Radio, Inc. Reprinted with permission. Chap. 5: Excerpt from Maya Angelou interview by Stephen Banker. Copyright © 1978 Tapes for Readers. Used with permission of Tapes for Readers, 4410 Lingan Road NW, Washington DC, 20007. Chap. 6: "Star Wars and the Mythological Hero," "Morning Edition," May 18, 1999. © 2005, National Public Radio, Inc. Reprinted with permission. Chap. 7: From interview with Mark Plotkin by Marti Moss-Coane, "Fresh Air,", Sept. 21, 1993, WHYY, Philadelphia, National Public Radio. Reprinted by permission of Mark Plotkin, Ph.D./Amazon Conservation Team. Chap. 8: "Gaviotas: A Utopian Community" by Alan Wiseman, "All Things Considered," 1994. © 2005, National Public Radio, Inc. Reprinted with permission.

NOTES

NOTES

NOTES

 **NOTES**